FEAR, the Accuser

Dan Gillmor

FEAR,

the

accuser

Abelard-Schuman, New York

Printed in the
United States of America

For

my Children

Acknowledgments

This book is the product of one man. This is not to say, however, that the author is not greatly indebted to others for their priceless assistance. Three researchers labored at different times to supply much of the raw material. Several attorneys gave freely of their time and professional advice concerning the legal aspects of the problems presented. Three ladies, including the author's secretary, converted a typographical mare's nest into a typescript certain to gladden any printer's eye. Two friends, good and true, diligently read the result, offering many useful comments and, above all, unfailing encouragement when it was most needed. Finally, though it may not be customary, the author must express his admiration for the publisher and editor of Abelard-Schuman, Inc., who, in these times, took up the challenge presented by a book on this subject.

EDWARD LIVINGSTON, II

Friday, July 23, 1954

Contents

Contents

"Those who won our independence . . . valued liberty both as an end and as a means."

—Mr. Justice Louis D. Brandeis

1 | THE FEAR ITSELF

"There are two obvious places we could go. One is to war. The other is broke. There must be another alternative."
—HENRY FORD II

IT WAS A COLD, raw day. On Capitol Hill, members of Congress and plain citizens pushed their way through a light drizzle as they hurried toward the Capitol. Inside the big, white-domed building, symbol of representative government for one hundred and sixty-six years, a workman removed the word "Minority" from a door. In gilt lettering he replaced it with "Majority." In the Senate chamber, Republican floor-leader Robert A. Taft took his seat, dressed in a cutaway for the occasion. On the rostrum, Vice President Alben W. Barkley gallantly kissed the hand of Senator Margaret Chase Smith of Maine as she escorted her junior colleague from that state, Frederick G. Payne, to take his oath of office. Senator Wayne Morse of Oregon, a former Republican who was the only Independent, walked down the aisle carrying a small folding chair. The Secretary of the Senate advised him to take his usual seat in the front row on the Republican side. As he continued down the aisle, still clutching the chair, members on each side cordially shook his hand.

At noon, the retiring Vice President called the Senate

to order. Forty-seven Democrats, forty-eight Republicans and one Independent responded to the roll call.

In the other wing of the Capitol, the Clerk of the House of Representatives rapped for order. He presided over the election of the new Speaker of the House and then stepped down. The new Speaker, Joseph W. Martin of Massachusetts, was given the oath of office by a fellow Representative. In turn he administered the oath to the assembled members.

Before one o'clock, both Houses had named committees to notify the President that the Eighty-Third Congress of the United States had assembled. It was the first time in twenty years that a Republican Congress, elected with a Republican President, had convened to represent the people of the United States.

In his address to the House, Speaker Martin declared that "a new order" was taking over in Washington. Then he went on to speak of the fears uppermost in the minds of many:

"... For the past half century the world has been caught up in a political tidal wave that already has drowned out the lamps of liberty in two score countries and has dimmed them in every other nation on the face of the globe, including the United States," he declared. "We call this political malady Marxism, a doctrine which has spawned those twin evils, socialism and communism. By either name it has only one goal: to deliver the people once more into the hands of the State; to deliver the power of decision once more to the few instead of the many. Were it not for Marxism, Europe today might be peaceful and happy. China might be free ... We in Congress would make a tragic error if we did not fully comprehend that Marxism is the greatest enemy of representative government the world has ever known ..."

America, it seemed, might be losing not only her sense of humor but her sense of proportion. The "lie detector" was increasingly resorted to in government, beginning with the top employees of the 13,000-man Central Intelligence Agency. Later all CIA employees were tested. By the end of the year, its use was so widespread that officials felt called upon to explain that employees were submitting to it on a "voluntary" basis only. In private, civil servants referred to the "lie detector" as the "soul-washer."

Security officers were charging government workers with taking part in a discussion in which an (unnamed) individual said: "Who cares about the Constitution"; with patronizing a book store which "may be" the successor to an allegedly communist enterprise; with "attending meetings of a radical group" (unnamed) at which the employee was "ever willing to defend the cause of communism"; with associating with someone whose brother-in-law "is said to have communistic tendencies" and whose wife "is said to have subscribed to [the defunct weekly edited by George Seldes] *In Fact.*"

The situation aroused Dean Carl W. Ackerman of the Columbia University School of Journalism in New York to declare bluntly that he would no longer cooperate with federal, state or police investigators except on written request and advice of counsel.

"Students are 'tried' secretly without their knowledge and without an opportunity of explaining or defending their records before employment by any governmental agency," the Dean said ". . . If a dean or professor should answer in a particular case that the student's views are 'left of center' the student will not likely be employed, even though the dean may add that Anne O'Hare McCormick [late editorial columnist of the New York

Times] once described President Roosevelt as being 'left of center.' Under President Roosevelt's administration, it was popular to be 'left of center.' Today that term is a red flag of suspicion."

Not even appointees of the new President were above suspicion. Mrs. Mildred McAfee Horton was denied her commission as chief delegate to the United Nations Social Commission, although she had been duly named by President Eisenhower. Just why was never made clear. Mrs. Horton was formerly president of Wellesley College and wartime commandant of the WAVES, but the New York *Times* reported that the House Committee on Un-American Activities had reported its "files disclosed" that Mrs. Horton had once signed a petition to end the "abuse of power" of such committees and another to encourage citizenship among the foreign born.

A year later the wartime scientific head of the atomic bomb project, J. Robert Oppenheimer, was charged with disloyalty and endangering security. A special three-man board appointed by the Atomic Energy Commission unanimously found him loyal, but voted 2-1 to condemn him as a security risk." On appeal the Commission upheld the decision.

As the end of the 83rd Congress approached, one could look back on two years of flamboyant manifestation of the fears expressed by Speaker Martin.

After a year's investigating, the House Committee reported "ever-increasing evidence" of a clear and present danger to the country resulting from "an international conspiracy" of which the U.S. Communist Party is a part.

In November, 1953, millions watched Attorney General Herbert Brownell declare to a televised hearing of the Senate Internal Security Subcommittee that former President Truman had promoted the late Harry Dexter White

knowing that he "was a communist spy." Senator William
E. Jenner, chairman of the subcommittee, began the hearing with the statement: "Nine important officials of government" in the previous administration "were implicated
in the communist underground organization directed by
Soviet superiors."

Later, the Committee heard former Assistant Secretary of State Spruille Braden in a March, 1954 hearing.
If Mr. Braden was less specific, he sounded even more
frightened:

"Swarms of state interventionists have been injected
or absorbed into the agencies having to do with our
foreign operations," he declared. "Behind them in the
wings, developing and pushing plans, infiltrating not only
our political structures but education, the press and elsewhere, exists an unidentifiable but nonetheless effective
'THEY.'

"Here is where we may expect to find the dangerous
communists and traitors. 'THEY' are diabolically in-
genious and effective in both plans and methods . . . The
state interventionists and 'do-gooders' often turn out to
be the puppets who can be juggled by 'THEY.' If the
United States and, therefore, civilization are to survive,
this anonymous 'THEY' must be rendered impotent."
Braden urged the committee to expose the patterns which
demonstrate "the existence of exotic influences and the
degrees to which these United States have departed from
the principles laid down by the founding fathers . . ."

Not to be outdone, the chairman of the Senate's Investigations Subcommittee, Senator Joseph R. McCarthy,
added his bit to the fearful atmosphere: "Competent
estimates of men in military intelligence," he told a
Kansas audience in April, 1954, "are that less than fifty
. . . traitors could secrete atomic or hydrogen bombs in

key spots in these United States and at a given moment explode them and completely destroy this nation's power to resist. In other words, in a matter of hours ... just a few traitors could end our free civilization."

Repeatedly he told millions watching the televised hearings of the Army-McCarthy dispute that the administrations of Presidents Roosevelt and Truman were "twenty years of treason"; that the Central Intelligence Agency is infiltrated with communists, that there would be no point in turning over the names of "one hundred and thirty-five communists in defense plants" to the Defense Department because the Department would do nothing about it. He hinted that some in the Eisenhower administration had "something to hide." To cap the climax, the Senator casually indicated that he had revised his version of the history of modern times by mentioning the past "twenty, twenty-one" years of treason.

Amid the increasing din, Attorney General Brownell declared that the remaining U.S. communists were a "greater menace now than at any time before." If so, their power to menace the United States had increased in inverse proportion to their numbers, or in direct ratio to the size of the FBI. The end of former President Herbert Hoover's administration was the high point of U.S. communist strength. In the 1932 elections, 102,000 people voted Communist. In 1932 there were a mere 801 FBI employees, and the Bureau's appropriation was $2,978,000. By 1952, 15,181 FBI personnel were authorized by Congress to spend $90,000,000 annually; yet, according to FBI Director J. Edgar Hoover there were some 25,000 U.S. communists in 1953.

Was this curiously contradictory situation to be explained as some kind of crowd madness? There were those who said no. They pointed to the tremendous expansion of that part of the world beyond our shores which has come under the control of communist governments since the war. This increase in the strength of the communist world necessitated our preparing for the worst.

There were others who said that the increasing emphasis on the "communist conspiracy" is a "political racket," designed to distract attention from the real social and economic problems of our times, and to create a unity based on conformity rather than conviction. The true fear in the minds of those who continually sound the "communist" alarm is not so much a fear of communism, according to this view. It is a fear of the future. It is the fear that we must indeed either "go to war" or "go broke."

Whatever fear operated at a particular moment, the sum of these fears combined to make a record for the first two years of Speaker Martin's "new order" in the amount of time, money and attention lavished on investigations of communism, subversion, espionage and other menaces to the Republic, real or imaginary.

"Such a power as this ... may be employed to ransack the most distant states and to drag citizens before the Senate all the way from Wisconsin or from South Carolina ..."
—CHARLES SUMNER protesting a Senate investigation in 1860.

THERE IS AS MUCH TALK—and as little done—about investigations as there is about the weather. Investigations have been with us since before the first settlers arrived. In England, they began in the 16th century. The American colonial legislatures investigated. After the Revolution, the state legislatures investigated. So, beginning in 1792, did Congress.

There were always objections. The ill-fated expedition of General St. Clair against the Indians of the northwest resulted in the first congressional inquiry. It was opposed on the ground that the probe would invade the area of the government under presidential control. To this, a congressman replied: "An inquiry into the expenditures of public money [is] the indispensable duty of this House." The House voted 35-10 to investigate.

Since then, the right of federal and state legislatures to conduct such inquiries has never been seriously challenged. Practically every one concerned has agreed that there are at least two excellent reasons why investigations are necessary: to enable Congress to carry out its "watch-dog" functions over government spending and the execution of the law; and to obtain information so that it can decide what laws need enactment.

There is much less agreement on a third justification for investigations. This argument, a comparatively new one, asserts that Congress has an "information" function. One of its jobs, in other words, is to inform the American people. This may be done whether or not the information in question could lead to legislation.

The "disclosure" argument has often served in the defense of the House Committee on Un-American Activities, especially since the committee has been responsible for very little legislation. Representative (now Senator) Karl E. Mundt stated the case very neatly in 1946 as he sought funds for the committee from the House:

"Our task—to which you members of this House assigned us," he said, "is to seek out and *to expose those activities which, although legal,* are nonetheless un-American, subversive, and contrary to the American concept." (My emphasis.)

But if the right to investigate has been conceded, the way in which the investigations are conducted has always been the subject of bitter debate. Each time a major inquiry gets under way there is a hue and cry. It always comes from those who expect their cause to get hurt. Meanwhile, the other side thumbs the law books for well-turned phrases in support of the probe.

Sides have been known to reverse with remarkable and sometimes embarrassing swiftness. In 1860, Southern senators were happily investigating the supposedly subversive activities of anti-slavery Yankees. The latter, led by Senator Charles Sumner, a leader of the six-year-old Republican Party, protested bitterly.

"I know it is said this power [of investigation] is necessary in aid of legislation," Sumner told the Senate. "I deny the necessity. Convenient at times it may be; but necessary never . . . Such a power as this—which, without sanction of law, and merely at the will of a partisan majority, may be employed to ransack the most distant states, and to drag citizens before the Senate all the way from Wisconsin or from South Carolina—may be convenient, and, to certain persons, may seem to be necessary. An alleged necessity has, throughout all time, been the apology for wrong:

" 'So spoke the Fiend, and with necessity,
The tyrant's plea excused his devilish deeds.' "

Neither the Senator's eloquence nor his familiarity with Milton availed him anything. The investigation was voted, but hardly eighteen months elapsed before the erstwhile investigators were leading a rebellion, while the Republicans were defending the Union with their lives.

In our time, Fate has indulged in her own practical jokes at the expense of liberal and conservative alike. Less than twenty years ago, Supreme Court Justice Hugo Black, then a Senator, was busy conducting a senatorial investigation into the lobbying activities of the utility companies. Democrats defended his committee; Republicans denounced it. The chairman of a "committee of public utility executives," Philip H. Gadsden, declared that the committee was "a wicked example of government terrorism." The Senator, he said, was "not an investigator into facts, but a prosecutor who stoops to misstatement and insinuation to blacken the character of any witness testifying before him." To a balky witness, Senator Black uttered these now-familiar warnings: "This committee is determined that it will no longer permit the practice of this witness of evading questions by making speeches or criticism of the committee, or by asking questions, or by going far beyond the scope of the question in the answer, and by continuing to talk after he is called to order." Today, Mr. Justice Black is consistently found among those members of the Court who vote against encroachment on individual rights by governmental or legislative bodies.

Republican Congressman Frederic R. Coudert of New York has also tried on both pro- and anti-investigatorial shoes and found each comfortable at different times, depending upon who was investigating whom. In 1929, Mr. Coudert wrote a law review article entitled "Congressional Inquisitions v. Individual Liberty." A few years later, Mr. Coudert hit the headlines as co-chairman of a New York state legislative inquiry into communism. As Congressman, the gentleman from New York regularly votes for appropriations for the House Committee on Un-American Activities. Nevertheless, in 1929, he roundly attacked congressional investigations and looked hopefully to the courts to cramp their style.

When he wrote his piece on "inquisitions," Mr. Coudert could hardly have had investigations into subversion or "un-Americanism" in mind. There were none at that time. The Rapp-Coudert Committee conducted one of the first of the many state Red hunts to be held in the last two decades. The House Committee was not created until 1938, becoming in 1945 the first congressional body whose permanent job is to investigate subversion—or, to be exact, "subversive or un-American propaganda" activities.

There were, of course, sporadic special investigations of subversion on federal or state levels. Looking back on them with all the benefits of hindsight, we can observe a curious fact about committees mandated to look into whatever was currently considered subversive or un-American: they had a habit of looking the other way. Just before the Civil War, for example, several senators busied themselves investigating the Post Office. They wanted to know whether it was being used to undermine a certain good old American institution by carrying anti-slavery propaganda in the mails. Another Senate inquiry sought to connect the free-soil and anti-slavery movements in general with John Brown's Harper's Ferry raid. No legislators saw fit to inquire into secessionist propaganda.

A state investigating committee went even further afield, just a century ago. In 1854, Massachusetts elected, to its subsequent regret, a "Know Nothing" legislature. The newly elected members promptly decided to investigate "Popery" throughout the state. They created a seven-man committee headed by one Joseph Hiss and commanded it to look into the nunneries of the Commonwealth. The "Nunnery Committee" would have set forth at once, had not an unusually bright member pointed out that Massachusetts contained nary a convent. Determined to root out Romanism, the legislature enlarged the committee's mandate. The committeemen were now authorized to visit "such theological seminaries, boarding schools, academies, nunneries, convents and other institutions of like character as they may deem necessary."

The investigators adopted an extremely generous view of this already broad grant of power. They departed forthwith on a grand tour of the state's Catholic institutions. In Worcester, the members visited Holy Cross College and a local purveyor of wines. The probers must have investigated both with festive impartiality. After passing the check over to the state treasurer, the anti-Catholic legislators reported favorably on the Jesuit college and on the wines.

Perhaps to make up for their lack of severity toward Holy Cross, the committee next descended in force on a Catholic children's boarding school. Though the committee numbered but seven, twenty solons tramped about the building, frightening the children and insulting the nuns. They poked in closets and under beds for some derogatory evidence of "Popery." The exhausted investigators then repaired to a champagne supper. Once more they quaffed freely at state expense, though champagne was prohibited by state law.

By the time the probers reached Lowell, they were feeling the effects of their efforts to save Massachusetts from the "Catholic menace." They made only the most cursory inspection of the local institution. Once more they refreshed themselves with state-provided liquid conviviality. There spirits revived, they called on a lady "answering to the name of Mrs. Patterson." The record shows that the modest fees for Mrs. Patterson's professional services—sometimes called the world's oldest—were also charged to committee expenses.

In fact, the record revealed it too plainly, even for the "Know Nothings." Chairman Hiss, though exonerated of any misconduct toward Catholic believers, was expelled from the legislature. Some 150 members stayed away rather than vote against him, but the remainder concluded that Mr. Hiss need not have carried his investigation to quite that extent. The legislature then voted itself increased salaries and eventually passed into history as the Commonwealth's most expensive and least productive.

3 | ABOLITIONISTS, SOCIALISTS, AND RED REPUBLICANS

"To lay sudden and violent hands upon this ark of a people's safety [the Constitution] may be regarded as a sort of sacrilege..."
—THADDEUS HYATT defending himself against charges of contempt of the Senate for refusing to testify, 1860.

THE TIME WAS LATE in 1859. The country was swept by such an uproar of excitement, suspicion, and mistrust as has never been known before or since. One region accused another. Neighbor suspected neighbor. After a senator was assaulted by a colleague, congressmen began appearing in their respective chambers armed with pistols, knives, or leaded canes.

Even Boston, the center of abolitionism, was angrily divided. Many recalled the mayor's earlier denunciation of "irresponsible revolutionaries." There were others who still agreed with the Boston *Pilot's* assertion that "whenever you found an abolitionist [you also found] an anti-hanging man, woman's rights man, an infidel frequently, bigoted Protestant always, a socialist, a red republican ..."

At the height of the tension, John Brown led an "army" of twenty-one men into the town of Harper's Ferry, Virginia, and seized the federal arsenal. Brown's force was subdued the next day by U. S. soldiers led by Colonel

Robert E. Lee and a lieutenant named J. E. B. Stuart.
Five men escaped. Seven, including Brown, were tried for
treason and murder in a Virginia court, and hanged.

John Brown's body was hardly cold in the grave before
Senator James M. Mason of Virginia proposed the creation of a special investigating committee. Senator Mason,
the "Mr. Democrat" of his time, wanted the committee
empowered to reinvestigate the incident, although the trial
had gone into it thoroughly. In addition, his resolution
proposed that the committee inquire "whether any citizens
of the United States not present were implicated therein,
or accessory thereto."

Anxious to go along with their southern colleagues,
most of the opposition at first confined themselves to
attempting to limit the scope of the inquiry. Senator
Trumbull, of Illinois, said he hoped the investigation
would "disabuse . . . that portion of the Union which feels
most sensitive on this subject of the idea that the outbreak at Harper's Ferry received any countenance or support from any considerable number of persons . . ."

But Mason was not willing to let well enough alone.
If the Republicans knew as much about it as he did, he
declared, "they would not be so confident that [Brown]
had no participators and aiders and abettors . . ." This
ignited smouldering passions. Senator Trumbull proposed an amendment ordering the committee to investigate the seizure of arms in 1855 by a pro-slavery group
which had raided an arsenal at Liberty, Missouri. Rhode
Island's Senator Simmons declared that the investigation
would be a "most singular institution—an inquisition in a
free country."

"I suppose," he continued, "that those who feel most
intensely on this subject . . . if they could find a dozen
men who had contributed to John Brown, would deem

that sufficient evidence to fasten the imputation on the
party to which they belonged ... As soon as the thing
happened [at Harper's Ferry], nearly the entire press of
one party attempted to charge this crime as instigated by
the other, there happening to be three or four important
state elections pending, and these are the witnesses who
are to be examined—those who have already made the
charge; and they will hunt up something in order to sustain it. I say such an inquiry, with such an avowed object,
would be the most pernicious ... ever carried on by any
deliberative body in the world . . ."

For a week, the slavery issue in all its envenomed com-
plexity was once more discussed. Senators charged that
Mason's true purpose was to implicate not only the Republican Party but also sections of the northern Democratic Party in acts of "treason." In the end, the southern
majority had their way. Senator Trumbull's amendment
was defeated; Senator Mason's resolution was overwhelm-
ingly approved. A committee was appointed, composed
of Senators Mason, Jefferson Davis, and G. N. Fitch for
the majority, and Senators J. Collamer and J. R. Doolittle
for the minority.

The committee set to work immediately, and the familiar pattern of such investigations began to unfold. Colonel
Lee and a group of slave-owning Virginia gentlemen from
the area around Harper's Ferry were called to testify.
Their testimony was no more nor less than a repetition of
what had been brought out in the trial of Brown and his
confederates and spread across the front page of every
newspaper.

One Richard Realf was ordered summoned from Aus-
tin, Texas, "by telegraph or otherwise, as the Chairman
may direct." Realf had defected from Brown's group
shortly after the close of a convention held in Canada by

Brown, his followers, and a group of Canadian Negroes.

"I had not been at all satisfied with the condition of the Negroes in Canada," Realf told the committee. Dispatched to New York by Brown, Realf decamped to England, where, he admitted, he lectured on the abolitionist movement. He denied that he collected money there for Brown, "or, that if I did, they did not get it; which, so far as implicating me is concerned, amounts to about the same thing." After lecturing on the same subject in France, he sailed for New Orleans, where he "immediately joined the Catholic Church" and expressed his intention of becoming a Jesuit priest.

An ex-abolitionist might be expected to cooperate with the southern investigators, and he did.

"Was Brown's intercourse with [a Negro member of the group] of a character to show that he treated him as an equal and an associate?" Senator Mason inquired.

"It certainly was. To prove it, I will simply state that, having to wait twelve hours at Chicago, in order to make railroad connection from Chicago to Detroit, and to Canada, we necessarily had to breakfast and dine. We went into one of the hotels in order to breakfast. We took this colored man, Richardson, to table with us. The keeper of the hotel explained to us that it could not be allowed. We did not eat our breakfast. We went to another hotel, where we could take a colored man with us and sit down to breakfast."

In what was surely a voice laden with sarcasm, Mason added: "Where you could enjoy your rights, I suppose?"

The Senator then turned to a subject dear to all investigators: names. Realf was not much help. He could supply only the vaguest sort of information regarding the participants in the convention in Canada. In addition, he named one or two New England contributors to Brown's earlier efforts in Kansas, but these were apparently already known to the committee and had been subpoenaed.

"I may as well state, once for all," he said at last, "that I do not believe John Brown would intrust to any man, no matter how intimate his friendship might be, more than barely sufficient of his schemes to secure his cooperation and support."

In vain the chairman asked him repeatedly to dredge his memory.

QUESTION: ... Do you know of any other persons with whom Brown was in communication upon the subject of getting money?

ANSWER: I understood that ... Thomas Wentworth Higginson ... was an intimate friend of John Brown, and that he ... was one of those who supplied him with funds ... in behalf of freedom in Kansas ...

QUESTION: Can you recollect any others?

ANSWER: I cannot.

QUESTION: Can you remember the names of any persons, in any of the states, with whom Brown ... was in correspondence?

ANSWER: No, sir ...

The chairman, assisted by Senator Davis, hammered away at "unfriendly" witnesses in the quest for names. Samuel G. Howe, a Boston physician whom Realf had mentioned, was called. He was questioned regarding a letter written to Brown by the Massachusetts State Kansas Committee. The committee, in which Howe was prominent, had raised thousands of dollars to aid settlers in Kansas Territory and supplied them with arms to resist raids from pro-slavery bands across the Missouri border. Howe freely testified to his relationship with John Brown, but at one point he balked:

QUESTION: Who ... wrote the letter you refer to?

ANSWER: I should prefer not to answer that question.

THE CHAIRMAN: I see no reason why you should not answer the question.

THE WITNESS: I am here to answer as to all I have done myself, freely and frankly, but I would respectfully ask to be excused from answering any question touching the actions of anybody else . . .

MR. DAVIS: The witness confounds his position. He is not here arraigned to answer for what he did, but to give information as to what everybody did.

Each "unfriendly" witness was asked to name others, but they firmly avoided mentioning any whose names they were not certain were already disclosed. The cashier of a Hartford, Connecticut, bank who had known Brown in Ohio, proved less than helpful:

QUESTION: Can you give the names of any of the contributors?

ANSWER: I cannot at present . . .

QUESTION: It would be desirable to learn the names of any of those persons who contributed, if you can recollect them, with safety to your memory, of course.

ANSWER: I cannot recollect them.

QUESTION: Was no list kept of them?

ANSWER: No, sir . . .

A Boston attorney, John A. Andrew, was also summoned. The committee knew he had obtained counsel to defend Brown in hostile Virginia, but Chairman Mason wanted to know more:

". . . What I want to know," the Senator said, "is at whose instance were counsel employed . . . and who furnished the compensation to the counsel?"

Lawyer Andrew replied boldly, but names were conspicuously absent from his answer:

" ... When the intelligence reached Boston ... that the local court in ... Virginia was proceeding to the trial of John Brown and one of his associates with such speed and hurried action on its part as to render it probable that there was to be no sufficient opportunity to make a full and complete defense, and under such circumstances as that the physical condition of the men themselves seemed to render it entirely improbable that they could prepare a defense ... it struck my mind, and the minds of various other gentlemen whom I met with in the ordinary avocations of my business, in the street, the office, the court rooms, and otherwise, as being a judicial outrage. I certainly felt it to be such ...

"Various gentlemen said to me, without respect of party or person, 'You, Mr. Andrew, are known to be a lawyer of anti-slavery sentiments, or of Republican sentiments, and of considerable readiness to act on any occasion which seems to you to be proper; why do not you go to Virginia and volunteer to defend Captain Brown?' Without remembering the names of the persons who spoke to me, I should not think it strange if twenty men, of all shades of opinion, might have made that remark . . . I said to others, and said to myself, 'If I should go to Virginia, I, a Republican lawyer and a Massachusetts man, should be before a court and jury so little in sympathy with myself that I should be quite as much on trial as my client would be ...'"

Andrew described how he had instead arranged for a Washington attorney, familiar with Virginia law, to take the case for a fee of $1,000.

QUESTION: Will you state how this money was furnished and by whom ...?

ANSWER: ... I accepted the drafts [from Brown's defense counsel] as they were drawn on me, and the money was furnished by A, B, and C, whom I might happen to meet in business, or in pleasure, or at church.

But Andrew was quite willing to say he had himself given Brown money in the spring of the year of the Harper's Ferry incident.

". . . I sent him $25," he told the Senator from Virginia bluntly, "and in parting with him, as I heard he was a poor man, I expressed my gratitude to him for having fought for a great cause with earnestness, fidelity and conscientiousness, while I had been quietly at home earning my money and supporting my family in Boston under my own vine and fig tree, with nobody to molest or make me afraid."

The investigators summoned Brown's defense counsel, Samuel Chilton, and questioned him, over minority objections, not only on how he had been retained, but on what John Brown had said to him:

QUESTION: . . . Did he disclose to you . . . the names of any persons . . . who were connected with him in this assault upon Harper's Ferry, other than those who were present . . . ?

ANSWER: He did not. I did not ask him any questions. I listened to whatever he chose to communicate . .

MR. COLLAMER [senior minority member]: . . . Really, ought we to ask counsel as to communications from his client?

THE CHAIRMAN: . . . Whether we could ask him . . . anything his client told him in reference to the matter pending before the court . . . is one question, but as to matters unconnected with his trial, is a different question.

* * * * *

THE WITNESS: I was going to remark that . . . if a

question were asked me, the answer to which would disclose anything of that sort, I should very respectfully decline to answer it . . . I think it is much shorter to say that . . . whilst he gave me a long narrative of his life pretty much in the general—an interesting one too —he did not mention the name of a single individual . . .

The investigation dragged on through January and February of 1860. For the first—but not the last—time in congressional history, the investigators began to explore the now familiar topic of associations and organizations. Former Representative Joshua R. Giddings, for 21 years a congressman from an Ohio county on the mainline of the "underground railroad," was called. Giddings testified that he had been asked for money by John Brown's son as he was on his way to lecture in a neighboring town. "These were the circumstances," he said. ". . . I had started, actually got as far as my door, when he stopped me and told me . . . that his father was in want. I dare say I should not have given more than a dollar if I had the change, but three dollars was the lowest I had, and I gave it without any hesitation."

He went on to explain how he was in the habit of lecturing throughout the state to associations "for aiding in all those charitable and humane purposes connected with the escape of slaves fleeing from bondage."

QUESTION [by Mason]: Were you a member of any of those associations?

ANSWER [by Giddings]: I never was a member of any association of that kind . . .

QUESTION: Will you state . . . what were the . . . objects of the associations . . . ?

ANSWER: I would not be willing to undertake to say . . .

The investigators then began exploring Giddings' beliefs and opinions. The Republican minority entered mild objections, the milder, perhaps, because they knew Giddings' prowess as a debater. Jefferson Davis was interrogating Giddings at that point, and finally a minority member remonstrated:

MR. DOOLITTLE: Right here, Colonel Davis, I must interpose. I think, although this colloquy between you and Mr. Giddings is very instructive to us all, perhaps it is no evidence. You are simply asking for his opinion.

MR. DAVIS: It is evidence only in this sense, that I wish to get at the sentiment which was inculcated by the lecturer and received with approbation, as connected with our present inquiry as to how far combinations exist to destroy the institutions of the country. That is the object.

THE WITNESS: Propound your question directly, Colonel Davis. I will take great pleasure is answering it.

MR. DAVIS: Did the doctrine inculcated teach that it was right to liberate any person who was restrained by the laws of the land from those liberties which you say belong to all as the endowment of nature?

THE WITNESS: Permit me, with all due deference, to suggest, so that I may understand you, do you intend to inquire whether those lectures would indicate whether your slaves of the slave states had a right at all times to their liberty?

MR. DAVIS: I will put the question in that form if you like it.

ANSWER: My lectures [asserted] the right of every human soul ... charged with no crime or offense, to maintain his life, his liberty, the pursuit of his own happiness ... In all my lectures I inculcated the right

of the Africans in the United States to their liberty,
as standing upon precisely the same level that the
claim of Americans enslaved by Africans stood at the
time we sent our navy to Algiers.

* * * * *

QUESTION: But who is to judge whether the laws of
the land violate or conform to the laws of nature?

ANSWER: In our nation the people are made the
judges. Our government was based upon the doctrine
that it was constituted to secure the people in the
enjoyment of life, liberty, and happiness; that whenever
any form of government becomes destructive of life,
of liberty, or of happiness, it is the right and the duty
of the people to alter or abolish it, and reorganize
its powers in such form as to them shall seem most
likely to secure their interest and happiness. They do
this in our government in the regularly constituted
mode of turning out such officers as disregard the
laws of nature, and placing those who hold to the
doctrines asserted by the founders of our republic.

This was enough. The former representative was asked
to step down. As other witnesses took the stand, the investigators revealed less and less inclination to stick to
the point. A lawyer from Oberlin, Ohio, who had served
a jail term for violation of the Fugitive Slave Act was
questioned about his association with men in no way
connected with Brown:

QUESTION: Did you know a man named L. S. Leary?
ANSWER: I did.
QUESTION: Was he a white man or a Negro?
ANSWER: He was a Negro.
QUESTION: Where did he live?

ANSWER: He lived in Oberlin.

QUESTION: Did Leary apply to you at any time in the fall of 1859 for money?

ANSWER: He did.

QUESTION: What did he want with the money?

ANSWER: I understood that he wanted to engage in assisting slaves to escape.

QUESTION: Did he say that?

ANSWER: No, sir; he did not.

QUESTION: Did he tell you what plans he had?

ANSWER: No, sir; he did not tell me any particular plans he had in view.... In the community where I live we are in the habit of giving money for aiding slaves to escape, and whenever application is made to us for that purpose, there is but little said. If we are satisfied it is wanted for that purpose, and can give it, we give it.

* * * * *

QUESTION: Is it your custom to give the money without inquiring in what way it is to be used, except the object to which it is to be applied?

ANSWER: Certainly. We do not know the ways in which it is to be used. The object is the only thing. We are not in favor of promoting insurrections, and had no such thought or intention, and should never give any money for that purpose in our community.

* * * * *

QUESTION: How are they to know it is to be so applied [to aid fugitive slaves] if you do not tell them so?

ANSWER: We know each other well, and have confidence that whatever is wanted in this way is properly applied.

QUESTION: Why is not the use that is to be made of it disclosed to each other?

ANSWER: Well, the opposition to the practice of aiding slaves to escape, on the part of some of our citizens, is such that it is not thought advisable to say anything about it.

Towards the end of the hearings, the southern senators made more and more strenuous efforts to implicate the anti-slavery movement. They questioned George L. Stearns, chairman of the Massachusetts State Kansas Committee with an insistence born of frustration.

QUESTION: You saw John Brown the elder, in Boston, some time in the spring of 1859. Will you state under what circumstances you saw him there; what brought him there, so far as you know?

ANSWER: He came to Boston . . . to get money for anti-slavery purposes.

QUESTION: What were those anti-slavery purposes? Did he disclose them?

ANSWER: No, sir.

QUESTION: Did you give him any money at that time?

ANSWER: Yes, sir.

QUESTION: How much?

ANSWER: I do not recollect how much. I have no means of knowing—some hundreds of dollars.

QUESTION: Will you state to the committee what were the anti-slavery purposes to which you intended that money to be devoted—what sort of purposes?

ANSWER: Well, my object in giving him the money was because I considered that so long as Kansas was not a free state, John Brown might again be a useful man there. That was one object. Another was a very high personal respect for him ... I gave him money to enable him to live or to do whatever he thought was right ...

But the southerners' suspicions would not be downed by such frank answers. They sought without success to implicate the witness by pure association:

QUESTION: There is a letter from John Brown, jr., ... in which he says: 'While in Boston I improved the time in making the acquaintance of these staunch friends of our friend Isaac. First called on Dr. H———. He gave me a letter to the friend who does business on Milk Street.'

Is your place of business on Milk Street?

ANSWER: Yes, sir.

QUESTION: He goes on: 'Went with him to his house, at Medford, and took dinner.' Do you recollect whether he brought you a letter from Howe?

ANSWER: I think he did.

QUESTION: He continues: 'The last word he said to me was, "Tell friend Isaac that we have the fullest confidence in his endeavor whatever may be the result."' Do you remember that message sent to his father?

ANSWER: No, sir, I do not. I recollect sending a complimentary message to his father that I had confidence in him; but I have no recollection of that.

MR. DAVIS: Was it his father who was called Isaac?

ANSWER: I do not know.

THE CHAIRMAN: I was going to ask you whether you did or did not know that the father at that time passed by the name of Isaac, or Isaac Smith?

ANSWER: I did not.

The questioning grew more and more hostile. Stearns

recalled seeing the elder John Brown at a dinner at
Parker House in the company of Dr. Howe and another
man. Senator Mason pursued the quest for more "conspirators":

QUESTION: Can you recollect none others who were
there except the two whom you have mentioned?

ANSWER: No, sir, I think they were the only two
that I knew personally...

Senator Davis disclosed his ignorance of Boston's famous
hostelry:

QUESTION: What kind of a house is this Parker
House?

ANSWER: It is one of the best eating houses in the
town ... a place where everybody goes for a good dinner ... a place where you can get the rarities of the
season, and cooked in the best manner.

* * * * *

QUESTION: Do you remember the names of any
prominent contributors ... any men connected with the
United States government in any capacity?

ANSWER: No, sir; I think that those men would not
contribute at all.

QUESTION: Not local officers, but members of Congress or any other body?

ANSWER: No, sir; you can see that in our operations
we did not go in that way. Instead of getting money
as you would in a political contest, in large sums from
individuals, to distribute among the people, we went
to the lower class of people. Our dependence was upon
the laborers, the mechanics, the farmers, and such persons, much more than it was upon the professional
men and merchants ...

QUESTION: There was no return of names then anywhere?

ANSWER: None, whatever.

Meanwhile, the investigators were having worse troubles with other witnesses. The Senate, at Mr. Mason's
request, issued warrants for the arrest of four men. The
Sergeant-at-Arms reported that one could not be found.
Another was arrested by a deputy of the Sergeant-at-Arms
and as promptly released by a Massachusetts court. A
third, John Brown, Jr., had armed himself and was protected by armed friends who promised to resist any attempt to seize him. The Senate declined to give its Sergeant-at-Arms authority to use force. The fourth witness,
Thaddeus Hyatt, presented himself, but refused to take the
stand. Mason had him brought before the Senate and demanded that he give his reasons for refusing and that he
promise to testify. Republican Senator John P. Hale of
New Hampshire opposed him. He said that Hyatt, a New
York merchant, must have been called solely in connection with the committee's mandate to inquire "whether
any citizens . . . not present were implicated" in the Brown
affair.

". . . . I contend that this is strictly and literally a
judicial power," he declared. "It is a power to which the
judiciary is perfectly competent . . . Congress can only
inquire in reference to the necessity of passing general
laws . . ."

The southern majority voted solidly to bring Hyatt
to book. In a sworn statement, Hyatt declared to the
Senate:

". . . The undersigned would respectfully observe
that, while admitting the justice and propriety of investigating committees . . . he is constrained to regard [the

Mason] committee as . . . a tribunal with powers such as
were never known before or contemplated in this Republican government; powers that are inimical to freedom, subversive of liberty; and in violation of the fundamental
law of the land . . . To lay sudden and violent hands upon
this ark of a people's safety [the Constitution] may be
regarded as a sort of sacrilege . . ."

The Senate did not think so. It ordered its Sergeant-
at-Arms to throw Hyatt in the District of Columbia jail.

Two months passed. As the hearings drew to a close,
Senator Charles Sumner presented a petition from "citizens of the Commonwealth of Massachusetts of African
descent" asking for better jail conditions for Hyatt. It
was referred to the Mason committee. Mr. Mason's majority voted to return it "to the Senator who presented it."

It was a face-saving gesture. Hyatt's arrest and im-
prisonment were ample "vindication of the authority of
the Senate," said the Senator from Virginia. He declared
that, since the committee no longer required the man's
testimony, he saw no further reason to keep him in jail.

The minority and the majority agreed no legislation
could be recommended by the investigators. But the
minority went on to point a moral to the proceeding:

". . . The committee, by its majority, seem to regard
it as their duty to inquire whether there are any citizens
who, though not 'implicated' in this affair, yet hold such
opinions and pursue such courses on the subject of slavery
as are dangerous to the national tranquillity, even although Congress has no power to take any action in relation thereto . . . Witnesses, and especially those known
or suspected of ultra-abolition sentiments, have been
freely examined as to their personal sentiments, theories,
purposes, conduct, charities, contributions, lectures and
speeches . . . We feel bound to protest against all the con-

clusions which the same spirit of suspicion which could call such testimony will seek to deduce from it."

These comments fell on deaf ears. The majority found "most persuasive proof of the utter insecurity of the peace and safety of some of the states of this Union, in the existing condition of the public mind and its purposes in the non-slaveholding states." Yet it was "not prepared to suggest any legislation." The best it could do was to conclude on a grimly threatening note:

"If the several states, whether from motives of policy or a desire to preserve the peace of the union . . . do not hold it incumbent on them . . . to guard in future by appropriate legislation against [similar] occurrences . . . the committee can find no guarantee . . . for the security of peace between the states . . ."

It was no idle threat. Little more than a year later, the principal investigators were leading an armed rebellion against the Union. Mr. Mason's fellow Virginians were planning the seizure of the same arsenal at Harper's Ferry. Jefferson Davis was named provisional President of the rebellious states. Former Colonel Lee had accepted the command of the armed forces of the rebellion and named former Lieutenant "Jeb" Stuart as his cavalry general. "John Brown" was no longer a despised name, but the first words of a battle song.

Of the conflict, ex-Senator Mason said sadly: "I look upon it, then, sir, as a war of sentiment and opinion by one form of society against another form of society."

So had been the investigation, but he did not see it that way. Only New Hampshire's Senator Hale had had sufficient vision to predict the outcome. During the debate on the resolution to create the inquiry he observed to his unheeding colleagues:

"I do not believe exactly that the resolution is germane to any legislation . . . nor do I believe that when the resolution is passed, and the investigation is had, and the report is made, the gentlemen who have moved it will be very swift to ask for any Federal action, and I will tell you why, sir:

"It is a very good thing to have Federal action if we could always have it on our side . . . When the gentlemen come . . . to look at the question and see the results to which it may lead . . . they will come to the conclusion that although a little Federal action might be wholesome just about this time, for this particular case, yet . . . it may be invoked and employed on the other side of the question."

4 | FROM BEER TO BOLSHEVISM

"We may well wonder ... whether con-
stitutional government as heretofore main-
tained in this republic could survive an-
other great war even victoriously waged."
—CHARLES EVANS HUGHES addressing the
alumni of Harvard Law School in 1920.

CONGRESSIONAL INQUIRY into "per-
sonal sentiments, theories, purposes, conduct, charities, contributions, lectures, and speeches" is curiously
rare in American history. The Democratic exploration
into abolitionist and, by association, Republican subversion was enough of that sort of thing to suit Congress
for fifty-nine years—if minor senatorial and House adventures are excepted, for seventy-eight years.

In the intervening half to three-quarters of a century, the country survived an armed rebellion, panics,
major and minor wars, and the great depression. It did
so without the assistance of committees investigating subversion. During the Civil War, there were no investigations of that kind whatsoever. Not a single congressman
or senator descended on the colleges to inquire whether
the professors were open or secret advocates of the overthrow of the government by armed rebellion, though such
a rebellion was actually in progress. Congress questioned
no one regarding his pro-slavery or anti-Union teaching,

33

opinions or associations. Individual Confederate sympathizers were suppressed, sometimes ruthlessly, and often
unfairly, but congressional committees played no part in
the process.

The same picture holds for times of external danger
or internal economic crisis through which the United
States has passed. During World War I, there were vigorous efforts to punish individuals who were charged
with being "pro-German" or with obstructing the war effort. Congressional committees, however, were again conspicuously absent from the scene. There were no inquiries
into un-American Prussianism. It was not until after the
war ended that the Senate created a select committee
to investigate German brewing and liquor interests in
order to determine what, if any, connection they might
have had with the Kaiser's propaganda in this country.

Under the chairmanship of Senator Lee S. Overman
of North Carolina, the committee plodded along noise-
lessly. Suddenly the Senate sent it new orders. Two
theatre rallies in support of the new Soviet government
of Russia had been held in Washington. The Senate
ordered the Overman committee to investigate "any efforts being made to propagate in this country the principle of any party exercising or claiming to exercise
authority in Russia . . . and further to inquire into any
effort to incite the overthrow of the government of this
country . . . by force . . ."

The investigators asked the Attorney General to investigate and report to it. That official testified that he
had already begun an investigation before the senators
had asked it of him. The overthrow or subversion of the
government had not been advocated, he reported. The
committee ignored him and proceeded to hold seventeen
fairly spectacular, if inconclusive hearings. Finally it

issued an anticlimactic report under the two-headed title of "Brewing and Liquor Interests and German and Bolshevik Propaganda." Oblivious to the fact that Congress could not conceivably legislate on the subject, the senators reported at great length on what was occurring inside Russia.

The "beer and bolshevism" committee must get the credit for a new investigating technique, however. In its report, it referred for the first time to the testimony of unnamed witnesses who appeared at secret sessions. The committee also helped to keep boiling the tensions and intolerances generated by the war to make the world safe for democracy. It was the time of the "Red scare," when aliens were rounded up by raids ordered by Attorney General A. Mitchell Palmer and carried out by J. Edgar Hoover.

The Senate Judiciary Committee subsequently investigated the conduct of the raids. Testimony before the committee revealed that men and women had been arrested, often without warrants; their homes had been illegally searched. They had been held without bail, refused permission to obtain a lawyer, questioned without being informed of their rights, and locked up under inhumanly crowded and insanitary conditions for days at a time. In the end, the majority of those seized by agents of the Bureau of Investigation, usually in the small hours of the morning, had to be set free for lack of any evidence against them.

No investigation of subversion was directly involved in the affair, however, unless actions of the Department of Justice could be regarded as subversive. A group of twelve distinguished lawyers thought they came very close to being just that. Charles Evans Hughes, a former Republican presidential candidate, and later

Chief Justice of the United States, practically said so. In
an address at Harvard Law School, Hughes commented:
". . . Perhaps to an extent unparalleled in our history, the
essentials of liberty are being disregarded. Very recently
. . . violations of personal rights [have occurred] which
savor of the worst practices of tyranny . . ."

After the Overman Committee filed its report, on
which no action was taken, the investigatorial talents of
Congress turned in other directions for a full decade.
The doings of the Attorney General, the Secretary of the
Interior and other officials in connection with the Teapot
Dome scandal were explored. If ever justification was required, the results vindicated the usefulness of such investigations. Three cabinet members were forced to resign. Secretary of the Interior Albert B. Fall and oil
magnate Harry F. Sinclair were imprisoned. Unhappily,
two suicides also resulted.

Meanwhile, the nation prospered as never before.
President Hoover declared that the American system was
within practical attainment of man's ancient goal of
abolishing poverty. We had reached "a permanently high
plateau" of economic prosperity. Just as it seemed that
the "plateau" had a gentle upward slope, the economic
machine with its millions of passengers suddenly plunged
over the edge of a precipice. In a year, millions were
without work and without hope of obtaining it. Existence
was a grim problem even for the employed. Living in the
fear of losing their jobs, they accepted repeated cuts in
pay. If ever there was a time when the shadow of bloody
revolution might fall over the land, the early 1930's was
such a time.

One might suppose that such conditions would bring
on an investigation to determine the extent to which

discontent had radicalized America. So they did. In 1930, the House authorized Representative Hamilton Fish of New York to head a select committee to "investigate communist propaganda in the United States." The committee was also to look into charges brought by New York Police Commissioner Grover Whalen that the Amtorg Trading Corporation, a U. S. corporation organized in New York by Soviet commercial representatives, was disseminating red propaganda.

Logic did not prove to be one of the Fish Committee's strongest points. It reported that Whalen's charges were not supported by the evidence. The communist movement, it said, was pitifully weak in this country. Nevertheless, it recommended that Congress outlaw the U. S. Communist Party.

In 1934, the House created another special investigating committee under Representative John McCormack of Massachusetts. After holding twenty-four executive and seven public hearings, the committee discreetly reported that the American people were not exactly delighted with either communist or fascist ideology, even in that bitter depression year. Of its several mild recommendations for legislation, the committee enjoys the distinction of having had one enacted into law, the Foreign Agents Registration Act.

It was not until 1938, when war clouds began to form perceptibly on overseas horizons, that Congress got back into the business of investigating subversion. Although the committee which was created, the House Special Committee on Un-American Activities, was expected at the time to be a one-Congress affair, it has been investigating ever since. Its mandate as a special committee was renewed repeatedly and, in 1945, it became the first

permanent congressional committee investigating subversion.*

The pre-war committee behaved in the familiar fashion of such investigating committees. Like the ante-bel-
lum senator from Virginia, Representative Martin Dies
of Texas studiously turned his attention away from the
nazi, fascist and Japanese thunderclouds. The committee
devoted itself primarily to investigating "communism"
and various other "un-American" organizations. Among
the latter, it saw fit to list the Allied Voters against
Coudert, the American Committee for Anti-Nazi Literature, the American Friends of Spanish Democracy, the
American Investors Union, the American Labor Party,
the National Committee to Aid the Victims of German
Fascism, and the Milk Consumers' Protective Committee, to mention a mere handful of the 639 organizations
and 204 publications which eventually found their way into the committee's "subversive list."

Like the senators of the slave-holding south, committee members revealed by their comments and questions that they, too, were as interested in implicating
the opposition party as they were in subversion. In the
committee's first hearings, Republican Representative J.
Parnell Thomas, later its chairman, asked a witness: "Are
not many of the acts now being advocated or now being
enacted by the [Roosevelt administration] similar to the
steps which led to dictators in Soviet Russia, Germany
and Italy?"

* The story of the House Committee's endless inquiries is not only
worth telling, it has been well told in two books. The first, covering
the pre-war and war years, is *The Dies Committee*, by Father August R.
Ogden, Washington, Catholic University Press, 1945. The second covers
the post-war period. Written by Professor Robert K. Carr, it is called
The House Committee on Un-American Activities, 1945-50, Cornell
University Press, Ithaca, New York, 1952.

"Well, now . . . that is calling for a pure conclusion," the witness replied.

"This is not partisanship. This is un-American activity," Thomas declared. If anyone thought he might be referring to his own question, the confusion was dispelled when Mr. Thomas added that among the "un-American activities" he had in mind were "the Supreme Court packing bill and the reorganization bill."

Although the investigators occasionally mentioned nazism and fascism as equally "un-American" they developed a knack of condemning all anti-fascist efforts. The Hollywood Anti-Nazi League was derogated. Various committees proposing the boycott of Japanese goods were labeled "un-American." Others seeking to aid the Spanish Republican government in its unsuccessful efforts to suppress the rebellion supported by German supplies and Italian troops were branded "subversive."

In its first seven years the special committee published more than 15,000 pages of exhibits and transcripts of hearings, thirty-two volumes in all. It published fifteen reports. From this mountain came forth a single, short-lived mouse of legislation. Congress passed a rider to an appropriation bill forbidding the payment of the salaries of two government officials named by the committee. The rider was declared an unconstitutional bill of attainder by the Supreme Court.

The officials in question were not accused of being fascist, nazi, or Japanese agents. They were guilty of radicalism, or, in the phrase of the time, "premature anti-fascism." When the bombs fell on Pearl Harbor, anti-fascism ceased to be premature. The committee more or less subsided for the duration, but as the war ended, Congress unexpectedly made it the country's first standing or permanent investigating committee. The commit-

tee had become, in the words of Representative Mundt,
"the most powerful in Congress."

Except to the extent that Senate committees have
since moved into the field, the committee's power has not
subsequently lessened. By 1950, the committee's vast card-
file of names had grown to rival the files of the FBI in
size, though not in the secrecy with which they were kept.
More than 500,000 references to the activities and affiliations of Americans were indexed. There were reports
on some 25,000 persons and 1,768 organizations.

The millions of words of transcripts of hearings held
during the post-war period are filled with questions and
answers dealing with what the Republican minority called,
nearly a century ago, "personal sentiments, theories, purpose, conduct, charities, contributions, lectures and
speeches." Witnesses have been asked where their parents
were born, whether their parents were naturalized citizens,
what their salaries are or were, how old their "kiddies"
were, did they believe in the "common ownership of property," and how they voted in a presidential election.

Other not untypical questions: Aren't you interested
in the program of extending universal suffrage? Are you
a gentile or a Jewess [sic]? Are you an orthodox Jew? Are
you a member of any church? Do you recognize the
Supreme Being? Are you an atheist?

Among the sentiments, theories and purposes which
the committee has, over the years, indicated it thought
"un-American" or "subversive" are: criticism of the committee, of the FBI, of other congressmen; various New
Deal programs and policies; believing in a higher standard of living; favoring anti-poll-tax legislation; supporting the Morgenthau plan for the post-war German economy.

Nor have lectures and speeches been exempt from

the committee's scrutiny. Its investigators once demanded from radio networks the scripts of a list of—presumably "un-American"—radio commentators. Referring to articles written by a witness, Professor Frederick L. Schuman of Williams College, one committee member declared:

"We will have all of them before us and we will undertake to pass on them . . ."

In that distant time, the 1920's, the age of jazz, bathtub gin, and four-digit telephone numbers, Charles Evans Hughes little knew how forethoughtfully he spoke when he remarked to Harvard's lawyers: "We may well wonder . . . whether constitutional government as heretofore maintained in this republic could survive another great war even victoriously waged."

That second great war ended victoriously for America. Since then, the activity of investigating committees has steadily expanded, until, with the 83rd Congress, it reached record proportions.

5 THE INVESTIGATING CONGRESS

"Congressional information seekers will cover everything from the waterfront to the battlefront."
—Congressional Quarterly's "Weekly Report" commenting on the opening of the 83rd Congress, February 13, 1953.

WE HAVE COME ONCE AGAIN to the scene on Capitol Hill when the Republican Congress convened on a January day in 1953. The newly elected Speaker of the House, Joseph W. Martin, is delivering his opening remarks:

"... Not a single ... congressional function has escaped the abuse which [the] disciples of Marxism have heaped upon [Congress] ... We can dedicate ourselves to no higher goal than to restore the Congress of the United States to its full share of participation in ... government. All of us ... must never forget that this wondrous mechanism had worked best under a strong two-party system. If it were in my power to bring about the destruction of the Democratic Party, I would not exercise that power ... Let us join in a monumental effort to make this 83rd Congress the Congress which will go down in history as having served America and the oppressed people of the world everywhere ..."

The 83rd Congress seems certain to go down in history

as the "investigating Congress." Some 105 probes were launched in the first month, for which almost $4,000,000 were set aside. More than $1,000,000 were appropriated in the first session just for inquiries into subversion. In the first year, only about ten per cent of the roll-call votes were on key legislative questions.

The second session was, if anything, even balkier. April, 1954 arrived unaccompanied by showers of legislation. Only five out of 214 presidential recommendations had been enacted. Not all 214 were vital, of course, but the President indicated that his heart was set on eighteen major measures. As spring drew to a close, Congress had managed to pass three of them: the St. Lawrence seaway bill, the highway program, and extension of excise taxes. The last item was passed in a form opposed by Mr. Eisenhower. As the "Army-McCarthy" hearings continued, congressmen were quipping: "What is so rare as a legislative day in June?"

The "monumental effort" took place instead in the hearing rooms before the television cameras, not in the chambers of the Senate and House. It was not signally successful in achieving the high standards proposed by Speaker Martin. The effect of much of the investigating was not merely to restore Congress to equal responsibility for government, but to give it an edge over the Executive branch—in the varying language used by the President and key officials, to "undermine," "infringe on," or "usurp" functions and powers which belong, under the Constitution to the Chief Executive. The investigators accomplished this largely by investigating—or threatening to investigate—"communism" in the Executive departments.

The Speaker's promise not to "destroy the Democratic Party" held good as far as he was concerned, but the investigators did not follow his advice. They devoted no little effort to an attempt to discredit, if not destroy, the opposition. Their method: investigating "communist infiltration" of the previous Democratic administrations.

The division of labor was largely between Senators William E. Jenner of Indiana and Joseph R. McCarthy of Wisconsin. Senator Jenner heads the Senate Subcommittee to Investigate the Administration of the Internal Security Act. Senator McCarthy is chairman of the Committee on Government Operations and its Permanent Subcommittee on Investigations. Mr. Jenner's committee concentrated its efforts in two areas: "subversive influence in the educational process," and "interlocking subversion in government departments." The education hearings ended suddenly. On June 16, 1953, the Senator announced that further investigation would be left to local political and educational authorities. Thereafter, the subcommittee concentrated its efforts on questioning former officials, whether high or petty, of the Roosevelt and Truman administrations. Some were no longer in government service. Others had become employees of the United Nations.

The aim of the hearings was to demonstrate the existence of "red networks" within the Democratic administrations. At the April, 1953 opening of the first hearing, Senator Jenner said as much:

"The subcommittee has been impressed by the extent to which the communists it has exposed were able to move, often with great facility, from one government agency to another, spinning their web of intrigue and drawing with them in positions of power and influence their confederates and auxiliaries," he announced.

Four months later, the committee issued an interim report. In it, the conclusions varied slightly but significantly from those Mr. Jenner had announced in advance:

"Despite the fact that the Federal Bureau of Investigation and other security agencies had reported extensive information about this communist penetration," the report stated, "*little was done by the executive branch* to interrupt Soviet operatives in their ascent in government ... Powerful groups and individuals within the executive branch were at work obstructing and weakening the effort to eliminate Soviet agents ..." (My emphasis.)

In its final conclusion, the committee dropped a hint in the direction of the current occupant of the White House: "Policies and programs laid down by members of this Soviet conspiracy *are still in effect* ..."

Shortly before election day, the report, entitled "Interlocking Subversion in Government Departments," was reprinted by the Republican National Committee. Some 50,000 copies were purchased by McCarthy-backer and Texas oil multi-millionaire H. L. Hunt. Nevertheless, the Democrats scored definite victories in several states. Republican spokesmen conceded that their party was "in trouble." A special congressional election in California's 24th district was still to be held, however, and Attorney General Brownell came to the rescue. In a speech before the Executives Club of Chicago on November 6, Mr. Brownell declared:

"It is a source of humiliation to every American that during the period of the Truman administration the communists were so strikingly successful in infiltrating the government of the United States ... We are now confronted with this problem [of communist infiltration], not because there was any real lack of information available to our predecessors as to the identity of communists in government, but because of the unwillingness of the non-communists ... to face the facts ..."

Mr. Brownell then described the government career

of Harry Dexter White from his employment as a Treasury economist in 1934 to his prominent role as Assistant Secretary of the Treasury and chief technical expert for the government at the Bretton Woods Monetary Conference in 1944.

"Notwithstanding all this, Harry Dexter White was a Russian spy," Brownell declared. "He smuggled secret documents to Russian agents for transmission to Moscow. [He] was known to be a communist spy by the very people who appointed him to the most sensitive and important position he ever held in government service."

As the Attorney General continued to talk, it became increasingly clear that the "very people" to whom he was referring were former President Truman and his principal advisers. Later he flatly said so in response to questions asked him by Democratic Senator John L. McClellan of Arkansas:

QUESTION: When you used the term "people," it applied to former President Truman?

ANSWER: Yes.

QUESTION: That is whom you meant?

ANSWER: Yes.

In the uproar that immediately followed, the voice of the investigator was not wholly lost. Senator Jenner charged Mr. Truman with "trying to protect his cronies and pals even if they might be communists." Investigator Velde, without consulting his fellow committeemen, issued a series of subpoenas at five o'clock in the morning of November 10. The summonses ordered the former President, Supreme Court Justice Tom Clark, Governor James F. Byrnes of South Carolina, a former Secretary of State, and General Harry Vaughan, Mr. Truman's military aide, to appear. Two others, former Secretary of the Treasury, later Chief Justice, Fred M. Vinson and Harry Dexter

White, were beyond the reach of subpoenas. They were dead.

Later the Velde Committee's chief counsel, Robert M. Kunzig, was kind enough to let the Democratic members in on chairman Velde's doings. He told them that plans were afoot to hold a joint televised hearing on the White case with the Jenner Committee. This was regrettably necessary, he explained, because the Senate committee had managed to subpoena General Vaughan before Mr. Velde's process server could reach him. A joint hearing was the only way to "get in the act." Mr. Kunzig offered the congressmen a consolation. A joint inquiry should provide, at least, "a more juicy hearing."

"Hold on to your seats, gentlemen," Mr. Kunzig went on dramatically, "while I tell you about the two other subpoenas we have out. One is for Governor Byrnes and the other is for former President Truman." A process server, he said, was flying to Columbia, South Carolina, to serve Governor Byrnes "to beat the Senate to the punch."

Representative Francis E. Walter, a Democratic member of the committee from Pennsylvania, is the source of these quotations of Mr. Kunzig's unconscious humor. To Mr. Walter, the whole affair seemed not so funny. Long a conservative member of the committee, he declared that the summoning of the former President was the "most incredible, insulting, un-American thing that I have ever encountered in my twenty-one years in Congress."

At his press conference that week, President Eisenhower rebuked Mr. Velde. The President said that he personally would not have subpoenaed the former President. It was inconceivable, he declared, that Mr. Truman had knowingly done anything in the White case to damage

the United States. Attorney General Brownell issued a
new statement at the same time asserting that "there is
no intention of impugning the loyalty of any high official
of the prior administration."

Meanwhile, in Congress pressure was applied on Velde
from all sides. Byrnes, Clark, and Truman all declined
to honor the subpoenas. Senator Jenner rejected the proposal for joint hearings. Republican National Committee
chairman Leonard Hall telephoned Mr. Velde from California in an effort to undo the "confusion" following on
the issuance of the Truman subpoena. It soon became
clear that this was not an act of charity, but an effort
to place the investigation which was to follow in the hands
of Senator Jenner. The New York *Times'* Washington
correspondent, W. H. Lawrence, reported that, following
the severe criticism of Republicans as well as Democrats,
Mr. Velde had agreed to do nothing further until his full
committee could meet. "The Senate Internal Security
Subcommittee," Lawrence wrote on November 12, "has
won a clear field for opening the congressional investigation of the charge . . . that White was a Russian spy."
Flushed with victory, Senator Jenner declared: "The Internal Security Subcommittee is interested only in facts
and is not concerned with political by-play. We intend
to make a complete record of the White case and other
cases in the same careful manner in which our subcommittee has always operated and let Congress and the
American people be the judge of what the true facts are."

While Senator Jenner busied himself with "twenty
years of treason," Mr. McCarthy's subcommittee concentrated on what he later casually referred to as "twenty-
one years of treason." Sometimes the Senator blandly
declared that he was just trying to help his President
clean out the holdovers from the "Truman-Acheson re-

gime." At other moments, he frankly opposed Mr. Eisenhower.

One of these times was when, soon after he took office, the President nominated Charles E. Bohlen, a career diplomat, to be U. S. Ambassador to Moscow. The Senator's opposition failed to block the nomination but, in the process, he seemed to have acquired a taste for investigating the administration's foreign policies.

Shortly after the Bohlen affair ended, the Senator announced that he had negotiated an agreement with Greek ship owners to halt trade in their ships with China and other communist nations. Eisenhower's Mutual Security Agency director, Harold E. Stassen, appeared at a committee hearing and told McCarthy to his face that his action "undermines our enforcement . . . instead of helping our enforcement" of administration policy in the area of East-West trade. Mr. Stassen would have been better advised to check with the President before speaking so bluntly. Senator McCarthy denounced Stassen's remarks, and Eisenhower stated that it perhaps would have been better had Mr. Stassen used the word "infringes" instead of "undermines."

Meanwhile, two McCarthy Committee staff members, the now-famous Messrs. Cohn and Schine, were touring Europe "investigating" the work of government agencies abroad. Their performance was widely criticized in Europe by conservatives and radicals alike. In England, former Prime Minister Clement Attlee's remarks reflected the general impression created by this and other adventures of the committee and its chairman into the foreign policy field. Mr. Attlee wondered out loud who was the more powerful in matters involving foreign affairs, the President or the Senator. McCarthy replied with a demand that England apologize for Mr. Attlee's "cheap" attack on him.

The summer brought no respite. Senator McCarthy demanded and got the resignation of Theodore Kaghan, Deputy Director for Public Affairs of the U. S. High Commissioner for Germany. Subsequently, the Senator attacked the President's nominee for High Commissioner, former Harvard President Dr. James B. Conant. In July and August, he began an inquiry into the Central Intelligence Agency. CIA chief, Allen W. Dulles, brother of the Secretary of State, John Foster Dulles, protested with such vehemence that the Senator was temporarily rebuffed.

The setback held Senator McCarthy in check for only a brief interval. He took his one-man investigation on the road, hearing a disconnected assortment of witnesses in New York, Boston, and Albany. When the Senator was in New York's capital, former President Truman replied to Attorney General Brownell's spy story. He ended with a blast at "mccarthyism."

"It is now evident that the present Administration has fully embraced, for political advantage, mccarthyism," Mr. Truman declared. "I'm not referring to the Senator from Wisconsin—he's only important in that his name has taken on a dictionary meaning in the world. It is the corruption of truth, the abandonment of our historical devotion to fair play."

The Senator at once demanded and got network time for a reply. The speech turned out, however, to be as much an attack on the Eisenhower administration as it was on Mr. Truman.

"... Let's take a look at the Republican Party," the Senator suggested. "Unfortunately, in some cases, our batting average has not been too good. Before looking at some of the cases in which our batting average is zero, let me make it clear that I think that the new administration is doing a job so infinitely better than the Truman-Acheson regime that there is absolutely no comparison ... However, let us glance at a few cases where we struck out ..."

The first case proved to be that of John Paton Davies "on the payroll after eleven months of the Eisenhower administration." Mr. McCarthy's objections to Mr. Davies were that he was "one, part and parcel of the old Acheson-Lattimore-Vincent-White-Hiss group which did so much toward delivering our Chinese friends into communist hands"; and "two ... he lied under oath about his activities in trying to put—listen to this—in trying to put communists and espionage agents in key spots in the Central Intelligence Agency."

Seven months later, the Senator's interest in the CIA was unabated. In the "Army-McCarthy" hearings, he repeatedly referred to "communist infiltration" of the intelligence agency. Throughout the quarrelsome hearings, the Senator made use of the occasion to attack the agency as well as other Executive departments. He implied that only through the information supplied him by "confidential informants" within Mr. Eisenhower's governmental domain could the country be protected. The hearings were officially an inquiry into Army charges that the Senator and staff members Roy Cohn and Francis Carr had used undue influence in an effort to obtain a commission and other favors for former staff-member G. David Schine. The Senator counter-charged that the Army's civilian chief, Army Secretary Robert T. Stevens, had attempted to stop investigations of the Army, using Mr. Schine, an Army Private, as a "hostage." As the hearings drew to a close, he implied that the CIA would be high on the list of his investigations because "the worst situation that we have is not in the military—it is in the CIA." He also charged that the Eisenhower administration probably would have retained Alger Hiss as a State Department officer, if he were not already in prison serving out a sentence for perjury.

With Mr. McCarthy tied down in the four-month-long wrangle with Army Secretary Robert Stevens, it was Senator Jenner's turn to pick up the twenty-first year of "treason" theme. He did so with a cooperative witness. It was another investigation into "interlocking subversion" in the State Department.

"Would it be a fair statement," he asked his first witness, "to say in your relations with the State Department that, during your tour of service, from the memoranda you have received, the United States Department of State was pro-communist?"

The witness, former Assistant Secretary of State Spruille Braden, replied: "I don't know that I would say that..."

"If it was not pro-communist, there was something radically wrong?" Jenner prodded.

"My feeling was there were relatively few communists, but there were an awful lot of state interventionists, collectivists, 'do-gooders,' misinformed idealists and whatnot, that were easily led and were in effect the puppets of the unknown," Mr. Braden testified.

QUESTION: Do you not think there has been a reform since that time?

ANSWER: I haven't been able to see it. I don't think so...

QUESTION: By and large, do you still have the same people there?

ANSWER: I think so. That is my impression.

As the target date for adjournment of the 83rd Congress approached, Speaker Martin's hopes seemed thoroughly frustrated. The investigators had run away with the show.

6

MR. VELDE,
INVESTIGATOR-AT-LARGE

"MR. [ARTIE] SHAW: *I just wish you could come out on the road with me sometime and see—*
"[REP. KIT] CLARDY: *We have been on the road, too.*"
—Hearings, House Committee on Un-American Activities, Investigation of Communist Activities in the New York City Area, May 4, 1953.

HAROLD HIMMEL VELDE, chairman of the 83rd Congress' House Committee on Un-American Activities, doesn't talk much, or at least not much for a representative from Illinois. This may be because he is more in the habit of listening. He used to work for the FBI as a specialist in wire-tapping. Or it may be because when he does say something it frequently proves embarrassing.

As soon as he was made chairman of the House Committee, Mr. Velde announced how the committee would henceforth operate.

"It's a lot better to wrongly accuse one person of being a communist," he told a television audience on February 8, 1953, "than to allow so many to get away with such communist acts as those that have brought us to the point of World War III."

Robert L. Kunzig, chief counsel to the committee, seems to have applied his chairman's words literally. The committee's 1953 report declared that "*a majority* of the [280] witnesses subpoenaed refused to affirm or deny their alleged membership in the Communist Party." This was evidently too legalistic a wording for lawyer Kunzig. He subsequently informed a luncheon meeting of the All-American Conference to Combat Communism that, to quote a New York *Times* reporter, "*every one* of the 280 witnesses before the Velde Committee last year had either admitted communist activity or invoked the Fifth Amendment." (My emphasis in both quotations.) Yet in one hearing, a member moved to have "the record show ... that this committee has no record of any Communist Party affiliation or membership" by the witness. The motion carried unanimously. In another, the witness flatly denied past or present membership. Neither used the Fifth Amendment.

A soft-spoken, lanky six-footer, Mr. Velde has come a long way from his FBI days. He was a county judge for two years before he was elected Republican representative from Lincoln's Illinois congressional district in 1948. The little he has since had to say has been rather contradictory. In 1949, he and two other Republicans on the committee objected vigorously to a proposal to investigate alleged communist propaganda in textbooks.

"The committee [is] proceeding down the same road which led the Nazis to the infamous book-burnings," Mr. Velde and his Republican confrères charged.

Three years later, he introduced a bill requiring the Librarian of Congress to mark each of the Library's millions of books, pamphlets and recordings so as to identify which of them was "subversive" and to compile a list of them for the guidance of libraries throughout the country.

On another occasion he charged that "the influence of Mrs. Roosevelt in promotion of communism and immorality and indecency among so-called minority groups in Washington ought to be investigated . . ." Some of his colleagues took exception to this remark, so Mr. Velde, a month or so later, explained that he had not intended to say anything reflecting on the widow of the late President.

As the first session of the 83rd Congress got under way, the new chairman announced that educators would be investigated. Mrs. Agnes Meyer, wife of Eugene Meyer, publisher of the Washington *Post*, criticized this proposal. Mr. Velde promptly called Mrs. Meyer an "intellectual pinko" and accused her of expressing "profound admiration for the Soviet Union" in a signed letter published in Moscow's *Pravda*. Mrs. Meyer did some investigating of her own. The letter, she revealed, had been signed by a Mrs. G. S. Mayer, of British Columbia, Canada. Examining this evidence, the chairman reluctantly backed down, declaring, however, that the error was caused by a communist plot:

"Because of the tremendous underground network of the Communist Party which works through well-meaning individuals by deceit and treachery, honest mistakes are sometimes made in the investigation of communism," he told the press. He announced that he had fired the investigator responsible for misinforming him.

Later that year, Mr. Velde even incurred the wrath of Herbert Philbrick. Mr. Philbrick, an FBI agent within the Communist Party for nine years, testified at a secret committee hearing in New York City on July 6, 1953. Mr. Philbrick explained that he had "no legal evidence" of any clergyman's membership in the Communist Party, but he told the committee that three clergymen in the

Boston area were, respectively, "under Communist Party discipline . . . worked with us on Communist Party projects . . . [or] worked with the Communist Party . . ."

When the committee de-secretized the testimony, there was an explosion. The ministers hotly denied the accusations. Mr. Philbrick, it was reported, phoned the committee and "blew his top." He apparently got little satisfaction, for on September 30, 1953, he declared the disclosure was premature and a "bad mistake."

"I think they went off half cocked," he said. His testimony, he explained, was given "in the nature of leads and tips to be followed for further facts. My information was given in executive session. I didn't expect it to be released until all the facts had been assembled and the probe completed. The committee has played right into the hands of the communists, communist sympathizers and the left-wing element."

The witness' indignation is justified by the record.

"Mr. Philbrick," said committee counsel Kunzig at one point, "seeing as we are here in executive session, and this testimony being confidential, do you feel you could tell the committee the names of these ministers in the Boston area whom you, as you said, have a pretty good idea were the ones that you feel were the members of the Communist Party?"

Early in 1954, another row developed within the committee. It seemed that the chief investigator, Louis J. Russell, had borrowed money from screen actor Edward G. Robinson, who had testified before the committee in 1952. Cleared of communist taint, Robinson said Russell had borrowed $300 a year before his (Robinson's) last appearance as a "friendly witness." Mr. Velde once more was obliged to announce the firing of a staff man. The committee investigated. Later it announced that there was nothing wrong with the loan transaction and that the matter was therefore closed.

No sooner was one difficulty disposed of than another arose to plague "Judge" Velde, as he likes to be called. On March 24, Representative Bernard W. Kearney of New York, next in Republican rank to Mr. Velde, boiled over. The situation in the committee was "rotten and intolerable," he told the press. He said he believed reports that Leslie Scott, a committee staff-member receiving some $7,000 yearly, had been assigned to checking Mr. Velde's Illinois constituents in preparation for the chairman's campaign for re-election. The committee is overloaded with staff, the upstate New Yorker said, adding that about $200,000 of the $300,000 appropriated for 1954 had already been spent (by the end of March). Mr. Kearney declared that investigators were "jockeying for advantage over one another, trying to get raises which are undesirable and engaging in back-biting."

"We recently had two days of hearings in Chicago," the irate congressman said. "Five witnesses were questioned and five investigators went along at the committee's expense."

The "road-show" style of the committee's work is nothing new. At one of several appearances in New York City, the traveling showmanship of the committee was the subject of a friendly exchange between band leader and witness Artie Shaw, and Representative Kit Clardy, a Michigan Republican member. Mr. Shaw had been explaining the error of his earlier ways: "I hate to admit I was a dupe," he said. "I don't like the word, and I certainly don't like to have to admit publicly I wasn't responsible for my behavior, but I think that just about accurately states my position . . ."

MR. CLARDY: And now that your eyes are opened to how you have been duped and misled in the past, I take it that you do appreciate this opportunity of appearing before the committee and getting your story before the people of the United States?

MR. SHAW: I certainly do, sir. I welcomed the opportunity before I came here, and now that I am finished I am very glad that I had the opportunity to state my views and state my present status, my present position.

MR. CLARDY: I am unable to see why our invitation— the latchstring was always out—escaped you, but perhaps you have been so immersed in your musical career—

MR. SHAW: I just wish you could come out on the road with me some time and see—

MR. CLARDY: We have been on the road, too.

The committee stayed on the road. It held hearings in Los Angeles, San Francisco, New York, Albany, N. Y., Columbus, Ohio, Philadelphia, Pa., Chicago, and Lansing, Mich. Two of the members are from California, and there happen to be one each from New York, Ohio, Pennsylvania, Illinois, and Michigan. Some unkind critics have pointed to this coincidence as evidence that the committee is sometimes used for the personal political advantage of its members. During the 83rd Congress' lifetime, however, the committee held no hearings in the home states of two of its nine members, the gentlemen from Missouri and Tennessee.

The committee is not uninterested in showmanship itself. Moving into New York City last year, Mr. Velde announced: "During these hearings, the committee hopes to obtain valuable information relative to the extent and success of subversive influence in the field of entertainment and education ..."

The hearings in Gotham were fairly representative of Mr. Velde on the road. Thirty-two witnesses were heard in two separate sittings, one in May, another in July. All told, the hearings consumed nine days. At first, the committee divided its attention between entertainment and education.

The first witness was band leader Artie Shaw. Mr. Shaw was nothing if not entertaining.

"Are you aware, Mr. Shaw—I suppose you are—" a questioner asked, "that the committee has been making an investigation over a period of time of communist activities in the entertainment field with special reference to the moving picture enterprise?"

Mr. Shaw indicated that the examiner supposed rightly. Then the questioning got down to the serious business of the day. Frank S. Tavenner, assistant committee counsel, asked whether Mr. Shaw knew a Mr. Paul Perlin. Mr. Shaw could not remember him. Mr. Tavenner said that Mr. Perlin was a communist organizer of studio workers and a lecturer in Marxism.

MR. TAVENNER: ... Now, does that information relating to Paul Perlin help to refresh your recollection?

The entertainer was anxious to oblige:

MR. SHAW: I could say something ... which may easily implicate this man, but I never knew him by name if it is the same man ...

The band leader told a complicated story of how he came to attend meetings of individuals he supposed were communists at which matters of policy concerning the Screen Writers Guild were discussed. He had done so, he said, because an individual who did not give his name had called on him and asked him, "How would you like to see how [the group] operates? I would appreciate it if you would see how it operates, and you will see other people you know there."

"I thought, 'What can I lose?' I was curious. I'll be perfectly honest about it. I was curious," Shaw told the committee.

Shaw said that he "resented fiercely" the statement of the committee witness "who says I was a member because I was at these meetings." To protect its witness, the committee questioned Mr. Shaw sharply:

MR. CLARDY: . . . You had some sympathies with what you generally understood to be the communist objectives—

MR. SHAW: I don't think—

MR. CLARDY (*continuing*): Or you wouldn't have attended those meetings?

MR. SHAW: I don't think that is true, sir.

MR. CLARDY: Well, what sympathies did you have with what—

MR. SHAW: The Fair Employment Practices Committee—the FEPC.

MR. CLARDY: That is one specific thing. Is that all?

MR. SHAW: That was the main issue . . . The only other thing—temporary thing—was when Gerald L. K. Smith was coming to town. There was a big civic furor over that . . . That sort of thing I was very angry about. I just came out of the war, and I was very angry about a lot of things. There was a lot of black-marketeering and an awful lot of other things going on that I didn't like . . .

MR. CLARDY: And based on that you were willing at least to explore what the Communist Party had to offer?

MR. SHAW: Well, based on that and—

MR. CLARDY: Just answer the question directly . . .

MR. SHAW: That's right.

MR. CLARDY: And you did?

MR. SHAW: I did.

This settled, the committee reverted to the Marxist lecture which Mr. Shaw said he once attended. Would the band leader describe the substance of the lecture?

MR. SHAW: Well, yes, the substance of the last lecture meeting . . . It had to do with international policies of Stalin as against Roosevelt and Churchill—and it was all pretty big grand strategy stuff. I can't tell you what that was about because I have no experience on those matters. I have never been politically minded —a politically minded man, anyway, except on specific issues. I mean, I have joined organizations which had to do with words like democracy and peace. And I am at the point now where I am afraid to join any organization. I haven't joined an organization for three years because I don't know what any word stands for any more.

The questioning kept returning to the basic grist of the committee mill: names.

MR. TAVENNER: Did Hy Kraft attend any of these meetings?

MR. SHAW: Never. He was never at any of these meetings; but I would have suspected him of being a communist, although I didn't know he was a communist.

MR. CLARDY: You say you would have suspected him of being a communist?

MR. SHAW: I would have suspected him of being one, because there were—I felt—communists in the meetings . . .

＊ ＊ ＊ ＊ ＊

MR. VELDE: And you would be willing to give us the names of those you remember in executive session?

MR. SHAW: Actually they are names I am sure you know.

＊ ＊ ＊ ＊ ＊

MR. VELDE: Mr. Shaw . . . do you recall who it was who requested the use of your name as a sponsor to this organization?

MR. SHAW: Gee, I wish I could.

Endeavoring to explain how it happened that his name appeared as a sponsor of several organizations disapproved by the committee, Mr. Shaw got himself into difficulties with the committee but not with the audience.

MR. SHAW: . . . My mail is filled with such requests—anything from a non-ethereal symphony on up or down. I mean, I get these all the time. Some seem rather worthy causes, and it is very hard sometimes to turn them down . . . It may turn out to have been a mistake. I have now learned it is better to be sure . . . I had this discussion with a man not long ago, when he asked me how I could have been naive enough to join the Congress—the World Peace Congress—put my name on that. I said to him, 'Do you know any other peace congress I can join? I want peace.' He says, 'That is the com-

munist inspired one.' I said, 'Get me a Republican
Party inspired one and I'll join that. I don't care
which one.'—

MR. VELDE: The committee must have order—

MR. SHAW: That wasn't meant—

MR. VELDE (*continuing*): In the hearings, and we
will countenance no further demonstrations favorable
or unfavorable.

MR. SHAW: I wasn't bidding for any applause, I
assure you.

MR. VELDE: I am sure you weren't, Mr. Shaw.

MR. CLARDY: Well, Mr. Shaw, as these organizations
you joined were one by one shown to have been communist inspired, don't you think it would have been
the best wisdom to have in writing withdrawn and
disassociated yourself from them?

MR. SHAW: I see that now. I do see that now.

But the congressmen were not sure that the witness
did see it just he way he should:

MR. CLARDY: Didn't the fact the Russians were raising so much Cain with us . . . in some way alert you to
the fact that any organization dealing with friendship
. . . with Russia was suspect?

MR. SHAW: I can answer that by saying not since
then will you find my name on anything of any kind
outside of the American Federation of Musicians.

MR. CLARDY: What you are saying is you want us to
believe that you were extremely naive, shall we say,
at that time . . . and didn't investigate thoroughly
enough to understand what it was all about?

MR. SHAW: I investigated only to the extent of seeing
peoples' names on there that I thought were perfectly
all right and that I still do in most cases think they

are perfectly all right—and on the basis of that I put my name on it. Since then, I have never signed anything because, as I said earlier, I wouldn't sign anything today unless I had the advice of seven lawyers and the granting of permission or clearance by this committee.

MR. CLARDY: I take it your wastebasket is your biggest file on these things, things like this today?

MR. SHAW: Yes, sir, and it has been awfully full for three years now.

Gordon H. Scherer, Republican Representative from Ohio, a committee member, interposed:

MR. SCHERER: You realize then, Mr. Shaw, you were thoroughly duped by the communist group then, do you not?

MR. SHAW: In this communist thing, I certainly was.

MR. SCHERER: Not this particular thing, but in all of these matters?

MR. SHAW: Yes, sir...I am at a point today if someone says, "Here is a committee for personal freedom," I don't want any part of it...

Representative Clyde Doyle, California Democrat, is considered the most liberal member of the Committee. He seems to have thought the committee might profit by Mr. Shaw's advice, in view of his broad political experience:

MR. DOYLE: ...Have you any suggestions to make to the United States Congress...? Have you ever thought in the area of whether or not there is any remedial legislation which ought to be enacted by your Congress?

MR. SHAW: Yes, sir, I have ... It seems to me something could be done ... This haze of rumor started ... about three years ago. It began to affect me ... very seriously. At that time I was approached by various people in the radio and television ... fields ... and they would say, 'Do you realize the cloud you are under? Do you realize you ought to clear yourself of all this suspicion?' And I would ask every one of them, 'How do I clear myself? What way is there?' I have had to wait three years to ask to appear before this committee so I can clear myself in this sense, and I thought there ought to be somewhere some group, some responsible official party designated by the Congress of the United States to which people like I [sic] could come and appeal, without having to wait to be subpoenaed, where I could go and say, 'Could I come and testify as to my part in this so I can once and for all make it clear where I stand now, and where I stood at that time?'

* * * * *

MR. [DONALD L.] JACKSON [Republican of California]: ... The committee is just as interested in getting people out from under a cloud, if they are unjustly there, as they are in pointing out the truth and facts of the Communist Party membership when they exist. I think that is a very important fact which is sometimes overlooked by critics of the committee.

MR. SHAW: It is not being overlooked by me today, sir. I feel very glad, and I am actually—I suppose it's difficult to say—I hate to have to come in and plead any kind of exculpation because of what I have done in the past. I know ignorance is no excuse, but in these cases I have never broken laws. So I think I can plead ignorance in regard to having made a great mistake—or great mistakes—in judgment about what I was lending myself to.

MR. JACKSON: I wouldn't even sign a check without two thoughts these days.

In its report, the committee expressed "great appreciation" for the "full and informative testimony" of eleven of the witnesses who appeared in New York. Mr. Shaw, it must be reported, was not among them.

For three days more the committee took testimony, now from a teacher, now a writer, a producer, an actor. As always, names were sought from every witness who would answer. Some typical questions: "Who recruited you into the [Communist] Party? Do you recall any other names of members of that particular group? Will you list them clearly for the committee, please? Who else? Can you spell it? Any others? May I ask the counsel to inquire more specifically as to the identification of the person she is naming, if she can give other identification, such as the address, occupation? Did you know a Mr. Blank?"

In its report to Congress, the committee indicated that questioning of this kind had yielded the names of 229 persons "identified as Communist Party members during the . . . hearings in New York City." Two columns of names follow, the left-hand column, appropriately enough, being the list of those "identified," and the right-hand column showing which of the committee's friendly witnesses did the identifying. In some cases, the person is "identified," but the accuser is not named. Instead there appears to the right, the notation: "investigation identifying Mr. Blank as a member of the Communist Party has not been made public."

Witnesses who deny membership are listed just the

same. Lee Sabinson, a producer of Broadway plays, swore he was not a member of the Party, and stood on the Fifth Amendment regarding past membership. Mr. Sabinson demonstrated an independence of mind that may have damned him in the committee's book.

The producer testified that it was possible that he had publicly favored the seating of Simon W. Gerson in the City Council of New York. Mr. Gerson, a Communist, was proposed by his party to take the seat made vacant by the death of Communist Councilman Peter V. Cacchione. New York law provided that the unexpired term of a deceased councilman was to be served by a successor appointed by the late councilman's party. When Mr. Sabinson indicated his approval of the law, even when applied to communists, the committee was scandalized:

MR. SCHERER: You said today you would urge it?

MR. SABINSON: If the people elected a communist and that communist died, then I think he should be replaced by a communist.

MR. CLARDY: Today?

MR. SABINSON: Yes, if the people elected the man. That is the will of the American people in this instance.

MR. KUNZIG [committee counsel]: So, if the will of the American people were to elect communists and have a completely communist government of the United States of America, that would be entirely satisfactory to you?

MR. SABINSON: Whatever [is] the will of the American people is perfectly satisfactory to me.

MR. KUNZIG: Including a communist government in New York, Washington or anywhere?

MR. SABINSON: Whatever [is] the will of the American people is perfectly satisfactory with me, because the people are sovereign.

MR. KUNZIG: I think you have made your position completely clear.

On May 7th, Robert Rossen, a producer, director and writer of motion pictures, appeared as a voluntary witness. He had previously appeared on June 25, 1951, but had refused to answer questions.

Why had Mr. Rossen decided this time to answer? "I did a lot of thinking," he declared. "I don't think, after two years of thinking, that any one individual can even indulge himself in the luxury of individual morality ... It's my duty and my right to appear here today after much thinking and give you whatever information I have. It is not my right to judge as to whether or not that information has any value. This is in your hands."

In the testimony that followed, he was asked to identify as communists some 65 individuals.

Choreographer Jerome Robbins was also called. Mr. Robbins testified that one of the reasons he left the Communist Party was "that the artist was not free; that he wasn't—that he became a puppet to the communist line, communist propaganda." Later there was this exchange:

MR. DOYLE: ... Now, let me say this, too: you are in a wonderful place, through your art, your music, your talent, which God blessed you with, to perhaps be very vigorous and positive in promoting Americanism in contrast to communism. Let me suggest to you that you use that great talent ... to put into ballets in some way, to put into music in some way, that interpretation.

MR. ROBBINS: Sir, all my works have been acclaimed for its [sic] American quality, particularly.

MR. DOYLE: I realize that, but let me urge you to even put more of that in it where you can appropriately.

The record indicates that there was no response from the witness.

But the most spectacular witness was one whose declared desire to cooperate was not to Chairman Velde's liking. In vain, Mr. Velde endeavored to confine the witness, motion picture actor Lionel Stander, to brief answers.

MR. STANDER: I am not charged with anything, am I?

MR. VELDE: Now, Mr. Stander—

MR. STANDER: Does this committee charge me with being a communist?

MR. VELDE: Mr. Stander, will you let me tell you whether you are charged with being a communist? Will you be quiet just for a minute while I will tell you what you are here for?

MR. STANDER: Yes; I would like to hear.

MR. VELDE: You are here to give us information . . . which will enable us . . . to investigate reports regarding subversive activities in the United States.

MR. STANDER: Well, I am more than willing to cooperate—

MR. VELDE: Now, just a minute.

MR. STANDER: Because I have—I know of some subversive activities in the entertainment industry and, elsewhere in the country.

MR. VELDE: Mr. Stander, the committee is interested—

MR. STANDER: If you are interested, I can tell you some right now.

MR. VELDE: (continuing): Primarily in any subversive knowledge you have—

MR. STANDER: And I have knowledge of some subversive action.

MR. VELDE(*continuing*): In the overthrow of the
government.

MR. STANDER: I don't know about the overthrow of
the government. This committee has been investigating
15 years so far, and hasn't even found one act of
violence.

MR. VELDE: Now, the record will speak for itself.

MR. STANDER: Well, I have been reading the record.

MR. VELDE: That is entirely—

MR. STANDER: I know of some subversion, and I
can help the committee if it is really interested.

MR. VELDE: Mr. Stander—

MR. STANDER: I know of a group of fanatics who are
desperately trying to undermine the Constitution of the
United States by depriving artists and others of life,
liberty, and pursuit of happiness without due process
of law. If you are interested in that, I would like to
tell you about it. I can tell names, and I can cite
instances, and I am one of the first victims of it; and
if you are interested in that . . .

MR. VELDE: Now, Mr. Stander, let me—

MR. STANDER: And these people are engaged in the
conspiracy, outside all the legal processes, to undermine our very fundamental American concepts upon
which our entire system of jurisprudence exists—

MR. VELDE: Now, Mr. Stander—

MR. STANDER: And who also—

MR. VELDE: Let me tell you this: You are a witness
before this committee—

MR. STANDER: Well, if you are interested—

MR. VELDE (*continuing*): A committee of the Congress of the United States—

MR. STANDER (*continuing*): I am willing to tell you—

MR. VELDE (*continuing*): And you are in the same position as any other witness before this committee—

MR. STANDER (*continuing*): I am willing to tell you about these activities—

MR. VELDE (*continuing*): Regardless of your standing in the motion-picture world—

MR. STANDER (*continuing*): Which I think are subversive.

MR. VELDE: (*continuing*): Or for any other reason. No witness can come before this committee and insult the committee—

MR. STANDER: Is this an insult to the committee—

MR. VELDE (*continuing*): And continue to—

MR. STANDER (*continuing*): When I inform the committee I know of subversive activities which are contrary to the Constitution?

MR. VELDE: Now, Mr. Stander, unless you begin to answer these questions and act like a witness in a reasonable, dignified manner, under the rules of the committee, I will be forced to have you removed from this room.

MR. STANDER: Well, I—

MR. CLARDY: Mr. Stander, may I say—

MR. STANDER: I am deeply shocked, Mr. Chairman.

MR. CLARDY: Mr. Stander, let me—

MR. STANDER: Let me explain myself. I don't mean to be contemptuous of this committee at all.

MR. VELDE: Will you—

MR. STANDER: I want to cooperate with it. You said something—you said you would like me to cooperate with you in your attempt to unearth subversive activities. I know of such subversive activities. I began to tell you about them, and I am shocked by your cutting me off. You don't seem to be interested in the sort of subversive activities I know about.

MR. VELDE: You will be asked questions relative to subversive activities by counsel.

MR. STANDER: All right.

MR. VELDE: Just let him ask you.

MR. STANDER: All right. Let him ask me, and I will be glad to answer. And I am not a dupe, or a dope, or a moe, or a schmoe, and everything I did—I was absolutely conscious of what I was doing, and I am not ashamed of everything I said in public or private; and I am very proud of my war record, my private record as a citizen and my public record as an entertainer.

To be subpoenaed, Mr. Stander declared, is tantamount to being blacklisted in the television and motion picture industries.

MR. CLARDY: Why did you want to appear before the committee so badly then if that is the case?

MR. STANDER: Because I was told by my agent if I appeared before the committee and the committee was a fair committee and allowed me to refute Lawrence's testimony that I would be able to get back in television and motion pictures. I had made eleven television shows in a row and one of the biggest TV agencies and producers had told my agent that if I went—could get before the committee and could again swear under oath that I wasn't, I would have my own TV program which meant over $150,000 a year to me.

MR. CLARDY: Mr. Stander—

MR. STANDER: So I had a hundred and fifty thousand buck motive—

MR. CLARDY: Mr. Stander, will you subside?

MR. STANDER: For coming before the committee.

The chairman has more than once condemned this notion. The committee, he has said, is not interested in the blacklisting of any witness. At a Washington hearing, he rebuked Professor John H. Reynolds of Florida University on this point. The professor had cited the Fifth Amendment in response to questions regarding former membership in the Communist Party. He had also declared, however, that he did *not* think members of that Party should be free to teach in American universities, because they might be "biased or partisan." Professor Reynolds was opposed to the committee's intervention in such cases, however:

MR. REYNOLDS: . . .I think it would be up to the State University, or whatever university it was, to see for themselves. I think it is a question for the university itself, not a question for governmental authorities to investigate. I just don't agree with that. It means that the state interferes in the university itself. I just don't agree with it.

MR. DOYLE: Do you think our American universities in which you have taught are equipped ... to investigate subversive activities of members of the college staff, if there are such? ...

MR. REYNOLDS: I think they can tell what a teacher is.

MR. DOYLE: What?

MR. REYNOLDS: Tell by his teaching. The university can tell by his teaching.

MR. DOYLE: In other words, go into the classroom and sit there and police the person to see what he is teaching?

MR. REYNOLDS: I would prefer the university to do that rather than the committee. I really would. I don't mean any disrespect for this committee. I mean, I object to it on the ground of a governmental institution interfering with the university and its teaching staff.

MR. VELDE: I think, Professor, that you are trying to leave the inference that this committee is engaged in investigating un-American activities, subversive activities in colleges and universities for the purpose of acquiring or setting up a blacklist of teachers in the American colleges and universities. I assure you that the committee has no intention of doing anything like that at all . . .

In another hearing, the chairman made a similar pronouncement to a witness employed by United Press Associations as a TV script writer:

"But what the committee is doing is trying me by publicity and endangering my employment," the witness declared.

"I assure you the committee has no interest at all in your employment," Mr. Velde replied. Then, setting some kind of a record for instantaneous self-contradiction, he went on: "We are out to determine, to ascertain facts relative to subversive activities in this country; and I believe—of course, I cannot speak for United Press—if you would furnish us the information that we are asking that probably your job would be a lot more safe than it is at the present time—"

United Press fired the witness the day after he testified.

7

THE BISHOP AND
THE CONGRESSMEN

"The committee, in its work, accumulates all pertinent information relative to any given individual whose name is listed in the files. That is the only way by which one can determine the philosophical bent of any given individual."
—House Committee hearings, Donald L. Jackson in debate with Bishop G. Bromley Oxnam.

"JUDGE" VELDE'S FLAIR for saying the wrong thing brought the coals of ecclesiastical fire down on his head on another occasion last year. On the radio program "Reporters' Round-up," Chairman Velde unexpectedly announced that it was "entirely possible" that the House Committee would investigate the churches. There was, he declared, "a field" for investigation into religion. Such an inquiry would probably "include individual members of the cloth, including some who seem to have devoted more time to politics than they have to the ministry."

"We would not be investigating the churches, any more than we are now engaged in investigating the colleges and universities," he said. "We are engaged at present in investigating the extent of communists in colleges—for the benefit of the colleges themselves and the people—and we would be doing the same, in relation to churches."

The next day, members of the House Committee, whom Mr. Velde had not troubled to consult in advance regarding the proposed investigation, repudiated the chairman's statements. Mr. Velde shifted from high to low gear: "I want to make it clear that no investigation of communists among the clergy ... is ... contemplated at this time by me, or as far as I know, by any members of the committee ... This statement does not, however, preclude the possibility of such investigations in the future ..."

These words failed to allay the anger of some of Mr. Velde's fellow congressmen and of members of the clergy. The next day, Representative Franklin D. Roosevelt, Jr., a Democrat from New York, introduced a resolution in the House calling for the removal of Mr. Velde as committee chairman. Representative Francis E. Walter, senior Democratic member of the committee from Pennsylvania, took a compromise course of action. Calling on committee members of both parties, he put through a resolution in the committee barring the announcement or commencement of any new investigation without the approval of the full committee. Even Chairman Velde voted in favor of it.

Meanwhile, G. Bromley Oxnam, Methodist Bishop of Washington, D.C., had denounced Velde's proposed investigation. Bishop Oxnam wondered for the benefit of reporters whether the gentleman from Illinois' "new interest" had some connection with criticisms "recently made by the clergy of methods used in investigations." A week later, Republican committee member Donald L. Jackson of California took the floor of the House to attack Bishop Oxnam:

"Bishop Bromley Oxnam has been to the communist front what Man O'War was to thoroughbred horseracing," Mr. Jackson metaphorized, "and no one except the good Bishop pays much attention to his fulminations these days. Having served God on Sunday and the communist front for the balance of the week over such a long period of time, it is no great wonder that the Bishop sees an investigating committee in every vestry. If reprinting Bishop Oxnam's record of aid and comfort to the communist front would serve any useful purpose, I would ask permission to insert it here, but suffice it to say that the record is available to any member who cares to request it from the committee."

Someone besides the "good Bishop," however, did pay attention. Two days after he spoke, Mr. Jackson reversed himself by declining to make the Bishop's committee dossier public. Responding to a request for the record, the congressman wrote: "The detailed documentation is very voluminous and would be much too lengthy to include in a letter of this kind. However, in general, Bishop Oxnam is alleged to have been associated in the past with the following groups and organizations which have been cited as subversive and communist."

The influential Washington *Post* then entered the picture. It obtained the full committee dossier, turned it over to Bishop Oxnam and invited him to comment on each of 24 items that it contained. The Washington *Post* published the dossier with the Bishop's comments on it, and editorialized on the incident as follows:

"The Washington *Post* publishes today a calm, factual, detailed analysis by Bishop G. Bromley Oxnam of a dossier on himself in the files of the House Committee on Un-American Activities. Bishop Oxnam's point-by-point refutation of the accusations, innuendoes and insinuations contained in the dossier, his exposure of its slovenliness and downright fraudulence, reveal a dangerous sort of evil which the House of Representatives ought not to countenance. What is a committee of Congress doing with a compilation of this sort of groundless gossip about a distinguished minister of religion?"

The dossier was indeed a remarkable document. Among other things, it charged the Bishop with membership on the national committee of the American Civil Liberties Union, an organization which the committee itself had formerly declared "has never been cited as red dominated or as communist..." Much emphasis in the dossier was placed on the frequent occasions on which the Bishop has assailed "witch hunts" and criticized the committee. The dossier also listed him as having declared that the United States must not "flirt with Franco to stop Stalin" or "ally ourselves with political, economic or ecclesiastical reaction."

"The committee apparently regards as 'subversive' any opinion of which it disapproves. The dossier compiled on Bishop Oxnam is the kind of dossier compiled by the political police behind the Iron Curtain," the Post editorial concluded. "It does not represent investigation, it represents a naked and ugly attempt at intimidation."

Referring to the release of such a dossier, Bishop Oxnam suggested that the committee had an obligation to determine whether its contents were true or false.

"But nothing of the sort takes place. When pinned down and asked explicitly, and only then," the Bishop said, "committee members piously assert to an inquirer that the report 'carries no conclusion of this committee' and that the committee never vouches for the correctness of any newspaper item.

"This is deceit at its most vicious. What usually happens is demonstrated by the letter written last month by Representative Jackson in response to a request for the information which he said was available about me.

"He did not make the file available, but only hinted darkly at its detail and volume. He then went on to list the twelve agencies that appear in the summary of my [dossier], including those with which I never had any relationship. He included, of course, the *Daily Worker* and the *New Masses*, where my alleged relationship was the fact that my name appeared in some news item carried by them.

"The letter clearly conveys to the reader that 'detailed documentation,' which is 'very voluminous' lies back of these reports," the Bishop asserted. "This letter, on the stationery of the Congress of the United States, House of Representatives, signed by a congressman who is a member of the committee, is patently designed to convey the conclusion that the material is an opinion of the committee ... A citizen ... assumes that the material does in fact represent the judgment and conclusion of the committee ... These reports have been reprinted by private agencies and circulated as the judgment of the committee, as I have had occasion to know in my own case.

"The committee, I suggest, is using methods that in ordinary parlance would be called blackmail."

The Bishop demanded that he be given an opportunity to testify in his own defense.

The committee, meanwhile, pursued other investigatory interests. It looked as if, for once, the force of public opinion had prevailed, and that Mr. Velde meant what he said in declaring that no investigation of the clergy was contemplated. After its first appearance in New York, however, in May, 1953, the committee suddenly decided to return early in July. It conducted a series of secret sessions on July 6, 7 and 8 and again on July 13 and 14. Each day the press was duly informed—sometimes by a "reliable source," sometimes by a committee member—as to what was taking place behind the closed doors of the hearing room. "Several" American clergymen had been named as communists by two former communist officials, Benjamin Gitlow and Joseph Zack Kornfeder, the public was told. The press reported that Kornfeder was described as an "intimate of Stalin." Representative Clardy said that the testimony was of "extreme importance" and proved that the communists had "planned to and did infiltrate the clergy."

"We now have the names of a number of clergymen, some of them prominent," Representative Scherer told reporters, "in more than one denomination and in various parts of the country, who have been identified as communists or fellow travellers, though Bishop Oxnam said we could not name one."

Only then did the committee grant Bishop Oxnam a hearing in the following week—three months after Mr. Jackson's speech. The hearing began at 2:30 p.m. on July 21, 1953. It was a rare occasion. The entire committee was on hand to hear the Bishop. In addition to Chairman Velde, the Bishop gazed upon Republican members Bernard W. Kearney, of New York, Donald L. Jackson, of California, Kit Clardy of Michigan, Gordon H. Scherer of Ohio, and, on the Democratic side, Francis E. Walter of Pennsylvania, Morgan M. Moulder of Missouri, Clyde Doyle of California, and James B. Frazier, Jr., of Tennessee. When Mr. Velde rapped the gavel for the last time, announcing that the session was over, it was 12:20 a.m. on the following morning. The printed record contains more than 100,000 congressional and episcopal words, not to mention forty-two exhibits.

"Bishop Oxnam has informed the committee that information in its files relating to him is in error and that he has been in some way harmed as a result of public disclosure of such information," Chairman Velde announced for the benefit of the audience, all nine committee members, and six members of the staff gathered for the occasion. "... The hearing today should not be interpreted by anyone as an investigation initiated by the Congress into the field of religion. It is incidental to this hearing that the witness is a man of the cloth ..."

Taking the stand, the Bishop declared that his purpose in appearing was "to secure redress for the damage done to me by the release of information in the files of this committee ... If a member of the committee can be so misled by this material," he declared, referring to Representative Jackson, "it is no wonder that uninformed citizens are similarly misled."

The Bishop quoted Mr. Jackson as having said in a debate: "The committee, in its work, accumulates all pertinent information relative to any given individual whose name is listed in the files. That is the only way by which one can determine the philosophical bent of any given individual."

Bishop Oxnam did not question the propriety of the committee's determining "the philosophical bent" of Americans. He asked, instead, why, if that were the case, "the individual who clipped derogatory statements" neglected to include his membership on the wartime Civilian Advisory Committee to the Navy, his award of the Certificate of Appreciation from the Navy, the award of the Order of the Phoenix given him by the King of Greece, his membership on the President's Commission on Higher

Education, his offices in the Federal Council of the Churches of Christ, his co-presidency of the World Council of Churches, and his secretaryship of the Council of Bishops of the Methodist Church.

"This might be called pertinent information," he observed. ". . . . We cannot beat down the communist menace by bearing false witness against fellow Americans. The communist wants a divided America, an America whose citizens are suspicious of each other, an America without trust, an America open to infiltration. I believe this committee will wish to end a practice that plays into communist hands."

The Bishop's disillusionment was not long in coming. As soon as he had finished his statement, the grilling began. Not content to review the charges which the Bishop had already demolished in the Washington *Post,* committee counsel Kunzig served up a mixture of accusations, some already released, others entirely new. He introduced evidence that Bishop Oxnam had written an article for, and had been an editorial advisor to, a magazine variously called *The Protestant Digest* and *The Protestant.*

BISHOP OXNAM: I was never an editor. I was on the board called the Advisory Board. The board never met, as a matter of fact. One ought not to be related to any board that does not meet, but I was on that board. I did resign in 1942. I think the Attorney General's list came out, if I recall correctly, in December 1947.

MR. KUNZIG: I might add that the lists are retroactive.

BISHOP OXNAM: I have heard that but I have never been able to understand how a list can become retroactive in the sense of saying that an organization was subversive twenty years ago because somebody found it subversive twenty years later. I do not understand that...

Then Mr. Kunzig began reading excerpts from some of the secret testimony taken earlier in New York. It was the testimony of Manning Johnson, a witness who has often testified as a "friendly" ex-communist witness before committees and elsewhere. Johnson had testified that the magazine was, despite "minute" deviations from communist policy, essentially an exponent of "the line which the Party wanted to carry out in the religious field."

BISHOP OXNAM: May I answer, please? Might I ask first, is the counsel testifying? I heard all of this about *The Protestant*. What has it to do with me? I indicated when I resigned and why. And I do not quite understand this long recitation of a witness of a day or so ago.

MR. JACKSON: . . . It seems to me that your statement indicating that you ceased to be an editorial advisor before the citation of the publication as being communist-dominated in no way alters the substantial fact that *The Protestant* was before that date engaged in activities which later brought it under federal scrutiny.

BISHOP OXNAM: But when reference is made to the united front, and in 1935 there is a remark in an article where I have opposed it, that America must not accept communism in order to oppose fascism—

MR. VELDE: You are getting out of line, Bishop...

Another charge produced for the first time at the hearing was that the Bishop had written an article for *Soviet Russia Today*. The Bishop agreed that he had.

BISHOP OXNAM: It was published, sir, but the article that I sent to them differs from it considerably, and I would like both to be in your possession.

The Bishop explained that he had protested to the magazine. He had castigated its editor for making "editorial changes that eliminated any word critical in nature," and refused to write for it again.

MR. DOYLE: Mr. Chairman, my impression is that in view of the fact that the Bishop is being confronted with this, as I understand it, for the first time now, and that you are calling attention to the fact that the front page of this magazine lists him as "amongst recent contributors," I think it very pertinent to list some of the other contributors to the same magazine. I notice there are quite a few other recent contributors. There is a United States senator listed here, for instance— two of them. There are two of them listed here as recent contributors, and other well known names to the American public.

MR. VELDE: Does the gentleman want to investigate or to—

MR. DOYLE: No, I do not want to investigate.

MR. VELDE (continuing): Produce any United States senators?

MR. DOYLE: I have heard of senators and—

MR. VELDE: I think with all due respect to you, Mr. Doyle, we are getting out of the realm of this investigation.

MR. DOYLE: I do not think it is out of the realm of the investigation to show the actual fact. We are only naming one person as a recent contributor, and there are a dozen or two dozen in the same magazine. That is the purport of my question...

MR. CLARDY: ... You have no doubt in your mind

at all about the fact that that is a communist magazine, have you, regardless of who may have contributed
to it, good or bad?

In a procedure unusual in the transcribed hearings of
the committee, the names of other contributors were
finally read into the record. Among them were: William
Rose Benét, Millen Brand, former Ambassador Joseph E.
Davies, Harold L. Ickes, Senator James E. Murray, Senator Claude Pepper, Arthur Upham Pope, and Quentin
Reynolds. Other contributors were persons of left-wing
persuasion.

The committee's Representative Clardy could not let
the occasion pass without further comment.

MR. CLARDY: I want to ask Mr. Jackson if he did not
recognize a considerable number of those names, and
I am specifically excluding you, Bishop, from the question—a great many of those are already publicly identified as communists in the files of this committee ...

Committee counsel Kunzig then turned to the charge
that Bishop Oxnam had belonged to an organization
called the National Federation for Constitutional Liberties.

MR. KUNZIG: . . . As to this organization, you never
had anything to do with it at all?

BISHOP OXNAM: That is correct.

MR. KUNZIG: Did you have any knowledge that the
Marshall Foundation, which is a communist-cited fund,
gave $65,000 to this group and was a large financial
backer to this organization?

BISHOP OXNAM: Since I was not a member of it
and had no relationship with it, I had no knowledge
concerning this ...

MR. KUNZIG: Do you have any idea at all how your name came to be used and how your name was listed as a signer in both of these messages?

BISHOP OXNAM: No, sir.

MR. KUNZIG: During that period of time it was never brought to your attention so that you might disclaim it in any way?

BISHOP OXNAM: I have tried to say that I had no relationship that I recall at all with that organization.

❋ ❋ ❋ ❋ ❋

MR. KUNZIG: For the record, I should like to incorporate into the record, and to be brief, the communist background, the cited background of this organization—

BISHOP OXNAM: Mr. Chairman, why should that be in? Is that pertinent when I have said I do not belong to it? Why does he insert in my record a whole communist relationship to an organization I do not belong to?

MR. VELDE: Because we want to get the record straight . . .

This process of "getting the record straight" continued through hours of testimony. Even in the case of an organization, the Committee on Militarism in Education, Mr. Kunzig did his best to "straighten the record" —in a direction unfavorable to the witness.

MR. KUNZIG: . . . Now, you stated, I believe, in a Washington newspaper, sir, that you admitted belonging to the organization but saw there was nothing wrong with it . . .

BISHOP OXNAM: . . . The Committee on Militarism in Education has never been cited as a communist or

subversive organization. I did belong to it. I happen
to believe in a strong national defense, but I have
never been convinced that compulsory military training is a wise contribution to it . . .

*   *   *   *   *

MR. KUNZIG: You said the organization was not cited.
That is partially correct. Let me state for the record
that the Committee on Militarism in Education has not
been cited in the sense you said as a communist front;
however, it must be noted that the Committee on Militarism in Education was cited as a communist front
because the first United States Congress against War,
held in New York City, September 29 to October 1,
1933, *led directly to the formation of* the American
League against War and Fascism. That was cited by
the Massachusetts House Committee on Un-American
Activities. Also, I might note for the record, sir, that
the Garland G-a-r-l-a-n-d Fund, which is a cited communist group furnishing money to various organizations of the United States of America, furnished over
$10,000 to the Committee on Militarism in Education.
So the group was tied in one way or another, Mr.
Chairman, with subversive activities. (My emphasis.)

BISHOP OXNAM: I object very strenuously. Here was
a legitimate organization and now, by a series of associations, there is the apparent attempt to make it appear
that I was related to an organization about which there
was some question. There was no question about that
organization.

MR. VELDE: I previously asked that, when you answer
the questions, if you didn't belong to the organizations,
say so, and if you did, to say so.

*   *   *   *   *

BISHOP OXNAM: Are you ruling that I am denied the privilege of saying anything? I want to abide by your orders, sir, but that is not quite the way we do things in this country. The Garland Fund has been called communist by somebody. It makes a contribution to an organization. I would like to have the facts rather than these statements. That organization was a worthy organization. I did belong to it and I don't think the organization ought to have its reputation attacked in this fashion...

MR. VELDE: You did belong to the Garland—

BISHOP OXNAM: No, I had nothing to do with the Garland Fund, ever. I was a member of the Committee on Militarism in Education.

MR. JACKSON: Mr. Chairman, in order that the record may be absolutely clear, and I don't know at the moment the citation on the Garland Fund—

MR. KUNZIG: I have it right here, sir.

MR. JACKSON: I wouldn't question that.

MR. VELDE: Counsel, will you please read it?

And so the "citation" on the Garland Fund was read into the record, notwithstanding the fact that Bishop Oxnam had no connection whatever with it. This, as Mr. Jackson said, makes the record "absolutely clear." The Bishop found this hard to understand: "If someone asks if I belong to a certain organization and I say I do not... why do we have to have this long list of citations so that somebody can read that in relation to my name?" he inquired.

"It is in an attempt to clarify your complete record, your complete file, that we are asking you these questions," Mr. Velde explained, "because it has puzzled members of the committee as to how you could be listed as a sponsor for these various organizations, how you could be listed as a member of these various organizations, without some knowledge that they were communist organizations or communist-inspired organizations, and that is the thing we want to clarify—not only for your information but for your benefit as well."

Other efforts to benefit the Bishop followed:

BISHOP OXNAM: ... In the matter of the poll tax that was referred to earlier, I've been advised ... that Congressman Bender and Congressman Jennings were entertained in a banquet in Washington by this organization in 1947 at the Statler Hotel.

MR. WALTER: What does that prove?

BISHOP OXNAM: Yes, what does it prove in connection with me?

MR. WALTER: Yes.

BISHOP OXNAM: That's just the point.

MR. WALTER: That is it.

BISHOP OXNAM: I said I had no recollection of belonging to that organization but in 1947 reputable members of this body were involved. Now why does my name get tied up with these things and somebody says I have to explain? I can't understand it.

MR. VELDE: For this simple reason. There might be a few cases where communist members in politics, religion or any other field belong or have belonged to communist fronts; but it is very apparent to me, at least, that there are so many of these front groups with which you have been associated that we want to find out whether or not you had any knowledge of them or whether you were used as a tool or just what happened exactly. That is the reason we are trying to clear this matter up.

Representative Walter then launched into an attack on the Bishop for having criticized the application of the Walter-McCarran Act in the screening of aliens seeking to enter the country.

MR. WALTER: My question is, what useful purpose did you feel you were serving by making an unwarranted, unjustifiable attack on the law of this land?

BISHOP OXNAM: Mr. Walter, I would be happy to answer that if you would give me opportunity . . . You are handing me newspaper records, sir, and with the utmost respect to the newspaper profession, very few American reporters write shorthand. You will find quote marks put around statements that I personally at times do not wish to take responsibility for. If this committee would follow a policy, when you have a question of that kind—

MR. WALTER: Now let's not criticize the committee . . . every time you are asked a question.

BISHOP OXNAM: I am not criticizing the committee.

MR. WALTER: Let's answer the question.

BISHOP OXNAM: I am answering.

As the hearing went on into the late evening, the nerves of some of the members began to become rather frayed.

MR. DOYLE: I don't like the idea of us producing for this witness documents way back in the year 1923 for the first time . . .

MR. VELDE: Well, Mr. Doyle, may I remind you that the witness has requested . . . an opportunity to appear before the committee . . . and we are attempting to do the best we can to give him a full and complete hearing . . .

* * * * *

MR. WALTER: I don't know of any case where the witness has been told in advance of the type of evidence that this committee will discuss; and furthermore, we are here only because the Bishop has requested this hearing ...

The inquiry turned in short order to the matter of the American Civil Liberties Union. The Bishop was asked whether he was and remains a member.

BISHOP OXNAM: The American Civil Liberties Union—

MR. KUNZIG: I just asked you whether you were or weren't.

BISHOP OXNAM: Well, just a moment.

MR. KUNZIG: You can explain afterwards.

BISHOP OXNAM: Quite.

MR. KUNZIG: Were you or weren't you?

BISHOP OXNAM: Yes, sir, I was.

Only then was the Bishop permitted to explain. He had been a member for a short time in the '20s in California and had rejoined in about 1939 or 1940 in Boston. He praised the Union and mentioned statements in praise of it by Thomas E. Dewey, General MacArthur, President Truman, President Eisenhower, and others.

"I am a member of it," the Bishop concluded. Without the knowledge of the witness, the committee, in the printed record of the testimony, added a footnote quoting from the California Committee on Un-American Activities' 1948 Report to the State Legislature. It said, among other things, that the California committee reported "an anti-totalitarianism resolution within the ACLU during the Stalin-Hitler pact." According to the footnote, the comment of the California committee on this anti-communist, anti-fascist resolution of the Union was that "undoubtedly, the American Civil Liberties Union was resorting to drastic communist strategy..." The committee report, says the footnote, reaffirms the "communist character of the American Civil Liberties Union."

Mr. Kunzig, however, was interested in hurrying on to material closer to the committee's immediate interests. He asked the witness whether "a certain Harry P. Ward was chairman of the American Civil Liberties Union."

BISHOP OXNAM: I think it was Harry F. Ward.

MR. KUNZIG: Harry F. Ward?

BISHOP OXNAM: Yes.

MR. KUNZIG: You know he is a good friend of yours, is that right?

BISHOP OXNAM: Just a minute. Don't put answers in my mouth, please.

MR. KUNZIG: Just answer the question.

BISHOP OXNAM: I will.

MR. KUNZIG: Is he a good friend of yours?

In a long answer, the Bishop stated that Professor Ward "was an inspirational teacher, to whom I owe very, very much. He was a dear personal friend." Nevertheless the Bishop declared that he had broken with the reverend professor many years before. The Bishop said he had written in 1936 referring to Professor Ward: "He takes the communist position as to objective if not as to method."

The committee then launched into an undisguised discussion of the affairs of the Methodist Church and of the Methodist Federation for Social Service. Counsel Kunzig offered to read into the record the previously secret testimony of Manning Johnson.

BISHOP OXNAM: Mr. Chairman, does this involve me? I want to be alert if it does.

MR. KUNZIG: It involves Dr. Ward, sir.

MR. VELDE: Let counsel ask his question, please.

MR. KUNZIG: It involves Dr. Ward.

MR. MOULDER: May I ask if the Bishop was present—

MR. VELDE: Just a minute. Will you wait until the counsel states his question?

MR. FRAZIER: I object to its being read if the Bishop was not present and does not know anything about it.

MR. KUNZIG: Mr. Chairman . . . here is sworn testimony as to the fact that this man, Dr. Ward, was a communist. Dr. Ward, the testimony will show here, was an active member of the Methodist Federation for Social Service of which this witness was an active member, and this is most pertinent, sir.

MR. VELDE: Was an active member?

BISHOP OXNAM: Was my name mentioned in this testimony, may I ask . . . May I ask again, was my name mentioned?

MR. VELDE: Counsel will proceed to ask the questions.

BISHOP OXNAM: . . . Was my name mentioned in it?

MR. VELDE: I do not know whether it was or not, but it does not matter for this particular occasion . . .

The testimony was read. For good measure, Mr. Kunzig also read previously secret testimony in which Mr. Johnson accused the Reverend Mr. Jack Richard McMichael, executive secretary until 1953 of the Methodist Federation, of being a member of the Communist Party. Representative Clardy added an excerpt from the previously secret testimony of Benjamin Gitlow, also taken in New York.

"McMichael became the cell head [in the 1940's], but Dr. Ward continued to be prominent," Mr. Gitlow testified. "The Methodist Federation . . . was already in the grip of this Communist Party cell and was therefore

an instrument through which the Communist Party operated in the religious field."

Mr. Gitlow left the Communist Party in 1929 when
Mr. McMichael was twelve years of age.

Bishop Oxnam indicated that he considered that Mr.
McMichael "was so tied up with the communist group
that whether or not he were a communist, I couldn't prove
whether he was a member of the Communist Party or not,
but I was sure that that organization [the Federation]
ought not to be under that leadership any more and I
did everything I could. Others talked to Mr. McMichael.
He denied this completely ..."

MR. WALTER: What caused you to reach the conclusion that McMichael was a communist?

BISHOP OXNAM: Sir, I hope you will not press that
question. I will be glad to state it to this committee if
I could meet it in executive session ... I would be glad
to convey it to the chairman of this committee. I am
not hedging here at all, but I think I have an obligation
because the source was of such a nature—I think the
chairman would be the first to recognize this. I will not
refer to the source other than that.

MR. WALTER: You couldn't make it much plainer.

MR. VELDE: I don't think the witness should be
required to answer except in executive session. We
appreciate that.

BISHOP OXNAM: I will be very happy, sir, to give
you the source of that.

But the committee continued to press the Bishop.

MR. KUNZIG: During that period of time, McMichael
was active, Ward was active, both in leading positions,
and you had these viewpoints about them and what
you thought they believed. Why did you not try at

that time to get them out, all during those years?

The committee's acceptance of this testimony apparently overwhelmed the Bishop. He even went so far as to say that the testimony of ex-communist witnesses who repeatedly testify, often rather contradictorily, at the government's behest, "confirms the suspicions that some of us got [about Dr. Ward] and I recorded my own back there in 1936."

MR. WALTER: During what period of time did you have the suspicion that he was a communist while he was acting as a theological professor in Boston University and at Union [Theological Seminary, N. Y. C.]?

BISHOP OXNAM: I did not believe he was a communist. I did not believe he was a communist when he was at Boston University's School of Theology. I do not know he is a communist now. This testimony is quite overwhelming ...

Although the committee had called neither the Reverend Dr. Ward nor the Reverend Mr. McMichael to testify, members declared that the secret testimony "is irrefutable evidence that in the policy-making echelons of the Methodist Federation for Social Service there were those who were there to do the work of the Communist Party. It cannot be overlooked, I think, Bishop, that during at least a portion of the time that this was going on, you were also a member of the Methodist Federation, and, I believe, an officer of the Federation."

* * * * *

BISHOP OXNAM: Mr. Chairman, was Jack McMichael called before the committee? Did he have any opportunity to answer that question? I am not pleading for him, but did he have a chance to answer what was alleged?

MR. VELDE: As far as I am concerned, Mr. Jack McMichael has never been called before this committee.

BISHOP OXNAM: Then this is given to the public all over the nation before the man accused has had so much as an opportunity to answer.

MR. SCHERER: Do you concur that Reverend Mc-Michael is a member of the Communist Party today? You said so yourself.

BISHOP OXNAM: That isn't correct at all. I am dealing with procedures and I was dealing with procedures when I made the statement.

MR. SCHERER: On the basis of the testimony we had in New York, sworn testimony of any number of witnesses, and on that basis, how could any reasonable person come to any other conclusion than that Dr. Ward and Reverend McMichael are dangerous communists?

BISHOP OXNAM: That isn't it.

MR. SCHERER: What is it?

BISHOP OXNAM: That a man is accused before a decision is reached and I do not believe this is a court.

If it was not a court, that did not prevent the members of the committee from rendering judgments. For instance, Mr. Clardy referred to a book containing a series of lectures delivered at the Boston University Conference on Preaching in 1933.

"I have read this in its entirety many times," Mr. Clardy said. "There are five articles out of the twelve— one of which is by you—which deal with the question of economics, and every one of them takes the socialist stand . . ."

"I wish, sir, you had read my introduction to that book," Bishop Oxnam replied.

"I have, and do not misunderstand me," Mr. Clardy said. "I am not accusing you of being a communist or anything akin to it. Far from it: but I do think that you were muddled in your thinking and unclear in your understanding."

The committee unanimously agreed that it had nothing in its files indicating that the Bishop was a communist. When it came to its annual report, however, the committee was less generous. In a three-paragraph reference to the Bishop, the committee identified Bishop Oxnam's position in the church, related that a hearing had been held at his request and that the Bishop had stated that certain information in the committee's files was in error. The second paragraph declares that the committee is "pleased to take every reasonable step" to correct or clarify its information. The last paragraph, the only one which reflects any judgment on the more than two hundred pages of testimony and forty-two exhibits introduced at the hearing, reads in full:

"The committee believes that the full record of the hearing afforded Bishop Oxnam will now serve to correct and clarify any erroneous information that *might* have been contained in the files relating to him." (My emphasis.)

8

ONE MAN'S RELIGION, AN-OTHER MAN'S SUBVERSION

*"The House Committee... has conducted
no investigation of subversive infiltration
of the clergy or religion..."*
—Annual Report of the Committee, February 6, 1954, page 97.

H AVING OVERWHELMED the Bishop, the committee rested from its labors for a day, before announcing that it had subpoenaed the Reverend Mr. Jack R. McMichael.

The younger wearer of Methodist cloth was subjected to a hearing as lengthy and as harrowing as that held "for the benefit of" Bishop Oxnam. This time, however, there was not the slightest suggestion that Mr. McMichael was to be benefitted. The California minister denied present or former membership in the Communist Party or the Young Communist League. He swore that he had never, so far as he knew, attended a communist meeting. The committee then confronted Mr. McMichael with three witnesses, presumably those to whom Representative Scherer had referred in the hearing for Bishop Oxnam.

Only one of the three proved to be among those heard in the New York executive sessions. He was Manning Johnson, who had sworn that "during the period that [he] was a member of the Communist Party, during the 1930's, Jack McMichael was a member of the national committee of the Young Communist League, and he was also a member of the Communist Party . . . and he attended occasionally meetings of the national committee of the Communist Party . . ." Mr. McMichael "took a good look" at Mr. Johnson and denied knowing him.

The other two witnesses with whom the minister was confronted were a man-and-wife team of former undercover FBI agents. The inference was that they too had identified Mr. McMichael as a Red. Again Mr. McMichael swore that he did not recall ever having met them. An affidavit of the witnesses, John and Martha Edmiston, was read into the record. It told of a meeting of the Ohio Youth Congress "in May or June of 1940" at which, according to the Edmistons, Mr. McMichael was present and engaged in a conversation with a communist named Robert Thompson on the subject of "*alleged* attempts by FBI agents to infiltrate the American Youth Congress." (My emphasis.) Mr. Kunzig paused in his reading.

"It must be remembered," he interjected with unconscious irony, "this document was prepared and sworn to by two FBI agents."

Confronted by the Edmistons, the Reverend Mr. McMichael denied knowing either. He said in effect that it was possible that, as chairman of the American Youth Congress, he might have seen or met one or the other, though he did not recall it.

"It's my policy as a Christian minister," he told the congressmen, "to meet all kinds of people and all kinds of folks."

In their affidavit, the former undercover couple had not identified Mr. McMichael as a communist, but they followed Mr. McMichael to the stand. If those present expected the minister to be so identified they were disappointed. Neither could do so.

Mr. Doyle asked Mrs. Edmiston: "Well, did you make any effort to identify Reverend McMichael as a communist?"

"Certainly. We would lead him into conversations, but we couldn't ask overt questions—is Reverend McMichael a communist?"

"Well, then," said Mr. Doyle, "your answer is you made an effort, but failed?"

"Right."

When Mr. Edmiston's turn came, the committee avoided such questions.

> MR. KUNZIG: Is everything that is in your affidavit . . . true and correct to the best of your knowledge and belief?
>
> MR. EDMISTON: It is, sir.

Only when the transcripts of the secret testimony taken earlier in New York were released in September did it become entirely clear why no other witnesses were summoned to confront Mr. McMichael. One such witness, a former communist named Leonard Patterson, had sworn he knew Mr. McMichael only as a member of the "New York district" of the Young Communist League. Not only was this testimony somewhat contradictory to that of witness Johnson, but, as Mr. McMichael endeavored to point out over the pounding of Mr. Velde's gavel, the clergyman was, in 1934, a seventeen-year-old freshman at Emory University in Georgia.

As for the other New York witness who solemnly swore that Mr. McMichael headed a Communist Party "cell," he proved to have left the Communist Party when the minister was a vigorous young Bolshevik of twelve summers.

Yet it was those hearings about which Mr. Scherer was

moved to declare: "On the basis of the testimony we had in New York, sworn testimony of any number of witnesses, and on that basis, how could any reasonable person come to any other conclusion than that Dr. Ward and Reverend McMichael are dangerous communists?"

"It was the sense of the committee," chairman Velde commented on the McMichael hearing, "that it is not to be inferred by any one that this was an initiation of an investigation in the field of religion."

The "Judge" was speaking very precisely. The "initiation" had already taken place several weeks earlier in New York. The hearings began with the questioning of Herbert Philbrick. He was asked to give evidence of a "conspiracy of the Communist Party among the clergy." Mr. Philbrick obliged.

"I have no legal evidence which would stand in the United States court of law to prove that any of these individuals, members of the clergy, are in fact also members of the Communist Party," the witness testified. Nevertheless, believing that he was testifying in a confidential session, Mr. Philbrick named a number of clergymen whom he suspected of being Reds.

MR. PHILBRICK: ... I did learn from my pro group sources that there were perhaps seven to eight of these ministers in the Boston area ...

MR. KUNZIG: You don't know the names of these seven or eight?

MR. PHILBRICK: No. In my own mind I am pretty certain I know who they are, sir, but I have never had any direct legal knowledge as to their identity.

Later in the hearing, an article written by Mr. Philbrick was introduced in evidence. Entitled "The Communists Are After Your Church," it contained substantially

the same material as that to which Mr. Philbrick testified
—with a single noteworthy exception.

"I am not guessing about this," Mr. Philbrick wrote.
"I saw those ministers in action—ruthless communist leaders, prostituting the Christian ministry to the evil ends of
atheism and oppression . . ."

In the four days of executive sessions which followed,
the record singularly failed to support Chairman Velde's
contention that religion was not the subject of inquiry.
Witnesses were asked over and over again regarding their
knowledge of "infiltration of religious groups." The affairs
of the Russian Orthodox Church both in Russia and the
United States were discussed in detail.

MR. KUNZIG: Mr. Petrov, there are at least two
branches of the Russian Church here in America, are
there not?

MR. PETROV: Yes, that's right.

MR. KUNZIG: Are they pro-American and anti-
communist?

MR. PETROV: No, there are three jurisdictions, as
they call themselves, of the Russian Orthodox Church
in the United States. One is directed or directly under
the command of the Patriarch in Moscow. This may
safely be called pro-Soviet in this country . . .

* * * * *

MR. KUNZIG: The other American church does not
have this domination?

MR. PETROV: No. It is entirely independent. It is
politically one hundred per cent American . . .

Of another witness, ex-communist Benjamin Gitlow,
Mr. Kunzig inquired at one point: ". . . Would you in brief,
please, trace the position of the Communist Party on the

question of religion and its policies, if any, in the matter of communist infiltration of religious institutions?" Mr. Gitlow, it developed, had been expelled from the Communist Party in 1929 as the result of an internecine dispute regarding Marxist doctrine. This did not prevent his testifying at length as to events which occurred long after he left the Party.

MR. KUNZIG: When did the communist infiltration of religion become a major policy of the Communist Party of the United States?

MR. GITLOW: It certainly did. [sic] On August 20, 1935, with a full delegation of the Communist Party of the United States present, a resolution was adopted [in Moscow] unanimously . . . This resolution declared: "The establishment of a united front with social-democratic and reformist organizations (party, trade unions, cooperative, sport, and cultural educational organizations), and with the bulk of their members, as well as with mass national liberation, religious, democratic, and pacifist organizations and their adherents, is decisive in the struggle against war and its fascist instigators in all countries."

The mention of "religious organizations" in this resolution of the Communist International proves that "infiltration of the religious field" is a major Red policy in the United States, Mr. Gitlow explained.

MR. KUNZIG: Has communist activity in the youth field continued to be tied in with the communist conspiracy in the religious field?

MR. GITLOW: It has. Let me give you an example. On May 28, 1949, the Labor Youth League was organized. The chairman of the national organizing conference . . . was Leon Wofsy, a member and leader of the Communist Party. His report of the organization of the

Labor Youth League is printed in pamphlet form ...
This youth organization, launched in 1949, functioned
as the youth section of the Communist Party.

MR. KUNZIG: Did religious youth organizations par-
ticipate at the conference of the Labor Youth League?

MR. GITLOW: They did. I will read to you from
Wofsy's report: "... In this connection *we greet* the
recent statement of youth leaders opposing the North
Atlantic war pact. It is signed by outstanding national
leaders, as individuals, of the National Conference of
Methodist Youth, the National Council of Jewish Youth,
the Young Progressives of America, the National Student Council of the Young Men's Christian Association.
(My emphasis.)

Mr. Gitlow was certain that Mr. Wofsy's enthusiasm for
the prior statements of unnamed "youth leaders" showed
religious group participation in the Labor Youth League
conference: "This clearly indicates," he explained, "that
the intent remains communist infiltration of religious organizations."

With his expertise thus established, Mr. Gitlow proceeded with Mr. Kunzig to discuss what proved to be the
main business of the day.

MR. KUNZIG: Did the communists infiltrate the
Methodist Church?

MR. GITLOW: In the infiltration of the Methodist
Church, the communists were highly successful. To detail the extent of communist infiltration of the Methodist
Church, the people who serve the communists in the
church consciously and those who were its stooges,
would take several hundred pages of testimony.

The committee's counsel evidently felt that it would

suffice for Mr. Gitlow to fire a few shots at individuals in whom the committee apparently had a special interest.

MR. KUNZIG: Who were the principal individuals involved in communist infiltration of the Methodist Church?

Mr. Gitlow obliged with the names of six clergymen, a lady, and a professor whose death several years before he was apparently unaware of.

MR. KUNZIG: What organization, in your opinion, played a most important part in the communist infiltration of religion?

MR. GITLOW: In my opinion, the Methodist Federation for Social Action. First, it set the pattern for the setting up of similar organizations in other Protestant denominations. It, in fact, assumed the leadership of the so-called social action movement in the Christian churches, and greatly influenced their ideas and the programs they adopted and their activities. It maintained the closest relations with all of them and often collaborated with them . . .

MR. KUNZIG: The names of those you mentioned as the most important principals involved in the communist infiltration of the Methodist Church, were they affiliated with the Communist Party and communist front organizations?

MR. GITLOW: All of them have long records of affiliation and sponsorship and activities in communist front organizations.

The witness then went on to give the "records" of those he had named, although in no case did he testify to any information based upon his own experience as a communist in regard to them. Apparently, the information to which he testified was material taken either from his private dossiers on each of the reverend gentlemen, or perhaps from the committee's.

Still not conducting an investigation into religion, Mr. Kunzig continued to question the witness.

MR. KUNZIG: What do you consider the aims of the communist infiltration of religion?

MR. GITLOW: I think all the aims of the communist conspiracy in religion will become clear when the complete record of this conspiracy is exposed. I would like at this time to point out one of its central aims which is almost totally ignored.

MR. KUNZIG: Will you tell us what that is?

MR. GITLOW: Communist infiltration of the religious field aims to undermine faith in the American system. It seeks to subvert the religious spirit on the basis of social-economic creeds and seditious politics. It strives to poison the minds of a religious people with a destructive, atheistic ideology cloaked in the name of social action and religious interpretations based upon the Bible, that the religious agents of communist infiltration are wont to call prophetic religion.

MR. KUNZIG: Did the Methodist Federation for Social Action serve the communists in this purpose?

MR. GITLOW: The record proves that the Methodist Federation for Social Action served the communists ideally in this diabolic scheme. An examination of the findings of congressional investigations, research reports, and available historical data discloses that over three hundred Methodist clergymen from all parts of the country, including some of the church's most prominent Bishops, participated in communist front organizations, collaborated with Communist Party leaders and with communists who were leaders in these front organizations. The record proves how effective the

Methodist Federation for Social Action was in the Methodist Church.

MR. KUNZIG: Did the Methodist Federation for Social Action exert influence on the religious field?

MR. GITLOW: The Christian Social Action Movement which was the outgrowth of an action at the conference of ministers held in Chicago, April 1932, proves how influential the Federation was in the religious field.

*　*　*　*　*

MR. KUNZIG: What did the conference held at Chicago decide?

MR. GITLOW: Its approach to the social problems created by the depression was decidedly Marxist. The conference approved steps toward the realization of socialism. It concluded ... the following: "At the present time, most of them [ministers, presumably] believe that the declaration of principles and the economic aims of the Socialist Party of America most clearly coincide with these principles."

MR. KUNZIG: Did the conference tie in Christianity with socialism?

MR. GITLOW: It did, for on page 14 of the *Leader's Handbook* [issued as a result of the conference] the following appears: "While socialism and Christianity are not identical, socialism builds up the basic principles of the Christian religion."

The witness did his best to bring the subject matter a little closer to communism. In response to questions, he said that the conference, held in the last months of the Hoover administration, "accepted the communist class struggle theory ... [and] gave its support to communism under the guise of scientific planning, in other words, to the Soviet communist system of planned economy ..."

To prove this last point, the witness quoted from the *Leader's Handbook* as follows:

"That we commit ourselves to the principle of an economy based upon scientific planning as opposed to the principle of laissez-faire and the competition that makes for periodic chaos and conflict."

As Mr. Gitlow continued to testify, it appeared that he had done a good deal of homework. It just so happened that he had "prepared an analysis of copies of the Social Questions Bulletins" of the Methodist Federation "from 1941 to date."

MR. KUNZIG: Can you give us that analysis?

MR. GITLOW: Gladly.

Mr. Gitlow went through the Bulletins singling out here and there material to suit his purposes. Among other items he found a number of radical-sounding phrases which he quoted briefly and expatiated upon at length.

The "analysis" covers more than thirty pages. Only one 1941 Bulletin is mentioned. Mr. Gitlow found none of the Bulletins published in 1942 suitable for his testimony. As general interest in our wartime ally, Soviet Russia, mounted, Mr. Gitlow was rewarded in the Bulletin by more material. He quoted from two 1943 Social Questions Bulletins of the Federation; from five issues published in 1944; six in 1945; four in 1946; and none for the following years.

"The evidence, with every issue of the Social Questions Bulletin," the witness told the committee, "piles up overwhelming proof that the Methodist Federation for Social Action conforms to a definite pattern which can be defined as follows: it is a Marxist organization committed to the overthrow of the social-economic system and the political government which sustains it—the United States government . . ."

To reach this conclusion, Mr. Gitlow had to use a comb whose teeth were not of the finest. He found evidence of communism in the fact that the Federation favored "over-all price controls on consumer goods, rents, and raw materials . . . rationing and low profits . . . taxation as a measure to fight inflation . . . the Dumbarton Oaks proposals . . . severing diplomatic relations with Franco Spain . . . the Bretton Woods Economic Cooperation Agreement, the Murray Full-Employment Bill" and other legislation. Since the Communist Party also favored these things at one time or another, Gitlow reasoned, it followed that the Methodist Federation was communistic.

In some cases, Mr. Gitlow's reasoning was even more difficult to follow, but the effort is worth it. In the January 1944 Bulletin, the witness found an official statement of the Federation entitled "Stop Inflation."

"Unless the fascist tendencies in our national life can be checked," Mr. Gitlow read from the statement, "we will win the war overseas only to find ourselves under a modified form of fascism at home." The witness found in this January 1944 statement proof that the Federation was following "the line of the Communist Party" because "that is the line of the Communist Party as expressed in its 1945 National Convention resolution. It reads as follows: 'If the reactionary policy and the forces of monopoly capital are not checked and defeated, America and the world will be confronted with new aggressions and wars and the growth of reaction and fascism in the United States.'"

From this, Mr. Gitlow concluded: "Both the Communist Party and the Methodist Federation for Social Service see a future of wars and the growth of fascism at home."

"Analyzing" the March 1945 Bulletin, the witness somehow failed to note that the Methodist Federation was yet more prematurely communist.

"The editorial in this issue in support of [Henry] Wallace is used ... to put the Federation behind Wallace, whose position on domestic and international issues was being exploited at the time by the Communist Party ..." the witness said. To connect this March, 1945, statement of the Federation with communism, Mr. Gitlow ignored the fact that the Communist Party was, at that time, also supporting President Roosevelt (who died a month later), the war effort, and the policies of the government in general. He was content to quote statements favoring Mr. Wallace's viewpoint taken from a communist magazine, *Political Affairs,* in September 1946 and September 1947.

Mr. Gitlow's analysis of the leading article in the March 1945 Bulletin is perhaps worth quoting as the supreme example of his style of logic.

"The Reverend [Ernest Freemont] Tittle, treating with the role of the church in the post-war world, gives expression to this amazing statement: 'The Church although it is bound to be influenced to some extent by its social environment, must cease to be identical with liberal capitalism, with western culture, with civilization largely based on individual and national self-interest. Protestantism in particular must cease to be identical with "the American way of life" or the British way of life or any other contemporary way of life; it must proclaim and embody God's way of life—the only way that leads to life and not to economic chaos, mass unemployment, mass slaughter, and destruction.'

"If, as the Reverend Tittle states, undoubtedly with the approval of the Methodist Federation for Social Ac-

tion," Mr. Gitlow concluded, "that the church must break
with liberal capitalism, with western culture and the
American way of life, he necessarily implies that the
church must identify itself with an economic system that
is different from ours, with a culture that opposes western
culture and with a way of life that is different from the
American way of life. Since we live in a world of reality,
within definitely defined borders and not in the ethereal
regions of a befogged ivory tower, we can come to only
one conclusion on the Reverend Tittle's statement. It is,
that the alternative the Reverend Tittle and the Federation offers Protestantism is that it identify itself with the
forces operating in the world, whose economic philosophy,
cultural standards and way of life are diametrically opposed to our economic system, culture, and way of life.
What the Reverend Tittle and the Federation term 'God's
way of life,' is obviously the Marxist, the communist way
of life."

The most sensational of Mr. Gitlow's statements, however, was one in which he named nine men as "ministers
who carried out the instructions of the Communist Party
or collaborated with it."

"The outstanding ones among them were," Mr. Gitlow testified, "besides Dr. Harry Ward, Dr. William B.
Spofford, Jerome Davis, Reverend Tucker P. Smith, Reverend Irwin St. John Tucker, Rabbi Judal [sic] L. Magnes,
Reverend John Haynes Holmes, Reverend Sidney Strong,
Rabbi Stephen S. Wise." When this testimony was released in September, it was promptly denied. The Reverend Mr. Tucker told reporters that he had voted
Republican since 1932. He was the Protestant chaplain
of the Republican National Convention in Chicago
in 1944.

Rabbi Magnes had emigrated to Palestine in 1922

where he settled permanently, later becoming Chancellor of the Hebrew University there; he died in Jerusalem in 1951. Neither the late Rabbi Magnes nor Rabbi Wise (who died in 1949 in New York City) could defend himself from the grave, but the anti-communist American Jewish Congress as well as numerous laymen and clergymen promptly denounced the committee for releasing Mr. Gitlow's testimony.

Dr. Israel Goldstein, president of the Congress, and Rabbi Maurice N. Eisendrath, president of the Union of American Hebrew Congregations, at once condemned the committee's release of Mr. Gitlow's unsupported speculations regarding the dead rabbis. They called it "a shocking and frightening betrayal of elementary public responsibility and decency" revealing "the irresponsible character of the committee's procedures." Mr. Gitlow's accusations they termed "a contemptible and vile desecration of two of the most noble and revered names in American Jewish history."

The national board of the National Council of Churches of Christ joined their Jewish brothers. Commenting on the "utter disregard of the American tradition of fair play," the board declared that the late rabbis were "revered not only by their coreligionists but millions of other Americans."

Defending himself against these strictures, Mr. Gitlow wrote a letter published in the Peekskill (N.Y.) *Evening Star* in which he noticeably crossed over to the other side of Jordan. The late rabbis were no longer carrying out Communist Party instructions or collaborating with it, according to his letter.

"It was the purpose of this testimony to show how the communist movement . . . was able to attract a number of well-meaning, liberal and social-minded religious leaders such as Rabbis Magnes and Wise. The charge was not made that they were ever communists or members of the Communist Party," he wrote.

Other ex-communist witnesses of only slightly more recent vintage were summoned to enlighten the committee with their special brand of "expert testimony," as one of them termed it. One of these was Joseph Zack Kornfeder, a perennial witness at committee and other government hearings.

MR. SCHERER: The fact is that there are somewhere a few ministers who are actually members of the Party, is that not right?

MR. KORNFEDER: Yes . . .

MR. SCHERER: What do you know about the membership of ministers in communist front organizations?

MR. KORNFEDER: Oh, there you really find them in tremendous numbers. You have, for instance, such a spectacle as more than two thousand signing a petition, communist sponsored petition, in behalf of the Rosenbergs . . .

*　*　*　*　*

MR. SCHERER: Who instigated the petition for the Rosenbergs?

MR. KORNFEDER: That committee they had, Committee to Defend the Rosenbergs.

*　*　*　*　*

MR. SCHERER: . . . Among these two thousand ministers were, however, some just idealists and pacifists, were there not?

MR. KORNFEDER: I do not think so. I think that those two thousand were pretty close to the machine.

Of course, they may have been. It is always possible to have a few stray ones.

The witness offered to "put them in three categories, really, the preachers."

MR. SCHERER: I would like to hear what categories you put them in.

MR. KORNFEDER: I put them in the category of, first, the secret Party members. Those, I believe, will not exceed six hundred among the thousands that they inveigled into the various operations.

MR. SCHERER: You mean there are not more than six hundred members of the clergy throughout the United States who are Party members?

MR. KORNFEDER: Yes. That is my estimate on the basis of the knowledge I have in this field . . .

The other two categories proved to be "the fellow travelers who . . . are members of one of their infiltration organizations . . . [and] sympathizers who temporarily go along with one or another front for a period of time and then fade out."

Mr. Kornfeder was less convinced of the materialism of the clergy than Representative Scherer.

MR. SCHERER: Well, we have been talking about intellectuals, which includes, of course, the clergy. I am just wondering if it is not a fact that some of our intellectuals and some of our clergy who have an exceptionally good educational background are not a little dissatisfied with a system that pays them maybe a maximum of $5,000 a year and the corner grocer who has not had even a high-school education gets maybe $15,000 a year.

MR. KORNFEDER: Well, I would say they would retain the same point of view even if you pay them $8,000 a year.

MR. SCHERER: Would that viewpoint not change a little bit if they were paid $25,000 a year?

MR. KORNFEDER: It could be with some of them that it may. It may with some of them, yes, but the economic consideration, I think, is subsidiary to the influence of propaganda and agitation . . .

Manning Johnson also referred to the Rosenberg "petition" signed by 2,300 clergymen in his testimony, even though he had left the Communist Party in 1940. The witness effortlessly overcame this difficulty by referring to an article which appeared in a communist magazine in 1935.

MR. JOHNSON: . . . The date of this article is in 1935, and the reason why I call this to your attention is that the major plot to take over the religious organizations was really hatched during that particular period, and the fact that the communists in headlines in the *Daily Worker* can boast of 2,300 Protestant ministers supporting them is the result of this [plot] that began back in the '30's when I was a member of the Communist Party.

MR. KUNZIG: 2,300 people supporting them in what?

MR. JOHNSON: 2,300 clergymen have talks with Eisenhower for clemency for the Rosenbergs.

MR. CLARDY: That refers, does it not, to a petition or a series of petitions that were circulated in which it is alleged that the 2,300 joined in seeking clemency for the Rosenbergs.

MR. JOHNSON: That is correct.

That was no more "correct" than Mr. Kornfeder's assertion that the "petition" was sponsored by the Rosenberg committee.

It was not a petition. Dr. Bernard M. Loomer, Dean of the University of Chicago Divinity School, one of the signers, called it "a letter asking for executive clemency" for the Rosenberg couple. Nor were the signers subscribing to a Rosenberg committee petition. In a second communication to President Eisenhower, Dean Loomer said: "Our *unaffiliated group* represents an important segment of the Christian clergy of this country. Among us are members of 28 communions and citizens of all 48 states, the District of Columbia, the territories of Alaska, Hawaii and the Canal Zone and the Commonwealth of Puerto Rico." (My emphasis.)

Nor did the letter itself follow the dictates of the communists who contended throughout that the Rosenbergs were innocent and that their trial was a "frame-up."

"We *are not questioning* the justice of the trial," the clergymen wrote, "but we earnestly question the political and spiritual wisdom of the sentence." (My emphasis.)

The members of the committee evidently did not take the trouble to read the text of the letter, although it was put in evidence at the hearing. Even so, the witness' testimony seems to have troubled Mr. Doyle to a limited extent.

MR. DOYLE: . . . Now as to whether or not these alleged 2,300 other clergymen which this Dr. Loomer refers to—did they sign anything to your personal knowledge?

MR. JOHNSON: Not according to my personal knowledge, because I was not a member of that organization . . . I think it is of concern to the American people if it is true that the communists have 2,300 of our clergy who administer to the souls of men daily in our churches.

Mr. Doyle tried again, but in vain.

MR. DOYLE: . . . Of course, of your own knowledge, in view of your answer, you do not know whether or not any of these clergymen are members of faiths other than Protestant, do you?

MR. JOHNSON: I do not know what denominations they are because I have not seen the list. I am merely stating that on the basis of my knowledge and experience while in the Communist Party, the Communist Party made serious efforts to enlist clergymen in their activities to give it a cloak of religious respectability and that this conspiracy began not yesterday but a number of years ago, and over the course of years, they have made deeper and deeper inroads in the religious field that I am reluctant to discount the possibility of them actually having 2,300 clergymen.

Anticipating criticism of the inquiry, Mr. Johnson concluded his testimony as follows: "The communist strategy of using the cry of 'attack on religion' in order to stop an inquiry on their attack on religious life should not deter those in whose hands lie the responsibility of exposing this deadly danger to religion in America."

Mr. Kunzig, however, had found the best of all possible reasons why the committee should not be deterred.

"I think even more interesting, Mr. Chairman, is the editorial 'Freedom of Religion' on page 5 of the *Daily Worker* of Friday, July 10, 1953, just a few days ago . . . which argues in favor of freedom of religion . . ." he said. "When the *Daily Worker* is in support of something, methinks we should question it."

In the committee's annual report, some faint traces

of a reaction to the storm of criticism which followed release of this testimony were discernible.

"The subcommittee received considerable testimony relative to the efforts of the Communist Party to infiltrate religious groups. This testimony was furnished by witnesses who have been called by the government to testify against communist leaders charged with violation of the Smith Act. The committee was criticized in some religious quarters for releasing the testimony having to do with the infiltration of church groups and institutions, but it must be understood that the committee cannot place itself in a position of coaching witnesses or attempting to add or detract from the voluntary testimony being given under oath, no matter how unpopular to any group such testimony might be ..." Nevertheless, the committee firmly insisted that it had "conducted no investigation of subversive infiltration of the clergy or religion and no such investigation is contemplated."

Yet on February 18, 1954, the committee heard the testimony of the Reverend Dr. John A. Hutchinson, Professor of Religion at Williams College. They gave him a public hearing on March 18, at which he was told that the committee had secret testimony that he was a communist. Dr. Hutchinson swore that the testimony was false. Representative Jackson was chairman of the session. He said other clergymen would be called. The non-investigation of religion marched on.

The section of the 1953 report is entitled simply but eloquently "Religion." Under that heading, the committee warned: "The names of *too many men of the cloth* appear as sponsors, directors, or contributors to organizations which were established by the Communist Party to serve the communist ends even though the number is very small in comparison to loyal clergy ..." (My emphasis.)

"I mean exactly what I asked you, General, nothing else. And anyone with the brains of a five-year-old child can understand that question."
—Senator McCarthy speaking to Brig. Gen. Ralph W. Zwicker, Hearings, Senate Permanent Subcommittee on Investigations.

IN THE CONDUCT of congressional investigations, there are two standards: one for the witness who is expected to, and does testify in the way that the committee wishes; the other is applied to the accused or suspect witness. The "friendly" witness is listened to with rapt attention, while the "unfriendly" witness is interrupted with hostile questions, threats of citation for contempt, accusations of guilt, and inferences that he is a liar. Mr. Gitlow is permitted to testify at length regarding matters about which he cannot possibly have any first-hand knowledge, but Bishop Oxnam is asked why he criticized a law proposed by one of the committee members, is questioned about organizations he denies association with, and is accused of being a muddled thinker, and by inference, a fellow traveller. Witness Rossen, who has told the committee that he has given up the "luxury of individual morality" is praised in the committee's report.

Witness McMichael, who has denied accusations that he is a communist, is given a different treatment:

MR. KUNZIG: Have you ever met Manning Johnson, Reverend McMichael?

REVEREND MCMICHAEL: The name in unfamiliar to me. I would appreciate your producing him and let me look at him. Perhaps I would be able to recognize him by his face. Is he here in the room?

* * * * *

MR. CLARDY: Would you know him if you saw him?

REVEREND MCMICHAEL: I'll be glad to look at him.

MR. CLARDY: Answer my question: would you know him if you saw him?

REVEREND MCMICHAEL: How can I answer that question? I'll let the record show that the question—how unfair it is.

MR. CLARDY: If you were a truthful man, you would answer that question, sir.

MR. DOYLE: Well, now, Mr. Chairman—

REVEREND MCMICHAEL: What kind of a question—

MR. DOYLE: Just a minute, now. I don't want to differ with my distinguished colleagues, but I submit that sort of statement by a member of this committee is highly improper.

MR. CLARDY: I stand by it.

As it often the case in reading the transcripts of hearings, one is reminded of the famous trial of the Knave of Hearts in Lewis Carroll's *Alice in Wonderland*. At one point in the trial, a set of verses is read by the White Rabbit prosecutor. What happened next, put in the question-and-answer style of congressional hearings, would read like this:

JURYMAN: Are they in the prisoner's handwriting?

WHITE RABBIT: No, they're not, and that's the queerest thing about it.

THE KING: He must have imitated somebody else's hand.

THE KNAVE: Please, your Majesty, I didn't write it, and they can't prove I did; there's no name signed at the end.

THE KING: If you didn't sign it, that only makes the matter worse. You *must* have meant some mischief, or else you'd have signed your name like an honest man.

The Jack of Hearts, however, was a more timid witness than Mr. Jack McMichael. The Methodist minister took advantage of whatever opportunity he could to make himself heard, but always over the violent objections of committee counsel, chairman, and the other members of the committee.

MR. CLARDY: I ask that the witness be requested to desist. Will you remain silent?

REVEREND MCMICHAEL: Under the First Amendment to the Constitution, it says "Congress shall make no law respecting—"

MR. CLARDY: Mr. Chairman—

REVEREND MCMICHAEAL: "—and [sic] establishment of religion, or prohibiting the free exercise thereof—"

MR. JACKSON: I move—

REVEREND MCMICHAEL: "—or abridging the freedom of speech or of the press—"

MR. CLARDY: Mr. Chairman, I would like to—

REVEREND MCMICHAEL: "—or the right of the people peaceably to assemble and to petition the government for a redress of grievances."

MR. JACKSON: I move that the gratuitous statement just put on the record be stricken.

MR. VELDE: Without objection, it will be stricken.

Time after time the chairman prevented Mr. McMichael from speaking.

"There is no question pending," he would say to the unhappy witness. At one point, Mr. Velde declared: "As I admonished you yesterday, I would very much regret to have to ask you to leave the witness stand; but if further outbursts are made with no question pending—"

"Would you please refrain from making accusations, Mr. Chairman?" Mr. McMichael interrupted.

"—I shall have to ask the officers to escort you from the room," Mr. Velde said.

Mr. Doyle objected mildly at this point, and the minister offered to continue his rebuttal of the chairman's most recent accusation. He was not permitted to. But if the freedom of speech does not apply for the accused, it does for the accuser. When it came the turn of Mrs. Martha Edmiston to testify, a somewhat different standard prevailed.

MRS. EDMISTON: Sir, may I point out—

MR. VELDE: I am sorry, Mrs. Edmiston, there is no question pending.

MRS. EDMISTON: Oh.

MR. VELDE: Not because we don't want to hear what you have to say—

MR. SCHERER: May I ask a question?

MR. VELDE:—But because of the regular rules—

MR. SCHERER: May I ask a question?

MR. VELDE: Yes.

MR. SCHERER: What were you going to say, Mrs. Edmiston?

The investigators frequently make very thinly disguised attempts to apply pressure to witnesses by demanding testimony as to their source of livelihood. The House Committee is not alone in engaging in this practice. Senator Jenner's Subcommittee to Investigate the Administration of the Internal Security Act questioned a free-lance writer named Edward J. Fitzgerald along similar lines. Committee counsel Robert Morris was examining:

MR. MORRIS: For whom do you write? Who are some of your clients?

MR. FITZGERALD: Various magazines, such as *Saturday Review of Literature*, the *Herald Tribune* book section, sometimes the *Times* book section.

MR. MORRIS: When you say the *Times*, you mean the New York *Times?*

MR. FITZGERALD: The New York *Times*.

MR. MORRIS: For how long have you been a book reviewer?

MR. FITZGERALD: Two or three years.

MR. MORRIS: Is that principally the source of your income, Mr. Fitzgerald?

MR. FITZGERALD: That and other writings.

MR. MORRIS: Give us a general idea of what other writing you do.

MR. FITZGERALD: I have written fiction for *Confession Magazine*.

The fact that the hearings, according to the senator, dealt with the subject of "interlocking subversion in government" did not deter the chairman from introducing into the record letters from the book review editors of the New York *Times*, the *Herald Tribune*, and the *Saturday Re-*

view of Literature. The letters were written in reply to the "telephone request" of the subcommittee's director of research, Benjamin Mandel. Mr. Mandel had asked for a list of the books reviewed by Mr. Fitzgerald. The book review editor for the *Times* explained to Mr. Mandel that the witness' "reviews dealt only with fiction of secondary importance." Mrs. Irita Van Doren, editor of the New York *Herald Tribune Book Review,* wrote: "As I pointed out [in a telephone conversation] Mr. Fitzgerald has never been a member of the staff of the *Herald Tribune.* He was a free-lance writer and, with three exceptions, reviewed for the *Herald Tribune* only unimportant and non-political novels." These assurances—even couched in the past tense—were apparently not enough. After questioning the witness at length on his government employment, the committee returned to his literary endeavors.

MR. MORRIS: Will you tell us the circumstances leading up to your relationship, say, with the New York *Herald Tribune?* What were the circumstances leading up to your becoming a book reviewer to that publication?

MR. FITZGERALD: I asked to be allowed to do book reviews.

MR. MORRIS: Whom did you ask?

MR. FITZGERALD: Mrs. Van Doren, editor of the *Herald Tribune Book Review* section.

Committee counsel Morris also asked the witness the same question regarding his work for the *Saturday Review.* Mr. Fitzgerald, in response to a question, said that he had discussed with the editor the fact that he had been accused by Miss Elizabeth Bentley of being a member of a Soviet espionage ring. Asked whether he had denied to the editor the truth of those accusations, Mr. Fitzgerald invoked the Fifth Amendment. Following the hearing, the committee handed out mimeographed press releases in which this part of the testimony was duly emphasized: "Fitzgerald declared his principal source of income now is the writing of book reviews for the New York *Herald Tribune,* the New York *Times,* and the *Saturday Review of Literature,* and that he has written fiction for *Confession Magazine.*"

The publications are no longer a source of income, "principal" or nominal to Mr. Fitzgerald. They have given him no work since his committee appearance.

Behind the closed doors of executive sessions of the investigating committees, the questioners are even more aggressive in their efforts to break down witnesses. Not many such secret hearings are disclosed to public gaze, but occasionally such a transcript is allowed to reach the light of day. One of these is a 348-page printed record of a hearing of the Jenner Committee entitled "Communist Underground Printing Facilities and Illegal Propaganda." Among the witnesses questioned in secret session was a Chapel Hill, North Carolina, woman and her husband. The couple were accused of operating a left-wing book store and of permitting the use of the rear of the store as a site for a printing press and other equipment supposedly belonging to the Communist Party.

In the privacy of the hearing, however, the senators and committee staff members felt free to ask any question that came to mind. Among the questions asked were: How did you meet your husband? Who were the friends through whom you met him? Where was the social gathering of friends at which you met him? Did he come there with friends? How old were you at the time? Who was the host at the party where you met him? These questions related to events which took place twenty-three years prior to the hearing.

Other questions included: Have you made any contributions to the Red Cross? Have you made any contributions to any social clubs, to any church? Do you or your husband belong to a golf or bridge club? Tell this committee all of the organizations to which you and your husband belong. What is your church affiliation? Are you an atheist? Whom do you know on the faculty of the University of North Carolina?

The committee also interested itself in the relations between the witness and her attorney: Did you give me your lawyer's name? How long have you known him? How did you hear of him? Who is [the] person [who told you about him]? Give us her address. How does she spell her name? Where did you know her? Do you spend much time in Washington? Does she ever visit you in Chapel Hill? How many times? Are you paying your attorney or is someone else paying him for you? Are you paying him from your own funds?

The children of the witness were not exempt from the interest of the investigators: Have you any children? How many? How old are they?

The witness was able to, and did answer most of these questions, but when she was asked about the printing press which was supposed to have existed a decade or more earlier in the book store, she declined to answer. The senators at once bore down, with two Southern gentlemen taking the initiative. They were Senators James O. Eastland of Mississippi and the late Willis Smith of North Carolina, who was not a member of the subcommittee.

SENATOR EASTLAND: You don't want us to cite you for contempt of the Senate, do you?

THE WITNESS: No, sir.

SENATOR EASTLAND: Why don't you testify now? Your refusals do not come within a mile of letting you out if we were to cite you, regardless of what your lawyer says.

THE WITNESS: My lawyer isn't saying. I think they do.

SENATOR EASTLAND: We are going to have to cite you if you take this position. We do not want to. Now, just tell us frankly, did you have a printing press in the back of your book store?

When the witness persisted in declining to answer, the senators discussed briefly how they might break up the question.

SENATOR SMITH: . . . Did you have a printing press in the back of your bookshop?

THE WITNESS: Again I must decline to answer that question.

SENATOR SMITH: I think that would certainly be the basis for a contempt citation, although I do not want to see it happen.

SENATOR EASTLAND: Mr. Chairman, I request that you order the witness to answer the question under penalty of contempt of the Senate.

SENATOR JENNER: I direct that you answer the question directed to you by Senator Smith of North Carolina. The question was whether or not you had a printing press in the back of your book store at Chapel Hill, North Carolina.

THE WITNESS: I decline to answer the question, sir.

SENATOR [HERMAN] WELKER [Republican member of

Idaho]: Did you have any printer's ink in the back of your book store in Chapel Hill, North Carolina?

THE WITNESS: I must decline to answer that question on the grounds previously stated.

SENATOR WELKER: Did you have any printer's type in the back of your book store in Chapel Hill, North Carolina?

The witness again declined.

SENATOR WELKER: Did you have anything, madam, by which you could reproduce anything that would come out as printed matter in the back of your book store in Chapel Hill, North Carolina?

Over and over, such questions were asked in varying form, but the lady persisted in her refusal to answer. Occasionally, she conferred with her attorney. At one point, Senator Jenner commented: "Let the record show that the witness is consulting her attorney, and hesitated to answer the question." Asked if her refusal to answer the questions regarding the printing press was on the advice of her counsel, the witness said, "Yes." At once, the attorney was administered the oath.

"I would like to object to being put on the witness stand without subpoena or without notice or without an opportunity to consult counsel," the lawyer, David Rein, told the senators. Mr. Rein's objections were in vain. The committee proceeded to question him about his professional career in detail. He told the committee that he had been a member of the Legal Department of the National Labor Relations Board and the Office of Price Administration, as well as a United States marine during World War II. A graduate of Columbia Law School and Columbia College, Mr. Rein said that he had also served as an employee of a New York commission appointed by the

governor to prepare for a constitutional convention in
that state to revise its constitution. Still not satisfied, the
senators asked him such questions as: Now, has your name
always been Rein? Your birth certificate would show in the
New York City records, would it? . . . Have you ever represented, before any congressional committees, or before
the courts, any communists? Are you a member of the
Communist Party?

The secret hearing at which Brigadier General Ralph
W. Zwicker was angrily questioned also resulted in a scene
which demonstrated the double standard.

THE CHAIRMAN: [Senator McCarthy]: You have
a rather important job. I want to know how you feel
about getting rid of communists.

GENERAL ZWICKER: I am all for it.

THE CHAIRMAN: All right. You will answer [the
pending] question, unless you take the Fifth Amendment. I do not care how long we stay here, you are
going to answer it.

GENERAL ZWICKER: Do you mean how I feel toward
communists?

THE CHAIRMAN: I mean exactly what I asked you,
General, nothing else. And anyone with the brains of a
five-year-old child can understand that question. The
reporter will read it to you as often as you need to hear
it so that you can answer it, and then you will answer it.

The reporter then read the Senator's question. Senator
McCarthy wanted to know whether the General thought
that an officer responsible for permitting an alleged communist to receive an honorable discharge should be
removed from the military, "or do you think he should
be kept on in it?"

GENERAL ZWICKER: I do not think he should be removed from the military.

THE CHAIRMAN: Then, General, you should be removed from any command . . .

The senator then went on to question the General regarding his consultations with the Army's attorney who had accompanied him to the hearing. He declared that the much-decorated officer was "not fit to wear that uniform."

The same kind of treatment was accorded James A. Wechsler in an executive session later made public. Mr. Wechsler, briefly a member of the Young Communist League in the late 1930's, but since then a most outspoken anti-communist, was questioned at length regarding his writings, his newspaper and magazine employment. Even though Mr. Wechsler reluctantly gave the Senator from Wisconsin a list of names of fifteen persons whom, he said, he had known as communists in the 1930's, the senator nevertheless applied the double standard to him. Mr. Wechsler protested:

MR. WECHSLER: . . . I became editor of the *Post* in May, 1949. At that time, one of the great issues which the communists were fighting in America was the Marshall Plan. I was a vigorous supporter editorially of the Marshall Plan. I was a vigorous supporter of the Truman Doctrine. This is editorially; these are matters that are on the record. I would be happy to submit to this committee every editorial written since I became editor.

THE CHAIRMAN [Senator McCarthy]: I do not think I would care to read them.

MR. WECHSLER: Well, sir, you have made rather

strong judgments about me. I would think perhaps in fairness you ought to read them some day.

THE CHAIRMAN: I read enough of your stuff, Mr. Wechsler, to find that your paper, as far as I know, always leads the vanguard with the *Daily Worker*, follows the same line against anyone who is willing to expose communists in government ...

Mr. Wechsler did not hesitate to declare that various journalists with whom he had worked over the years were "following the communist line." It did no good. When he pointed out that a Communist Party resolution of December 28, 1952 was bitterly critical of him, Senator McCarthy had a question ready.

THE CHAIRMAN: Did you have anything to do with the passage of that resolution? Did you take a part in promoting the passage of that resolution?

MR. WECHSLER: Is this a serious question?

THE CHAIRMAN: Will you read the question to the witness? (Record read by reporter.)

Mr. Wechsler again explained to the Senator that the opposition of the Communist Party was "a tribute to the militant and vigorous anti-communism of the New York *Post*." Senator McCarthy nevertheless demanded that the editor answer.

"The answer is No, Senator," Mr. Wechsler said. If he was perplexed, the Senator later cleared up any possible misunderstanding:

"I may say, so that there is no doubt in your mind," Mr. McCarthy stated, "I have been following your record, not as closely as I would if you were in government, but, you being a newspaper editor, I have been following you somewhat. I am convinced you have done exactly what you would do if you were a member of the Communist Party, if you wanted to have a phony break and then use that phony break to the advantage of the Communist Party. I feel that you have not broken with communist ideals. I feel that you are serving them very, very actively . . ."

Further examples of the use of the double standard could fill a second book. The chairmen of committees, as a matter of routine, sign batches of subpoenas in blank, leaving the staff to fill in the names of witnesses. Summoned, usually on two or three days' notice, the "unfriendly" witness is told nothing concerning the subject of the inquiry or what information is specifically sought from him. Most of the committees permit the witness to be accompanied by a lawyer, but the uniform rule is that he shall be seen but not heard. He may only advise the witness in a whisper as to his legal rights. Committee members have threatened to throw lawyers out of hearings for attempting to address the committee, to offer an objection. One lawyer was accused by Chairman Velde of coaching his client, but when he tried to reply, the "Judge" silenced him.

A favorite device of the investigators is to go over everything in executive session. Sometimes the purpose is undoubtedly to protect the witness from unfair publicity but, at least as often, the secret hearing is used to "rehearse" for a later public one. At the open hearing, the uncooperative witness is asked only those questions which will be the most damaging. Another use of the executive session is for publicity. With reporters and the public barred, the investigator is free to give the press whatever version of the testimony suits his immediate purpose.

Commenting on these practices, Dean Erwin N. Griswold of Harvard Law School recently said:

" . . . I think it fair to say that a large section of the public has from time to time felt 'a sense of injustice' with respect to some of these hearings . . . A failure to appreciate the intimate relation between sound procedure and the preservation of liberty is implicit . . . in that saddest and most short-sighted remark of our times: 'I don't like the methods, but . . .' "

Defending the importance to government of congressional investigations, Dean Griswold told his Phi Beta Kappa audience at Mount Holyoke College, South Hadley, Massachusetts, that it was up to Congress to put a stop to the "private frolics of an individual member." Committee hearings, he said, "are an exercise of the power of a House of Congress for which every member of that House has a full and equal responsibility."

Dean Griswold is one of a number of distinguished Americans who have proposed a single standard by which all committees should be bound. He suggested the enactment by Congress of a code of practice for legislative investigations in order to "bring order and fairness into this field which has recently become so chaotic."

A devoted student of the bitter conflicts by which Americans have bought the liberties written into the Constitution, the Dean chose to conclude his speech to initiates to the honor society with these somber but hopeful words:

"We have been through struggles of this sort in the past, and justice and liberty have always eventually won out. Indeed we have been strengthened in our liberties by each such struggle . . . For myself, I have great faith in the sober second judgment of the people. The immediate reaction of the people, like that of any individual, may be hasty, emotional, irrational, or unsound. But when that phase is past, when we have had a real chance to think through our problems, I have confidence that the people will demand a better standard of conduct in legislative investigations than has been evidenced in the recent past ...

". . . It was Aeneas who heartened his men by saying to them: 'O passi graviora—Oh you who have lived through worse days . . .' It is not surprising that now, as in earlier times, there have been those who seek to exploit our fears. Nor should it be surprising that many people, at first at least, respond to such exploitation. But it is the way of life to have to meet new problems; and, while doing so, we should not give up old values ...

"The problems of our day may be useful problems. It is good I think that we should have to bestir ourselves from time to time to protect our liberties, as our ancestors did on many occasions in the past ... And so I would suggest that you not be discouraged, nor even be unduly concerned if basic human rights are under attack. These are rights which thrive in vindication, and each generation better understands them and their significance if it has to think them through for itself. We are given a great opportunity today, to which I think we will measure up, if the past is any guide ..."

"Governour, it is an impracticable thing for any man to accuse himself; thou knowst it very well."
— Printer William Bradford.

THIS IS A TALE of printers. One, a young man of twenty-six, stood accused before the Governor and Council of Pennsylvania. It was 1689. Printer William Bradford, who had introduced the art of printing into the colony, stood accused of subversion. He had reprinted the text of the Penn Charter. In that historic document, William Penn granted to the colonists of his domain some of the rights which we enjoy today as Americans.

After Governor Penn's death, the new governor showed an increasing tendency to ignore the provisions of the Charter. Aware of this, Printer Bradford decided to reprint the Charter, so that settlers might know what their rights were. Expecting trouble, he refrained from the usual practice of including his name on the cover as printer, but that did not save him from an angry governor.

QUESTION: Why, sir, I would know by what power of authority you thus print? Here is the Charter printed!

ANSWER: It was by Governour Penn's encouragement I came to this Province, and by his license I print.

QUESTION: What, sir, had you license to print the Charter? I desire to know from you, whether you did print the Charter or not, and who set you to work?

ANSWER: Governour, it is an impracticable thing for any man to accuse himself; thou knowst it very well.

QUESTION: Well I shall not much press you to it, but if you were so ingenuous as to confess, it should go the better with you.

ANSWER: Governour, I desire to know my accusers; I think it very hard to be put upon accusing myself.

QUESTION: Can you deny that you printed it? I do know you did print it, and by whose directions, and will prove it, and make you smart for it, too, since you are so stubborn.

QUESTION: [*by another member of the council*]: I am informed that one hundred and sixty were printed yesterday, and that Jos. Growden saith he gave twenty shillings for his part towards the printing it.

ANSWER: It's nothing to me what "Jos. Growden saith." Let me know my accusers, and I shall know the better how to make my defense.

More recently another American printer found himself before investigators: time, 1953; place, Capitol Hill. Idaho's Senator Herman Welker was conducting the closed-door hearing of the Senate Internal Security Subcommittee on "underground printing facilities." The witness, Jacob Hyams, testified that he was manager of Superior Press, Inc., a five-man job-printing firm in Washington. Much to the Senator's annoyance, Printer Hyams had no more enthusiasm for self-incrimination than Printer Bradford.

"You are one of these gentlemen," thundered the Senator from Idaho, "in my mind who are very anxious to take advantage of the Constitution that we all love and respect, yet, when we are trying to clean up a political philosophy that is dedicated to the ruination and the destruction of our country, you ... say 'I refuse to answer' ..."

In another Jenner committee hearing, committee counsel Robert Morris indicated a like exasperation:

"... Those witnesses who have appeared before our committee and who have been identified and about whom there has been evidence of their own Communist activity, when presented with the evidence or when asked questions about that evidence have invariably invoked their privilege against incrimination," he told Chairman Jenner. "At the same time, very often, as in the case of a university, they go back to the university and when asked by the university authorities whether or not they have been members of the Communist Party, we find that almost without exception they deny membership at that time, the difference being, of course, that when they are asked by the university officials they are not asked under oath and before a tribunal such as this to be held accountable in a court of law for denial if it can be proved to the contrary ..."

That is not by any means the only difference, as Mr. Morris, who is now a New York Municipal Court judge, is probably well aware. Another major difference is what lawyers and judges know as the "doctrine of waiver." In non-legal terms, this means simply that once a witness has answered *any* question regarding a particular subject he may have waived his right to refuse to answer further questions on that subject. Before an employer one's job is in danger, but before a committee, one ill-advised refusal to answer may result in a citation for contempt of Congress.

There is nothing imaginary or vague about this danger of waiving the privilege. It is not a case of legal hair-splitting. It explains why many witnesses have refused to answer such questions as "Have you ever taught communist doctrine in your classroom?" "Have you ever solicited students to join the Communist Party?" If the witness answers, he then may fear that he has opened the way to all questions regarding alleged "communist activity." He can expect to be asked not only about his own doings but the activities of others. He will have to decide on the spot, with all the pressure of a committee hearing bearing down upon him, whether refusing to answer will result in an acquittal or in a jail sentence for contempt.

Dean Erwin N. Griswold is among those who believe that this is the reason why so many witnesses rely on the Fifth Amendment.

". . . Counsel . . . may well hesitate to make his client bear the risk and expense of taking a case all the way to the Supreme Court," he told the Massachusetts Bar Association in 1953. ". . . The only safe advice may be to claim the privilege at the earliest possible moment, so as to be sure to avoid the charge of waiver."

The investigators are well aware of this. For instance, a witness was asked by counsel for the Jenner Committee whether he worked for the New Theatre School in 1936 and 1937.

"That is right," the witness answered.

Asked to describe the school, he invoked the Fifth Amendment.

"I want to be perfectly fair with you, Mr. Witness, and to your counsel," Senator Welker, sitting as a one-man subcommittee, immediately responded. "This committee has no desire whatsoever to get anyone in contempt of the committee, but you certainly, counsel, are familiar with the law, which definitely states that the witness, once he opens up a subject matter, cannot call a stopping place . . ."

Threatened with contempt, the witness answered the questions that followed.

In executive session, the investigators are sometimes quite obvious in their efforts to lead the witness into a situation from which he cannot retreat on pain of contempt. Printer Hyams is now on the stand:

QUESTION: You never served in the Communist Party with Mr. Super [a stockholder in Superior Press]?

ANSWER: I have never seen him.

QUESTION: You have served in the Party with Mr. Super?

ANSWER: I have never seen him.

QUESTION: Have you ever served with him in the Communist Party?

ANSWER: I think I have answered the question.

QUESTION: I direct you to answer the question. It is very simple.

SENATOR WELKER: Have you served in the Communist Party with Mr. Super?

ANSWER: I have never seen Mr. Super.

QUESTION: Will you answer the question yes or no? The chair directs you.

ANSWER: Never having seen Mr. Super, I find it impossible—

QUESTION: Have you ever served in the Communist Party with the chairman here today?

ANSWER: I have never seen the chairman before today.

QUESTION: Have you ever served in the Communist Party with him?

ANSWER: It is impossible to have done that.

QUESTION: You can give a yes or no answer to that, Mr. Hyams. Have you ever served in the Communist Party with the chairman?

ANSWER: I don't know how else I can answer the question.

Of course, every one knows how else Printer Hyams might answer such a question, but what might be involved in answering is another matter. Questioning of this kind is just the sort of guessing game at which a witness, under the tense situation of a committee hearing, may not prove to be skillful enough. Indeed, judging by Senator Welker's remarks in this hearing, the hope is that the witness will guess wrong. Later in the same hearing, Printer Hyams endeavored to help Senator Welker out a bit. He conceded that a Mr. Wood, identified by committee counsel as a local minor Communist official, had had some printing done at Superior Press, Inc. The committee at once began to pour questions through this breach.

MR. RICHARD ARENS [*staff director*]: Did Mr. Wood always pay you in cash when he purchased printing from your establishment?

MR. HYAMS: I'd like to refuse to answer that on the same grounds.

SENATOR WELKER: You will be directed to do it. I want to again call your attention and the attention of your counsel to the fact that you yourself voluntarily opened up the question of Mr. Wood and his business dealings with you, so you cannot, as a matter of law, decline to answer one phase of it when you opened up the subject matter. Therefore, I direct you to answer.

MR. HYAMS: I would still have to refuse, on the same grounds, sir.

SENATOR WELKER: I shall inform the committee that it is the chairman's intention at this time to ask a citation for you for contempt for your willful failure to answer a question directed to you by the acting chairman of this subcommittee when you yourself opened up the matter of inquiry. . . .

Another witness, the Chapel Hill, N.C. bookseller whom we have already met, was given like treatment by Senator Welker. The bookman was accused of having permitted the use of a rear room of his bookstore for "storing and operating a printing press . . . [for] the purpose of . . . getting out underground papers and literature in the event of a war between the Soviet Union and the United States, or other circumstances forcing underground conditions for the Communist Party." His accuser was one Paul Crouch, an ex-communist employee of the Department of Justice. Mr. Crouch's subsequent testimony elsewhere proved so flagrantly contradictory that the Attorney General finally announced he was studying the record to determine whether Mr. Crouch should be tried for perjury.

QUESTION: Do you think it unfair of this committee to ask you . . . while you are under oath, whether or not you ever consented to the operation of a printing press in the back room of your establishment leased and controlled by you, which printing press was to be used for the printing of communist literature? Do you think that unfair of this committee?

ANSWER: I refuse to answer that question on the

ground that the answer might tend to incriminate me.

Senator Welker kept trying. He and the committee's counsel asked by turns scores of questions on every conceivable subject. They asked him whether the Republican Party of North Carolina was controlled by communists; whether he was a member of a church; whether he had been identified with the Progressive Party; whether he belonged to the American Booksellers Association, the American Automobile Association; finally the Senator declared:

QUESTION: ... Why don't you stand up like a man and [say] "Senator, you know I didn't do it, and it is a dirty lie." Why don't you say that and come out and be an American for a change instead of hiding behind the Fifth Amendment?...

ANSWER: I refuse to answer that question on the grounds of my privilege granted to me under the Fifth Amendment.

QUESTION: Privilege granted you under the Fifth Amendment—a privilege where people like you, if you keep on, will soon destroy all of us. I will tell you that. I will let it go in the record straight across the board.

Turning to another witness, Senator Welker began by reminding him that he was the father of three hostages to Fortune.

QUESTION: Are you a man with a family ... ?
ANSWER: Yes, sir.
QUESTION What does it consist of?
ANWER: Three children.
QUESTION How old are they?
ANSWER: Four, six and ten.

SENATOR WELKER: You may proceed, counsel.

QUESTION: What is your occupation, if you please?

ANSWER: I am a printer.

Asked about communist activity and communism, the witness invoked the Fifth Amendment.

QUESTION: You realize, of course, that your declination to answer these questions is at your peril.

ANSWER: I state that I refuse to answer because of my constitutional right not to testify to anything which might incriminate me.

QUESTION: What do you mean by incriminate?

ANSWER: Which may have possible bad effects upon me.

QUESTION: What do you mean by bad effects? You mean, just embarrass you?

ANSWER: Bad effects of any nature, either to embarrass me or physical effects, or whatever effects it might be.

QUESTION: I will say to you right now, Mr. Witness, that that is not the law. Have you committed any crimes?

ANSWER: I do not believe so, sir.

QUESTION: When did you sever your connection with the Communist Party?

ANSWER: I refuse to answer that question, sir, on the same grounds.

* * * * *

QUESTION: In other words, you are taking advantage of the Fifth Amendment and you do not know why you are taking advantage of it?

ANSWER: To a certain extent, you might say that is true. I don't know or in what way the Fifth Amend-

ment and my right not to testify about anything concerning myself is protected by it, but I am asking protection under that amendment.

SENATOR WELKER: Let me say to you that the Fifth
Amendment protects the innocent as well [as] the
guilty and that it precludes, if you take advantage of it,
any witness giving testimony against himself which
might lead to possible incrimination. Now, certainly
you are not entitled to take advantage of that if your
answer would not tend to incriminate you. So, if you
were not a member of the Communist Party, you are
not entitled to take advantage of that Fifth Amendment.

ANSWER: I am just not the judge in this.

QUESTION: I understand you are not the judge.

ANSWER: I am more confused than anything else.

The investigators have added a good deal to the confusion. While Senator Welker declares that the Fifth
Amendment protects against any kind of incrimination,
his colleague, subcommittee chairman Jenner, has repeatedly declared that the privilege may not be invoked
unless the witness has committed a crime.

"The justification for invoking the Amendment," according to the Senator, "is that the witness asserts under
oath and in good faith that if he testifies in response
to a certain question, he will put into the record evidence
which will prove to be at least a link in a chain of evidence
that will ultimately lead to his conviction for *a crime
that he has committed.*" (My emphasis.)

Senator McCarthy refers quite simply to "Fifth Amend-
ment communists." On November 9, 1953, Dr. Nathan
Pusey, President of Harvard, in an exchange with
McCarthy, telegraphed him that much as he deplored the

"use of the Fifth Amendment . . . I do not regard the use of this Constitutional safeguard as a confession of guilt." McCarthy replied by telegraph the same day: "Even the most soft-hearted and fuzzy-minded cannot help but realize that a witness' refusal to answer whether he is or is not a communist on the ground that his answer would tend to incriminate him is the most positive proof obtainable that the witness is a communist."

Senator McCarthy's opinion is, not suprisingly, shared by Miss Gertrude S. Carraway, President-General of the Daughters of the American Revolution. Miss Carraway condemned those who "hide under the cloak of the Fifth Amendment of our Constitution, without being willing to defend and support the Consitution in its entirety." The lady said that the framers of the Constitution never intended that the Fifth Amendment be invoked "by those whose loyalty to our government . . . is in doubt . . ." She failed to state what was the source of her knowledge as to the intentions of those who, 165 years earlier, insisted on the inclusion of the guarantee against self-incrimination in the Constitution's first ten amendments.

Others have supposed, on the contrary, that the framers of the Bill of Rights were laboring to protect not criminals, subversives, spies, traitors, but the freedom of all Americans. The courts, as former Federal Judge Rifkind pointed out recently, instruct juries that invocation of the amendment is not to be considered an admission of guilt.

"Either the courts are all hypocrites," the jurist said, "or the public does not understand the significance of the Fifth Amendment. One thing is sure. We cannot play it both ways. A society which practices one set of ideals and preaches another is in the process of dissolution, or at least is suffering from a disease that may lead to its dissolution . . . There is something strange about the notion that one who has recourse to the Constitution thereby defies the Constitution and subverts it."

"MR. COHN: *Was there anybody else in the AVC you knew to be a Communist?*
"MR. BERNSTEIN: *This was the only one I know for a positive fact.*
"MR. COHN: *Let's forget the positive fact ...*"
—Hearings, Senate Permanent Subcommittee on Investigations.

THERE IS NOTHING in the Constitution that protects a witness from the effect on his employer and on his reputation of invoking the Fifth Amendment. Beyond a doubt, to do so nowadays is to risk the loss of one's good name and one's means of livelihood. Yet the alternatives are, to many, equally abhorrent. Witnesses may be quite willing to tell the investigators all about their own actions, past and present, but when it comes to naming others, their consciences sometimes call a halt. Under the waiver doctrine, that is just too bad. Once a witness has answered questions about himself, he cannot, legally speaking, balk at questions regarding others, no matter how certain he may be that they are innocent of any wrong-doing or criminal conduct. To refuse to answer at that point is to commit certain contempt, unless a court should later decide that the questions themselves were not relevant to the subject which Congress authorized the committee to investigate.

In the now-famous Fort Monmouth investigation conducted by Senator McCarthy, scientist Barry S. Bernstein was being questioned. He told the Senator that, as a member of the local American Veterans Committee chapter, he had known a man who "admitted to being a communist." He named him.

MR. [ROY] COHN [subcommittee counsel]: Was there anybody else in the AVC you knew to be a communist?

MR. BERNSTEIN: This was the only one I know for a positive fact.

MR. COHN: Let's forget the positive fact. There were some very heated discussions down at the AVC [regarding a proposal to expel communists from the organization]. From those, couldn't you make out a reasonable deduction concerning several there?

The witness remonstrated mildly. Those who had opposed the expulsion of communists from AVC were not necessarily Reds, he said. They were "interested in a democratic ideal and . . . for this reason offered an opinion against" expelling communist members of AVC.

MR. COHN: You said there were several others concerning whom you could make the deduction that they were communists.

MR. BERNSTEIN: I would say this, that the most I could say is that perhaps there were some of them that might have been sympathetic.

MR. COHN: Who were the several people you feel were sympathetic?

Mr. Bernstein reluctantly mentioned a name or two, whereupon counsel Cohn moved on to broader pastures:

MR. COHN: Was any one presently employed at Monmouth a member of AVC at that time?

MR. BERNSTEIN: Presently employed? Yes, there are some people that are presently employed.

MR. COHN: Let's have the names.

The junior Senator from Wisconsin is not alone in his interest in obtaining names. So, as we are already aware, is "Judge" Velde. In one of its reports last year, the Jenner committee also frankly declared that a major effort of the committee had been to get former communists to testify fully in executive session and, "by answering questions," to give evidence "of their willingness to take a position against the communist organization."

The naming of names was not insisted upon, the report asserted "except to ask for some sign or some willingness that would indicate genuine conversion ... Three witnesses who admitted [former] communist party membership and alleged their defection therefrom defied the subcommittee on the point of their willingness to testify about personalities and gave no other evidence of redemption. Consequently, these three were heard in open session." That the public testimony was for the purpose of bringing economic and other pressures to bear on the unredeemed was openly admitted.

Dr. Alex Benjamin Novikoff, Professor at the University of Vermont College of Medicine and cancer researcher, was questioned in executive session, talked to at length by committee member Senator Welker of Idaho, and then recalled for an open hearing. He testified that he had not been a communist for the five years since he had joined the faculty at the University of Vermont. As to the previous period, he invoked the Fifth Amendment.

"... I have gone over this period," he declared. "I don't know whether it is proper to reveal what came up in executive session, but you are bringing up all these matters. I indicated clearly then, I indicated to Senator Welker in a private letter, that people differ psychologically. Some are able to talk and name names; some are not. Unfortunately in some ways I belong to the second category. I cannot be an informer, and this is what I was asked to do, to show that I was really telling the truth when I said I no longer had—when I said I had no connections whatever with the Communist Party and had had none for any time during the time I was at the University of Vermont."

THE CHAIRMAN: In other words, Doctor, you are not willing to help this Committee in its task. Our task is primarily this: to show that there is a Communist conspiracy directed from Moscow to infiltrate the educational system of this country, to affect the lives of the youth of this nation, and yet you as a professor and an outstanding cancer research scientist will not help this Committee break this insidious conspiracy that is gnawing at the very vitals of this country.

MR. NOVIKOFF: I would help this Committee in every way I am able short of doing—

THE CHAIRMAN: Then all we ask you to do is to testify.

MR. NOVIKOFF: Short of doing the one thing that was asked of me. This was put to me that way, "You name names, and we will know you are telling the truth." That I cannot do.

In the questions which followed, Senator Jenner made no effort to conceal that applying economic pressure to the witness was one motive for re-questioning him in open session.

MR. NOVIKOFF: I have indicated to you—I remember what you asked and I want to make this clear. The

counsel is referring again to something which has occurred in private or executive session.

THE CHAIRMAN: Of course he is, because that is why
we had the private or executive session, so that you
might come in here and *protect your career* and tell
the Committee the truth. (My emphasis.)

Then Senator Welker took a hand. In a series of
statements which were confirmed by Professor Novikoff,
the Senator told what had gone before. He had conducted
the executive session at which the Professor was questioned. It had been conducted with "all the courtesy and
respect" that a witness would have in a court. Afterwards,
a conference, "a very personal conference," between Professor Novikoff and Senator Welker took place, at which
time the Professor was "bothered with [his] conscience."
Senator Welker had offered to give Professor Novikoff
two weeks' time to think over his testimony and later
agreed to a third week to permit him to attend a scientific
meeting in Chicago.

SENATOR WELKER: I informed you, Doctor, that if
you told the truth before the Committee in private
session that you could go forth with a clear conscience
back to the University of Vermont, your testimony
would remain private, and your reputation in no way
hurt. Am I correct in that?

MR. NOVIKOFF: Yes, sir. But I should make it clear
what telling the truth really meant in concrete terms.
You say telling the truth, but I had been told within
the first five minutes that I spoke to Mr. Morris that
that meant naming names.

SENATOR WELKER: Dr. Novikoff, how can this Committee tell whether or not a man has severed his con-

nection with the Communist Party unless he tells us all the truth? Can you tell me that?

MR. NOVIKOFF: I have thought of that as you know because I wished there were a way for you to examine my brain. There isn't. You have to take the sincerity of what I am saying; you have to look into what I have been doing. . . .

Other witnesses have decided to run the full risk of waiving their Fifth Amendment protection. The record of such hearings dramatically demonstrates the truth of the assertion that, once a witness begins to testify, the investigators want to know everything—especially the name, address and occupation of every person the witness can dredge from his memory, whether or not he has any reason to suspect his present or former associates of crime.

One such witness was a Chicago University professor who was subpoenaed by the Jenner committee, questioned in executive session, and then made to testify all over again in public. The witness had testified to his past membership in the Communist Party and had sworn he was no longer a member. The name hunt began at once.

MR. MORRIS: Mr. Horton, will you tell us who the senior faculty member of the [Communist] unit at the University of Pennsylvania was?

MR. HORTON: I regret to say that I must decline to answer this question on three grounds: one, on the ground of my privilege against self-incrimination under the Fifth Amendment of the Constitution; secondly, a moral ground that it is deeply repugnant to one of my strongest convictions to play the role of informer; and thirdly, because I challenge the authority of this Committee to conduct this inquiry.

(There was a demonstration by the audience.)

THE CHAIRMAN: We will have order or we will have
to clear the room. Now, Mr. Reporter, what was the
first ground?

(The record was read by the Reporter as follows: "On
the ground of my privilege against self-incrimination.")

THE CHAIRMAN: Very well. The Committee recognizes your right to refuse to answer this question under
the Fifth Amendment of the Constitution of the
United States, and that is the policy of this Committee,
but in this particular case *you have opened up this
field* of inquiry. You have stated that you were a member of the Communist Party; that you belonged to a cell
at the University of Pennsylvania; and when you went
to Yale you joined there, you belonged to a cell there;
in both of these cells there were students, professors,
and other people. Now, you have attorneys here. You
have opened up this field and I do not believe you are
allowed to be the judge when you will pull the curtain
down and refuse to give this Committee testimony.
You have opened the field up. We are entitled to
know. (My emphasis.)

(The witness confers with attorneys.)

THE CHAIRMAN: So I direct you to answer the question.

MR. HORTON: Mr. Chairman, I must decline to answer that question on the grounds previously stated,
all three of them.

MR. MORRIS: Mr. Horton, have you had ample time
to consult with your two attorneys on this particular
point?

MR. HORTON: Yes, I have.

MR. JENNER: [the witness' attorney]: Mr. Chairman,
I object on the ground that it is an invasion of the

privilege of relationship between attorney and client.

THE CHAIRMAN: The objection is overruled. The witness answered the question and he said yes, that he had.

Professor Horton persisted in refusing to supply the names desired at his own risk, for having once incriminated himself—to whatever extent his admission of past Communist membership is incriminating—he could not legally claim further protection from the Constitution. Morally, he might be right, but he nevertheless faced citation for contempt.

Harvard Associate Professor Wendell H. Furry also chose to face jail rather than supply the names of persons he regarded as innocent. In his case, the committee chairman, Senator McCarthy, left no doubt that he would seek to have the Professor indicted.

Professor Furry had invoked the Fifth Amendment at a previous hearing, but before Senator McCarthy he chose to testify to his own actions. He said he had formerly belonged to the Communist Party. After some argument he was permitted to explain his decision to testify:

"Our forefathers wrote into the Constitution the privilege of the Fifth Amendment to provide protection which good citizens may sometimes sorely need," the Professor told the Senator. "Innocent people who feel the threat of false, mistaken, or overzealous prosecution because of unpopular opinions have every right to invoke this protection. It is clear, however, that widespread misrepresentation has produced in many minds a distorted idea of the meaning of the constitutional privilege. Though its real purpose has always been to shield the innocent, many people have been misled into believing that the exer-

cise of the privilege is an admission of guilt. I have now
come to the belief that for me to continue to claim my
constitutional privilege would bring undue harm to me
and to the great institution with which I am connected.

"Although I am sure that my past claims to the privilege have been both legally justified and morally right,
I now intend to waive my constitutional rights and give
this Committee all the evidence it may legitimately seek
concerning my own activities and associations. I hope that
by telling my own political history I can help to dispel
suspicion and contribute to public understanding.

"Experience has taught me that the inquiry is likely
to concern other persons than myself. I feel obliged to
state now that I shall respectfully refuse to answer questions that bring in the names of other people. I wish to
make it clear, however, that if I knew of any person whose
conduct, as I saw it, was criminal, I should feel bound to
reveal the facts. I am not seeking to protect the guilty
from prosecution. I wish merely to shield the innocent
from persecution. I hope that on this matter the Committee will respect my conscience."

Professor Furry's hope was in vain.

"I want to assure you right now," the Senator replied,
"that you will not be allowed to protect any member of
the communist conspiracy because you think that they
are only innocent conspirators. You will be ordered to
answer the questions that we ask you and we will now proceed."

Senator McCarthy immediately launched into a line
of questioning designed to elicit names. He asked Professor Furry whether there were communists doing "secret
radar work" during World War II in a laboratory with
him. Professor Furry replied that there were five or six.

"They never in any way departed from the [security]

rules, to my knowledge," he declared, "or showed any inclination to regard any outside connections, including
that with the Communist Party, as having any bearing
on their work. They were devoted to the war effort. They
worked loyally, and I shall not reveal their names."

THE CHAIRMAN: What were their names?

MR. FURRY: I refuse to answer that, sir.

THE CHAIRMAN: You are ordered to answer.

MR. FURRY: I refuse.

* * * * *

THE CHAIRMAN: Where are they now?

MR. FURRY: To my best knowledge, and about only
one of them I have any real doubts as to where he
might be employed, none of them are working on any
government work.

THE CHAIRMAN: Do you know where the six are now
working?

MR. FURRY: Pretty well, but I shall not reveal it. It
might help to reveal their names.

* * * * *

Senator McCarthy then listed the unnamed individuals as numbers one through six and questioned Furry
regarding his knowledge of their whereabouts and how
recently he had had contact with them. A guessing game
followed, the Professor having asserted quite clearly that
they were all working in universities and, as far as he
knew, none of them were connected with war work.

The Senator then went on into other matters. He
asked Professor Furry whether he collected funds for one
Israel Halperin.

"I collected funds for the assistance of Mr. Halperin
and his family during their difficulties," the Professor
replied. The difficulties came from Halperin's having been

accused of espionage for Soviet Russia by the Royal Canadian Commission.

"Perhaps part of these funds, certainly collected by somebody, may have gone toward paying his attorney's fees. He had one of the most prominent conservative attorneys in Canada at his trial at which he was easily acquitted and the fees were very nominal..." Professor Furry testified. "By easy acquittal, I [mean] that the judge found for acquittal without hearing any case for the defense...."

Once again, the Committee asked for names.

THE CHAIRMAN: How much money did you collect for Halperin?

MR. FURRY: Not very much. Most of the collection was done by other people. I suppose I collected maybe something on the order of $300.

THE CHAIRMAN: Whom did you collect it from?

MR. FURRY: I can't remember all the names.

THE CHAIRMAN: Do you remember anyone whom you collected money from?

MR. FURRY: Well, sir, I know that this is an idea to get me to give names, and I know that it is not a good thing when people's names are brought up before such a Committee.

THE CHAIRMAN: This is no laughing matter. It is rather important to get the names of people collecting money to defend a communist spy, one who has been named as a spy under oath, one who was found to be a spy by the Royal Commission, one who got off only because his co-conspirators, for some mysterious reason, either because of a pay-off or some other reason, finally refused to testify...

MR. FURRY: Sir, to the best of my belief, none of the people that I know about who contributed to this were communists, never at any time, and I refuse to have them smeared.

THE CHAIRMAN: Who contributed the money?

MR. FURRY: I refuse to answer that question.

THE CHAIRMAN: You are ordered to answer it.

MR. FURRY: I refuse.

THE CHAIRMAN: Who else collected money for this man named as an espionage agent?

MR. FURRY: I refuse to answer that question.

THE CHAIRMAN: You are ordered to answer.

MR. FURRY: I refuse.

The Senator began a few questions on Professor Furry's political opinions, but he dropped the subject hastily when Furry said that he thought that the communist system "looks pretty inferior to ours." The Senator returned to the more familiar territory of names.

At one point, the Professor seized an opportunity to confirm what many thoughtful lawyers have supposed was the principal reason why witnesses reply using the Fifth Amendment to questions which do not appear on the face of it to be incriminating:

". . . I certainly have never attempted to indoctrinate any students with communist philosophy," Professor Furry said in answer to a question.

THE CHAIRMAN: When you told us [in a previous hearing] that you thought if you answered that question the answer might tend to incriminate you, at that time were you aware of the fact that you never had attempted to indoctrinate any students?

MR. FURRY: I was aware of it, and I also was aware of the doctrine of areas under the privilege which you had expounded very ably yourself, sir, and this certainly would have come under that area and would have been a waiver of my privilege. It is certainly a matter of law that a witness would have to refuse to answer all questions which come within such an area. That was, of course, my constitutional ground for invoking the privilege and, in fact, for having to invoke it...

Once more the Senator returned to the matter of names:

THE CHAIRMAN: Do you know of anyone connected with Harvard who is or was a member of the Communist Party?

MR. FURRY: Sir, I am not sorting people for the Committee.

THE CHAIRMAN: Answer the question.

MR. FURRY: Well, I would like to make this statement and that is that I have never at any time known anyone who held a permanent position on the Harvard faculty with the exception of myself or who has since come to hold or who now holds a permanent position on the Harvard faculty, to be a member of the Communist Party. Apart from that, I will refuse to answer the question.

THE CHAIRMAN: Your definition of permanent may be different than mine. . . . The question is do you know anyone in any way connected with Harvard who is a member of the Communist Party?

MR. FURRY: Sir, there are all sorts of difficulties with this business of naming and sorting names, and I am very glad that I am having nothing to do with it. One of them is that indications, opinions, impressions, and differences of people's statements come into it, and that makes it not only one of the most distasteful notions I can think of to engage in, but also an extremely dangerous one, and I am not going to answer that question.

In July 1954, the committee voted unanimously to ask the Senate to cite Professor Furry for contempt.

12

A SUBPOENA
FOR MR. SMITH

"The characters in this tale are fictitious. Any resemblance to any person, living or dead, is purely coincidental."

—Anonymous lawyer

PROFESSOR FURRY WAS, by his own avowal, a former communist. We are still left to wonder whether witnesses who have never been members of the Communist Party invoke the Fifth Amendment, and, if so, under what circumstances. One such circumstance may well be that the witness, as Dean Griswold has pointed out, "may be badly frightened, even though he is wholly innocent."

"It is not everyone who can safely venture on the witness stand, though entirely innocent of the charge against him," the Supreme Court has opined. "Excessive timidity, nervousness when facing others in attempting to explain transactions of a suspicious character and offenses charged against him will often confuse and embarrass him to such a degree as to increase rather than remove prejudices against him. It is not everyone, however honest, who would therefore willingly be placed on the witness stand."

The high court was speaking of judicial trials where at least the charges must be precise, the accused's lawyer can object to improper questions, and the witness can tell

162

his story in response to his own attorney's questions. A committee hearing is a very different setting. The accusations are sensational but often vague. The evidence against the witness is sometimes wholly unknown to him. His accusers may be anonymous, or if they have testified or later testify against him, neither he nor his lawyer may cross-question them.

Then there is the case of the witness who is following bad advice. If he testifies without counsel, he is as likely as not to be in this category. Even lawyers have their troubles, however, when it comes to counselling witnesses. One lawyer, when he got his first two or three cases of this kind, advised his clients to plead the Fifth Amendment even to such questions as "Have you ever engaged in espionage against the United States?" The witnesses had not. After he had more time to consider all angles of the problem, the attorney concluded that his own previous advice was not the best. The frightened witness, or one who is acting on bad advice, is thus likely to rely on the Fifth Amendment protection in response to many questions which, no doubt, could be freely answered. The millions of words of transcripts of congressional hearings contain many examples of such responses. Here, for instance, is the testimony of an obviously confused and frightened witness at a secret hearing of the Jenner committee:

QUESTION: Is there a Communist Party in the United States, to your knowledge?

ANSWER: I refuse to answer that question on the grounds of the Fifth Amendment. [The witness is, presumably, afraid of waiving his privilege should he answer.]

QUESTION: Is there a Progressive Party in the United States, to your knowledge?

ANSWER: I refuse to answer that question.

QUESTION: Is there a Socialist Party in the United States, to your knowledge?

ANSWER: The same answer.

QUESTION: Would it be the same if I asked you if there were [a] Republican or Democratic Party?

ANSWER: I refuse to answer either one of those questions on the same grounds.

Given an opportunity to consult his attorney, the witness later said he would like to change his answer to an affirmative one regarding the Progressive, Socialist, Republican and Democratic parties.

We are left with the well-counselled witness whose true answer to the famous "$64 question" would be "No." Do such witnesses nevertheless invoke the privilege of refraining from bearing witness against themselves? Do they do so legally? Or, as Messrs. Investigators are wont to declare, are they "hiding behind the Constitution"?

The answer is not easy to come by. The only practicable approach seems to be to employ a device dear to the hearts of professors of law: the hypothetical case. Our story of "Mr. Smith" which follows is such a hypothetical case. Wholly fictitious, it is however based on discussions with attorneys who have represented witnesses summoned before investigating committees, and others who are expert in constitutional law. As nearly as possible, it is told just as it might happen.

On the morning of May 12, 195-, John B. Smith, director of research for the Council of Economic Research, Inc., was served with a subpoena at the Council's offices.

"Greeting:" the subpoena announced in Old English type. "Pursuant to lawful authority, YOU ARE HEREBY COMMANDED to appear before the Subcommittee on

Domestic Tranquillity of the Committee on the Judiciary
of the Senate of the United States, on May 14, 195-, at
10 o'clock a.m., at their committee room, 1085 Senate
Office Building, Washington D.C., then and there to
testify what you may know relative to the subject matters
under consideration by said committee.

"Hereof fail not, as you will answer your default under
the pains and penalties in such cases made and provided.

"To George O'Haley, to serve and return.

"Given under my hand, by order of the committee
this 10th day of May, in the year of our Lord one
thousand nine hundred and fifty-blank.

James F. McCaley
Chairman, Senate Subcommittee
on Domestic Tranquillity"

Mr. Smith looked at the subpoena again. He had less
than forty-eight hours in which to consult a lawyer and
go to Washington. He phoned Charles C. Overby, a
member of the Council's board of directors who also
served as its attorney. An hour later he was sitting in the
lawyer's office.

"We couldn't possibly handle this sort of thing, John,"
Mr. Overby explained. "The firm specializes in tax matters, you know. I would gladly take it myself, but this
requires special knowledge. Since you called, I've done a
little phoning around. The man I think you should go to
is Robert Z. O'Brien. He's in the Empire State Building.
He has handled a number of these cases, several of them,
I am told, people in very much your situation. I really
think you ought to see him right away."

"Well, I came to you for advice," Mr. Smith said, "so
I suppose I'd better start following it."

"Good. I thought you would say that, and in view of

the limited time you have, I took the liberty of making an appointment for you at two."

Arriving at lawyer O'Brien's office, Mr. Smith was shown in at once. The lawyer glanced at the subpoena briefly.

"Sit down, won't you?" he said. "I feel reasonably sure we can arrange a postponement for at least a day or two. Daly, the committee's counsel, is not a bad sort, at least when it comes to that sort of arrangement, but we can't be absolutely sure. Have you any idea what they want with you?"

"I'm not sure," said Mr. Smith.

"Naturally. Well, let's go over your background and see if we can get some ideas. You are employed by the Council for Economic Research, I understand."

"Yes."

"Tell me about the Council and your job there, please."

"I'm director of research. That's the title, anyway. I have a staff of three under me. Besides supervising their work, I prepare most of the studies the Council undertakes, edit them and arrange for publication. I also edit the Council's monthly bulletin, *Economic Review*."

"How long have you been with them?"

"Since 1948. I started at $800 a month and I am now making $12,000 a year—before taxes, that is, of course."

"Does the bulletin deal with subjects that are controversial—politically controversial, I mean. For instance, east-west trade? The economic aspects of the defense program?"

"We haven't had much to say about foreign trade, certainly little or nothing about trade with the Iron Curtain countries. We deal more with the current situation in the domestic economy. Any discussion of the prospects or effects of east-west trade we would consider too much in the realm of speculation. The defense program has been mentioned, naturally. I have several times referred to the effect that a marked decline in the size of appropriations would have on other areas of the economy, for instance, but I don't think my comments are much different from the sort of thing you might read in the National City Bank *Bulletin*."

"All right, Mr. Smith. Let's put that aside for a moment," the lawyer said. "Anything else about you or your work that you think gives us some clue to this business?"

"Well, I'm not a Red, if that's what you mean, and never have been."

"Now, now, Mr. Smith," the lawyer said, "please don't confuse me with Senator McCaley. As a matter of fact, I don't find it necessary to ask that question. I can advise a witness without doing so, at least as far as his rights in a committee hearing are concerned. However, since you volunteered the information, let's begin at the beginning. Give me a brief rundown of your education, job experience, and the highlights of your life, as best you can."

The story of John Smith's life as it came out in lawyer O'Brien's office was more or less typical.

"I was born in 1910," he said. "My father owned a smallish hardware business and dabbled in stocks, the way most people did in the twenties if they had a few dollars. Fortunately, I was a good enough student in college so that, when the crash came in 1929, and father lost heavily, I was able to continue college by getting a scholarship and supplementing it with anything I could get to do. You know how it was."

"You were one of the lucky ones."

"Yes, I suppose I was. My father died in '31. The business was gone, but he left my sister and me a few thousand in life insurance which somehow he had managed not to borrow against. By the time I got my B.A., we were in the bottom of the depression. That was in 1932. There wasn't a chance of a job, so I decided I would invest what was left of the insurance money in as much graduate work as I could manage to stretch it to. I took a masters degree in economics the next year and started work toward a doctorate, but then my sister was injured in an accident. That took what was left. By that time Roosevelt was in the White House. One of the members of the economics faculty recommended me for a place as a junior economist with the AAA, and I got the job. I was in government work until 1948, and I think it must be that period the committee is interested in. Perhaps I should have brought it up with you at once, but I—"

Mr. O'Brien held up his hand to interrupt: "Don't apologize. Tell it just the way you have begun, and I'll just throw out a question when something is not clear to me."

"All right, but to be honest, I guess I wanted to form an opinion of you before I went into this part of it, and I have and—well, to continue: I was with the Department of Agriculture until 1939. The emphasis in Washington shifted rapidly away from recovery and toward defense, as you know, and eventually I shifted with it to a job in the Treasury."

"Who was your boss there?"

"I was about to say, it was Black—Lawrence Black."

"The famous Larry Black?"

"Yes, but of course I was not working directly under him at first. For a while I worked under Ronald Kupser and then later under Jim Rawlings."

"They are among the government people who were named as members of a so-called Soviet spy ring by that Miss Maitress, Mary Maitress."

"Yes, but I think her charges are absurd. I didn't know Black well, but I can't imagine him as a commie. He was a Keynesian, as much as he could be anything. Matter of fact, he was a Blackian. A very strong, very vigorous personality, Larry Black was. I don't think he ever took orders from anybody except the Secretary, and a good many of those he didn't take very gracefully, to tell the truth."

"What about Kupser and Rawlings."

"Nor them either. It's preposterous."

"Were you friendly with them, outside of professional contacts, I mean?"

"Well, I went to an occasional cocktail party at the Blacks', of course, and the same thing would apply to the others. It was not obligatory, but—"

"Yes, of course. I'm not suggesting that you had anything more than the normal social relations with them, but those are quite enough to interest our Senatorial friends, I assure you. This is most likely the subject of inquiry, but let's go back a bit. Did you have other friends during your government service who might be named in this business?"

"There is certainly one. A fellow named Paul Roe. I was a bachelor when I first went to Washington. Roe was a man of about my own age who had just come to work in the AAA. We were quite friendly for a number of years, and then there were several other men, most of them economists, whom I knew. We used to get together occasionally, sometimes for poker, sometimes for a bull session about government policy. There were some pretty hot arguments at times. Some were solid New Dealers.

Keynesians, as I said. Keynes was the foremost English economist, foremost Western economist of this half-century. Most of the New Deal economists more or less applied his theories to government policy—as much as they could, anyway. Well, as I started to say, others were pretty definitely Marxians. Thought the country would never recover from the depression except by outright socialization of heavy industry at least. Of course, history has proved them wrong, but at that time—"

"I'd like to hear about it sometime, Mr. Smith, but just now hadn't we—don't you think we'd better stay pretty close to the problem at hand? Would you call these discussions or arguments a 'study group'?"

"I never thought of it as such—not at the time, anyway."

"Did you study Karl Marx?"

"No, not in the ordinary sense. We were familiar enough with the general theory, but it's certainly true we argued pro and con about socialist versus New Deal economic policies."

"Were communists present at these discussions?"

"I think some of them were communists, yes. There was a fellow named Elbert Noyes, for instance."

"Was he a communist?"

"I assume he was. You've got to remember this was a long time ago—eighteen, nineteen, twenty years. As I remember it, Noyes was always arguing the straight Marxist position. I don't recall his saying he was a member of the Communist Party, but it wouldn't surprise me. In those days, nobody thought a thing of associating with Reds. Then there was Roe."

"Tell me more about him, please."

"He more or less organized the thing, I guess you could say. He was the one who first began inviting the

boys to get together. We often gathered at his apartment, one of those converted stables in a back alley in
Georgetown. Washington is full of them. Anyway, Roe
was frankly and obviously a left-winger. He had the
Daily Worker and other communist publications lying
around his place. Other periodicals too, of course. He
had a superb economics library. Everybody you could
think of. I borrowed many a book from him. We knew
each other quite well for several years. We even double-
dated. Then I got married. My wife is a Washington
girl, and I more or less drifted into her circle of acquaintances. That was in 1938. He was certainly very
pro-Soviet. When they had those trials over there—the
purge trials—we used to kid him a good deal about it.
He insisted that the Soviets were just protecting themselves against espionage."

"Aside from the discussions in his apartment, what
other connection did you have with Roe?"

"Not only in *his* apartment. Some of the other boys
played host on occasion. To answer your question: I
recall giving him money for Spain, several times, at
least."

"At public meetings?"

"No, I gave it to him. Sometimes when the bunch
of us got together he would ask for contributions, and I
was glad to pitch in."

"How did you know that the money was going to be
used to help Spain, as you say?"

"I'm afraid I just assumed that he would transmit
the money to the medical aid committee that was raising
funds at that time to help the Spanish loyalists."

"Did you give him a check?"

"I can't remember. I might have."

"If you had given him a check, would it have been payable to the committee or to Roe?"

"The committee, I should think, but I'm not certain. Most likely the committee."

"Did you and Roe remain friendly right up to the time you left government service?"

"No, we didn't. He would come to dinner once in a while. He got married not long after Ruth and I did. We invited them to dinner now and then, and vice versa. One date was set for shortly after Labor Day in—when was it—1939. The point is, that in the meantime the Russians and the Nazis signed the famous Pact and Hitler invaded Poland. The dinner was a very unpleasant business. My wife was pretty sore at me afterwards, and I guess I should have kept my temper, but Roe began cackling about how the Nazi-Soviet deal served the British right. He said the British had been playing fast and loose with the Russians, hoping to turn the Germans against them, and so forth. He made a lot of remarks that seemed to me then—still do, for that matter—disgustingly cynical. He didn't seem to give a damn what happened to England or Western Europe, and only a few weeks before he was talking about collective security and all the rest of it. Well, to make it brief, I blew up and invited him to leave my house and suggested it would be fine with me if he didn't turn up again."

"Did you see him again after that?"

"As a matter of fact, yes, I did," Mr. Smith said a little sheepishly. "I don't know how this will look to you, but—well, first of all, he attempted to get in touch with me several times. I told him that as far as I was concerned I was still anti-fascist even if he wasn't. He would go into a long-winded explanation, and at least once I just hung up on him. Then one day about three years later, he called me up at the Treasury. By this time he had a rather important job at the Board of Economic Warfare. It so happened that some work we were doing had to be closely coordinated with BEW. In the war period everybody short-cut the red tape as much as possible. Roe never mentioned the row we had had, and I felt it would be discourteous of me to carry a grudge all that time, especially since there was a war on, and it was important that we cooperate in working out this particular policy. It had to do with various rather technical foreign exchange problems. Later we were put on an inter-departmental committee and met a number of times in that. As I recall it, Nancy Roe called up Ruth a week or so later to invite us to a cocktail party, but we didn't go. I lunched with Roe and others at times, when we were working together on the exchange problem and other Treasury-BEW matters."

"Have you seen him since you left Washington?"

"No, I haven't, but I have heard of him, unfortunately. He wrote a book recently, a thing called *Monopoly Capital Since World War II,* if I remember rightly."

"Who published it?"

"That's just it. The communist publishing house, International Publishers."

"Was Roe ever named as a member of one of these spy rings or in any other connection by our friend, Miss Maitress?"

"I think so, but I haven't followed it closely."

"Did you ever use him as a reference?"

"Not that I recall. I might have in transferring from Agriculture to Treasury, but I doubt it. I think I put down my immediate superiors as references, by and large. That was what Civil Service preferred. They wanted references who knew about you in terms of the work you performed."

"What about Black, Kupser and Rawlings?"

"I gave their names to the Council here when I applied for the job. It was purely a routine application, however, since they asked me to come on."

"Why did you leave the Treasury Department?"

"I was offered the job I have now. The salary was attractive and I thought I had better take it."

"Who signed your efficiency ratings there, do you know?"

"Larry Black, or Ron or Jim, depending upon who was my immediate superior."

"All right, now let me ask a few personal questions. Your wife, I presume, is not a communist?"

"And never was."

"Are you familiar with the Attorney General's list of subversive organizations?"

"Well, sort of, Mr. O'Brien. I've read references to it at one time or another in the papers. Of course, when I was in government, toward the end, I signed a loyalty form. The list was attached to that, but I don't remember the specific names."

"You mentioned contributing money to Spain. What was the name of the committee?"

"Committee to Aid Spanish Democracy—something like that."

"I'm afraid that is now on the list. Were you a member?"

"I may have agreed to be on the Washington committee, Mr. O'Brien. I really can't remember. It seems to me Leon Henderson was on it, not to mention various Congressmen and others."

"That may well be, but the committee will be inter-

ested not in who else was on it but in the fact that *you*
were. When you go home tonight ask your wife what she
remembers, look through your old correspondence, try to
refresh your recollection, as the lawyers say. Were you a
member of any other such organization, or did you make
contributions to any?"

"Not that I remember, though I occasionally contributed to war relief committees and that sort of thing."

"Is there anything else, especially, that you want to
tell me that you think might have some bearing on this
subpoena?"

John Smith thought a moment.

"I can't think of anything. I'm glad we had this discussion. I'm less concerned. There doesn't seem to be
much for me to worry about. I can't see what questions
they might ask that would make much of a problem for
me, can you?"

"Yes, I can. You have quite a few problems, my
friend. There's your friendly association with Roe, to begin with. That was pretty generally known among your
other economist associates there, wasn't it?"

"Yes."

"If Roe was or is a communist, your friendship has
probably created considerable suspicion of you as a communist or a fellow-traveler in the eyes of some of the
government investigators. Then, as a New Deal economist associated with Black, you have most likely been
listed in various committee and FBI dossiers as a possible member of one of the groupings which included
Black."

"That's ridiculous!" Mr. Smith replied angrily. "Nobody can call me a communist. I have never been one
and I'm perfectly willing to swear to it."

"It is not as simple as that, Mr. Smith," the lawyer

said. "I want to go over this carefully with you, before we decide how to approach these problems."

"If you're talking about my pleading the Fifth Amendment, I—I won't consider it. If I did that, the Council would be seriously hurt. It could easily cost me my job. Anyway, why should I? I've committed no crimes. I'm not a commie. There's no answer to any question they could ask that would incriminate me. I won't consider the Fifth!"

"Mr. Smith, you're a likeable fellow and I respect your ability as an economist. I will, of course, undertake to advise you even if you insist on pursuing this course, but after all I *am* the lawyer here. It's my duty to tell you, to the best of my ability, what you are up against. Then, if you still want to insist on your own view, that is entirely up to you. For the present, however, why don't we consider all the angles before you decide?"

"I'm sorry," Mr. Smith said. "You're perfectly right. Go ahead."

"We can't anticipate all the questions they will ask, of course, but we can guess at some of them. They will almost certainly inquire as to membership in the Communist Party. Now, you would like to answer 'no' to that, I presume."

"I certainly would."

"You can if you insist, but I think you are running very serious risks in—"

"But why, Mr. O'Brien! It's the simple truth."

"I know, but the situation is not simple. Suppose you answer 'no.' Then the next query is: 'Have you ever been a member?' You answer that negatively. Then there are a series of questions they may follow up with. 'Did you know Larry Black? Did you attend cocktail parties at his house? Did you meet Kupser and Rawlings there?

Were you acquainted with Paul Roe? Did you ever give him any money? Did you in 1936, say, give him a check for $25? Did you write in the Council's bulletin that the Korean truce might create a disturbance in the domestic economy? Did you sponsor the Washington Committee to Aid Democratic Spain?' There will almost certainly be others which we can't anticipate.

"Now then, let us suppose you answer all these questions. You knew Larry Black very well, indeed, as a matter of fact. You did attend cocktail parties at his home. You probably met Kupser and Rawlings there. You knew Paul Roe. You attended discussions in his apartment. Some of the discussions dealt with Marxism, communism, and so forth. You don't recall whether you gave him a check, but you may have, and they may have a microfilmed record of it. In any case, you gave him money. Almost certainly some quotations from the Council for Economic Research's bulletin can be singled out to indicate that your views are to the left of President McKinley's. You did sponsor the Washington Spanish Committee.

"You know what circumstantial evidence is, Mr. Smith. If you answer all these questions, you will be helping to create the impression that your denial of present or past Party membership is nothing less than perjury. Miss Maitress, remember, has already testified that Black, Kupser, Rawlings and Roe were members of this so-called communist ring. Don't you see that if you answer questions as to your personal acquaintanceship with any of them, you are giving evidence, as they say in English detective stories, that may be used against you?"

"Yes, I'm beginning to see what you mean."

"Unfortunately, that's only part of the story. If you answer those questions about communist membership,

you will be practically forced to go into the matter of
your relationship with Roe, Black, and the others, as well
as into your sponsorship of the Committee, your contributions, the discussion group and so forth, in order to explain how it could be that you were not a communist,
even though you had these associations. Once you do
that, then you cannot refuse to answer any question about
the matters to which you have already begun to testify.
They will almost certainly ask you if Roe was a communist, if he subscribed to the *Daily Worker*, and anything
else they might like to know. Similarly, they will want to
know all you know about your former Treasury associates,
about everyone who attended even one of these discussions at Roe's apartment, and so on. Are you prepared to
do that?"

"No. They haven't done anything criminal that I
know of. Even Roe, if he's a commie, there's no law
against it. Paul was a screwball, as far as I'm concerned,
but I just—well, it—"

"You don't want to be an informer. But if you were
asked about his attitude toward the Nazi-Soviet Pact,
about his political opinions before and after that event,
and before and after the Nazi invasion of Russia, you
would have to give testimony that would be used against
him."

"What about free speech, Mr. O'Brien? Isn't what
Roe may have said to me at lunch or in my home protected by that?"

"By the First Amendment? Not under the decisions
of the courts so far. You could refuse to answer the questions, if you wanted to, either on that ground, or perhaps
on the ground that the question was not pertinent to the
subject under inquiry. Witnesses who have tried it have
had a contempt trial and from six months to a year in

jail handed to them for their pains, but it is still possible that you might win on appeal to the Supreme Court."

"What would that cost me?"

"Somewhere between $5,000 and $15,000, depending on various factors."

"Good Lord, that's more than my savings and the equity in my house combined."

"Yes, that is one of the aspects of this problem that irritates me a good deal at times. When I hear this fellow or that one say, 'Why doesn't he answer the question, instead of hiding behind the Fifth?' I feel like saying, 'Okay, he'll do just that, and you support his family and pay his legal expenses while he battles it out in the courts.' Well, let's go on. We have other problems. We don't know what Miss Maitress may testify to, either in this hearing, in a secret session earlier, or later."

"About me? She can't testify to anything. She doesn't know me."

"Very true, but, frankly, that doesn't matter in the least, Mr. Smith. Look at what happened to Owen Lattimore: He not only denied he was a communist, he denied at length that he was a communist sympathizer. The witness against him, Louis Budenz, declared that at Communist Party meetings Mr. Lattimore was discussed as though he were a communist, and that there had been circulated within the Party an onion skin paper on which, in code, Lattimore's name was listed as a communist. He said this in 1950 under oath to the Tydings Committee, although in something like three thousand hours of previous consultation with the FBI he never mentioned Lattimore as a suspect. Lattimore's attorneys also discovered that in an interview with an editor of *Collier's* magazine, Budenz had flatly declared he was not suggesting that Lattimore had acted as a communist agent. Budenz

himself admitted that he has never met Lattimore, and
had no previous direct knowledge that he was a communist. He was indicted for perjury just the same.

"So you see, the mere fact that you know nothing
about Miss Maitress doesn't exclude the possibility that
she may testify that somebody said you were a communist,
or a Soviet agent, or what have you.

"There's something else we have to consider here, too,
I'm afraid. The paid government witnesses create still
another problem. It's not an easy thing for an American
to face, but the fact is there is a good deal of evidence
suggesting that these informants employed by congressional committees and the Department of Justice are,
shall we say, not too exact about the truth of what they
testify to. Some of them have very flexible memories.
There are three of them, for instance, who are the subject of a Department of Justice investigation because
their testimony in loyalty board and immigration hearings or in Federal courts appears to be plainly perjurious.
One of them, Paul Crouch, for instance, testified in a
Federal trial in California that he had never heard of a
man named Davis. Several years later, he was called by
the Department of Justice as a witness in a Philadelphia
Smith Act case involving Davis. He testified he knew
Davis very well, told of Communist Party meetings at
which he had seen Davis, and identified him as a communist. Obviously, he had to be lying either in California
or in Philadelphia. Matter of fact, the evidence, as you
can well imagine, has to be pretty strong for the Department to be persuaded to investigate its own witnesses.

"What I am trying to point out to you is that your
personal sense of integrity is not enough in this situation.
I don't like to say it, but, frankly, you have to face the
fact that if Owen Lattimore can get into trouble, you can

hardly regard yourself as immune. I don't even go so far as to say these informants are deliberately committing perjury in every case. They are under tremendous pressure to please the government and committee attorneys who not only hire them as 'experts' and as witnesses, but who, in many cases, hold over them the threat of prosecution for various offenses. You can see how powerful the temptation must be to 'remember' something about a person like yourself in such a situation, if the committee is especially anxious to get such testimony.

"Now, as I understand the law of the land, the Constitution protects you and me from having to make guinea pigs of ourselves. We are not required deliberately to subject ourselves to a trial in which the truth or falsity of our testimony, as opposed to that of such a government witness, is the issue. The Constitution, you might say, is against bullying. It says, in effect, that it is up to the government to pick the fights. It says the Department of Justice, if it wants to get tough, has to produce the goods, has to convince a grand jury that the evidence it has is enough to justify placing an American on trial. It says that the government can't bully you into helping it produce any such evidence. It says that, if you are subjected to a process which is clearly designed to get you into a situation where you can be prosecuted, you have a right to refuse to cooperate in your own destruction."

"What about the possibility that they may ask me if I have given away government secrets or committed espionage, though? What do I do then?"

"I'm glad you asked me that," lawyer O'Brien replied. "You should answer those questions."

"Now you've got me kind of confused, Mr. O'Brien. What is the difference?"

"Between such a question and the others we have been discussing? It goes to the very heart of the matter. Unauthorized disclosure of government secrets and espionage are very specific crimes. To prove them, the government has to come in with very concrete evidence. This is something altogether different from a charge which rests, fundamentally, on finding out what your political and philosophical convictions are. What I mean is, proving whether or not a man is a communist or a fellow-traveler involves evidence largely concerning his beliefs and opinions. Such evidence inevitably covers a lot of territory and the prosecution tends to try to get it from the defendant—from you, in other words. If you testify at length to the kinds of questions we have been anticipating you give them just such circumstantial evidence. Unauthorized disclosure or espionage requires proof of definite acts by the accused, not just his opinions and beliefs."

"In other words, there is no alternative to pleading the Fifth Amendment to questions like those, except the espionage and classified document type of question?"

"Yes, there is an alternative, Mr. Smith," the lawyer said. "You can either answer the communist membership questions, or you could cite the First Amendment and question the pertinency of the subject in refusing to answer. In either case, you are running grave risks. If you answer them, and refuse to answer other questions which the committee will claim are related, you run both the risk of a contempt citation *and* a possible perjury trial. If you refuse to answer on First Amendment grounds and on the basis that the question is not pertinent to the subject of inquiry, you are practically asking for a contempt citation. You have children, don't you?"

"Two."

"Own a house? A car?"

"Yes."

"And both are paid for in full?"

"Neither one, I'm afraid."

"Well, there you are. Even if you keep your job, taking that line is risking a long, expensive contempt trial
and possibly a perjury trial as well. Of course, if you feel
it's your—"

"I'm afraid I have very little of the martyr in me,
Mr. O'Brien, or desire to become a *cause célèbre*. All
right, I'm sold, but what about my employers? It won't
sit well with them."

"We'll do the best we can with them. If you lose your
job, at least you'll be out of jail and able to find something to support your family on. I know that's poor consolation, my friend, but it's the best I can offer, except
that I'll be happy to go over the whole matter with Mr.
Overby in an effort to explain the reasons behind your
refusal to answer. That may help."

"Yes, I'm sure it will, though it may not be enough.
Have you and Charles known each other a long time?"

"I don't know him at all."

"Then how did he happen to recommend you?"

"The usual way. When you told him the situation,
he phoned a number of acquaintances in the legal profession. Two of them happened to know that I have had,
by now, considerable experience in this type of problem,
so he called me to ask if I would handle it."

"Will you be able to go to Washington with me day
after tomorrow?"

"No, I have a case in court, but I'm sure I can per-
suade Daly to postpone your appearance for a day or
two longer."

"What about your fee for this, Mr. O'Brien?"

"If you want me to accompany you to the hearing, my fee will be $500 for the hearing and this preliminary conference. If they want us to stay over for another day —and that's quite possible—my fee will be an additional $150. You will receive a mileage allowance from the government for your travel to and from Washington, as well as $9 per day for your other expenses, but the government will not reimburse you for legal fees or my traveling and other expenses."

"It could run over $1,000 then, couldn't it?"

"I'm afraid so," the lawyer said. "Even if nothing else happens, a subpoena is a pretty expensive piece of paper."

13

MR. SMITH
TAKES THE STAND

MR. DALY: *Is the testimony of Mary Maitress which you have heard true?*

MR. SMITH: *I decline to answer that question on the ground it might tend to incriminate me.*
—from the hearing of "Mr. Smith" before the Senate Subcommittee on Domestic Tranquillity.

W E NOW ACCOMPANY our hypothetical witness and his non-existent lawyer to a purely imaginary hearing of the wholly fictitious Senate Subcommittee on Domestic Tranquillity. Mr. O'Brien succeeded in getting a postponement of economist John Smith's appearance for an additional two days. Four days later we find them on the early morning plane to Washington. After the "No Smoking" sign went off, lawyer O'Brien spoke:

"I ought to brief you on the committee's rules, I think. This committee recognizes the right of a witness to have counsel present and to consult him, but that is as far as it goes. I am not allowed to make any objections to questions, express legal opinions, offer argument in support of them, or any of the sort of thing familiar to court procedure. I am not even supposed to offer you advice. You have to ask for it. I hope your shins are in

good condition, because I intend to advise you whenever it seems necessary."

"I don't get it," John Smith said. He looked at his
lawyer and then both of them laughed a bit ruefully.

"Another thing," lawyer O'Brien went on. "A favorite
device of some examiners is the multiple question. You
know the sort of thing: 'At the time you were employed
by the old Morgenthau Treasury Department, did you,
as a member of a communist espionage ring, ever stop
beating your wife?' The way to deal with such questions
is to break them down into their parts. The question I
made up involves employment in Treasury, communist
membership, espionage, and membership in an espionage ring. You can answer each item separately, invoking
the Fifth Amendment as to the part of the question
dealing with communism."

"You forgot the part about wife-beating," Mr. Smith
said wryly.

"So I did. You decide that one. I'm glad to see you
in good spirits, Mr. Smith. Some witnesses are so appre-
hensive and frightened that they get terribly confused
on the stand, but I think you are going to do very well.
By the way, in all seriousness, you don't have to answer
any questions relating to anything that took place between
you and your wife."

When the two men arrived in Washington, they taxied
to the Senate Office Building on Capitol Hill and reported to room 1085. John Smith, they learned, was
scheduled as the first witness. After a short wait, Senator
McCaley rapped the gavel for order and the hearing
began. Some months later, the hearing was issued in
printed form. It looked like what follows, except that the
discussions between witness and attorney which appear in
brackets, are not, of course, part of a printed record:

INTERCONNECTING SUBVERSION IN GOVERNMENT

Thursday, May 16, 195–

United States Senate,
Subcommittee to Investigate the Administration of the
Domestic Tranquillity Act of the Committee on Public
Safety.

Washington, D. C.

The subcommittee met, pursuant to call, at 10 a.m.,
in room 1085, Senate Office Building, Senator James F.
McCaley (chairman of the subcommittee) presiding.

Present: Senators McCaley, Ailey, Bailey, and Cailey.

Also present: James Daly, subcommittee counsel; Robert Faley, director of research; and George O'Haley,
staff member.

THE CHAIRMAN: The committee will come to order.
The Senate Domestic Tranquillity Subcommittee, under
the authority conferred on it by the United States Senate
to investigate "the degree, nature and effects of subversive
activities in the United States," has been uncovering
evidence of widespread subversive, communist infiltration
in government. The purpose of this series of hearings is
to find out and expose the pattern by which communist
agents were able to permeate the government. The subcommittee hopes that all persons with knowledge of this
devious design will assist the subcommittee in its purpose.

We will now call the first witness.

Mr. Smith, will you stand and be sworn please? Do
you solemnly swear that the testimony you shall give
in this hearing before the subcommittee will be the truth,
the whole truth, and nothing but the truth, so help you
God?

MR. SMITH: I do.

TESTIMONY OF JOHN B. SMITH, 116 West NINTH STREET, NEW YORK, N. Y., ACCOMPANIED BY ROBERT Z. O'BRIEN, ATTORNEY AT LAW, NEW YORK, N. Y.

THE CHAIRMAN: You may state your full name to the committee.

MR. SMITH: John B. Smith.

THE CHAIRMAN: Where do you reside?

MR. SMITH: 116 West Ninth St., New York City.

THE CHAIRMAN: Proceed, Mr. Daly.

MR. DALY: What is your business or profession?

MR. SMITH: I am an economist.

MR. DALY: Where are you now employed?

MR. SMITH: I am employed by the Council for Economic Research.

MR. DALY: Where is that located?

MR. SMITH: 22 West 42d Street, New York City.

MR. DALY: Let the record show that Mr. Smith is before the committee with his attorney, Mr. O'Brien. Will you give your full name, please?

MR. O'BRIEN: Robert Z. O'Brien, 350 Fifth Avenue, New York City.

MR. DALY: Will you briefly describe to the committee your educational background?

[The witness repeated to the committe what we already know about his education. Then a series of questions followed in which Mr. Smith's governmental career from 1934 to 1948 was brought out in his answers. Then the committee got down to business.]

MR. DALY: When did you transfer to the Treasury Department?

MR. SMITH: I went there in 1939.

MR. DALY: Your transfer was by pre-arrangement?

MR. SMITH: No, it was not.

MR. DALY: Did you discuss the matter with Lawrence Black prior to your transfer?

MR. SMITH: May I consult with my counsel?

THE CHAIRMAN: You may.

(Witness consults his counsel.)

[SMITH: Is this one of them? O'BRIEN: Yes. If you say you did not, you may be opening the way for all questions about your relationship to Black.]

MR. SMITH: I decline, very respectfully, to answer that question on the ground that it might tend to incriminate me.

THE CHAIRMAN: How would answering that question tend to incriminate you?

MR. SMITH: May I consult Mr. O'Brien here?

THE CHAIRMAN: Yes.

(Witness consults his counsel.)

[O'BRIEN: That's a trick question. If you answer, you will be giving the answer to the previous question which you refused. SMITH: So, what do I do, invoke the Fifth? O'BRIEN: Yes.]

MR. SMITH: I must again respectfully decline to answer on the same grounds.

THE CHAIRMAN: Are you refusing to answer because you knew that Black was a Soviet spy at that time? You may consult your counsel if you wish.

(Witness consults his counsel.)

[SMITH: This is the same thing, isn't it? O'BRIEN: Yes. The Senator is trying to get you started answering questions regarding Black so that you can't turn back, and at the same time he is phrasing the question so as to make your refusal as damaging as possible to you.]

MR. SMITH: I refuse to answer on the same grounds, Senator.

THE CHAIRMAN: What other reason could there be for the fact that you believe that your answer might tend to incriminate you?

MR. SMITH: I must again decline to answer for the same reasons.

THE CHAIRMAN: You knew he was a criminal at that time, did you?

MR. SMITH: I respectfully decline to answer for the same reasons.

THE CHAIRMAN: Had he told you at that time of activities in which he was engaged that might classify him as a criminal so that you would feel that your acquaintanceship with him would amount to such information as would tend to incriminate you if you told us about it?

MR. SMITH: I refuse to answer that question, sir, on the same grounds.

MR. DALY: Is it your testimony that so far as you know, no one made any pre-arrangements regarding your employment in the Treasury Department?

MR. SMITH: Yes, sir.

MR. DALY: Was Ronald L. Kupser employed there at that time?

MR. SMITH: I refuse to answer on the same grounds.

MR. DALY: On the grounds that it might incriminate you?

MR. SMITH: Yes.

SENATOR BAILEY: Who was the Secretary of the Treasury at that time?

MR. SMITH: Mr. Morgenthau.

SENATOR BAILEY: Who was the Undersecretary?

MR. SMITH: I think it would be Mr. Bell at that time.

SENATOR BAILEY: Who was your immediate superior at that time?

MR. SMITH: I must respectfully decline to answer that question.

SENATOR BAILEY: Was Larry Black your immediate superior?

MR. SMITH: I decline to answer on the same grounds.

SENATOR BAILEY: Was Ronald Kupser your immediate superior?

MR. SMITH: I decline to answer on the same grounds, Senator.

MR. DALY: Did Paul Roe arrange with Mr. Kupser for your transfer from Agriculture to the Treasury?

MR. SMITH: I must respectfully decline to answer that, sir, on the same grounds.

MR. DALY: Do you or did you ever know Paul N. Roe?

MR. SMITH: I decline to answer on the same grounds.

MR. DALY: Now, when you were a senior economist with the Treasury Department, you were given a foreign assignment, were you not?

MR. SMITH: I was originally assigned to make an analysis of our trade—

MR. DALY: Mr. Chairman, I submit the witness can answer that question "Yes" or "No."

THE CHAIRMAN: You can answer that just "Yes" or "No," Mr. Smith. Make your explanations afterwards, if you wish.

MR. SMITH: Yes.

MR. DALY: Your answer is "Yes?"

MR. SMITH: Yes.

MR. DALY: And where were you assigned?

MR. O'BRIEN: Just a minute, there, Mr.—

THE CHAIRMAN: Now, Mr. Attorney, you know the committee's rules. We will not hear from counsel. You know that. You have been here before.

MR. SMITH: May I consult?

THE CHAIRMAN: Very well, you may.

(Witness consults his counsel.)

THE CHAIRMAN: Let the record show that the witness is consulting his counsel on each occasion when he does so.

[SMITH: What is it? O'BRIEN: He said you might explain your answer on the foreign assignment question. What's the story? SMITH: I was originally assigned to analyze our trade agreement with Iran, and when a mission was sent there to advise the Iranian government, naturally I was selected to go. O'BRIEN: Tell them you want to explain your answer to the previous question.]

MR. SMITH: Senator, I would like to make a further explanation—explain my answer to the previous question.

THE CHAIRMAN: Go ahead.

MR. SMITH: My original assignment with the Treasury department had to do with making an analysis of our trade relations with Iran. When a U.S. mission was sent to that country to advise the Iranian government, I was sent as the Treasury member.

MR. DALY: Who selected you?

(Witness consults his counsel.)

[SMITH: Black assigned me to that. O'BRIEN: Fifth Amendment, then.]

MR. SMITH: I respectfully decline to answer that on the same grounds.

MR. DALY: You won't tell this committee who in the Treasury selected you to go on this important mission?

MR. SMITH: I think I have already answered that, sir.

MR. DALY: As a matter of fact, Lawrence Black selected you, did he not?

MR. SMITH: I decline to answer on the grounds stated, sir.

MR. DALY: At that time, at the time you were sent to Iran, what position did Lawrence Black have?

MR. SMITH: I refuse to answer on the same grounds.

MR. DALY: You refuse to tell us what position Black, Larry Black, who later became an Assistant Secretary, had?

THE CHAIRMAN: You may consult.

(Witness consults his counsel.)

[SMITH: Was that the wrong answer? O'BRIEN: He is trying to get you to talk about Black, but the question he just asked may not necessarily open that up. Ask him if he is asking for your formal knowledge, as a member of the Department.]

MR. SMITH: Are you inquiring as to my formal knowledge of various—of who held various positions in the Department when I was employed in it?

MR. DALY: Yes, your formal knowledge.

MR. SMITH: I believe Mr. Black was then Director of the Research and Statistical Division.

MR. DALY: And who was next in line, under Larry Black?

MR. SMITH: My formal knowledge?

MR. DALY: Your formal knowledge.

MR. SMITH: Ronald Kupser.

MR. DALY: Did Mr. Kupser play any part in arranging that you be assigned to the Iranian mission?

MR. SMITH: I refuse to answer that question on the same grounds.

MR. DALY: At that time were you a member of the Communist Party?

MR. SMITH: I refuse to answer on the grounds already given.

MR. DALY: Were you engaged in espionage against the United States and on behalf of the Soviet Union at that time?

MR. SMITH: No. Not at that time or at any other, and

if I knew of anyone so engaged I would have reported it to the authorities.

MR. DALY: Did you associate with James E. Rawlings?

MR. SMITH: I decline to answer that question on the same grounds.

MR. DALY: Do you play chess?

MR. SMITH: I beg your pardon?

MR. DALY: Do you play the game of chess?

MR. SMITH: Yes, not very well, though.

MR. DALY: You say you have never been a member of a communist espionage ring?

MR. SMITH: May I consult?

(Witness consults his counsel.)

[SMITH: That's one of those double questions? O'BRIEN: Yes, answer it in the two parts, espionage and communist. No, on second thought, just reply to the espionage part and see what they do. By the way, what about chess? Did you ever play chess with any of these people? SMITH: No. I used to play at college, but I dropped it and didn't take it up again until I came to New York.]

MR. SMITH: Would you repeat the question, please?

MR. DALY: I'll withdraw it. Mr. Chairman, we have testimony before this committee in executive session that this witness has been actively engaged in espionage activities as a member of a communist spy ring. I have here the transcript of the testimony of Miss Mary Maitress, who, as you know, has testified that she was liaison for a Soviet spy ring engaged in supplying secrets, vital information about our government to the Soviet intelligence. Mr. Chairman, with your permission, I will now read the pertinent excerpts of the Mary Maitress testimony into the record.

THE CHAIRMAN: Read it.

MR. DALY: (*reading*):

MR. DALY: Now, Miss Maitress, who else other than Mr. Black was a member of this ring in the Treasury?

MISS MAITRESS: Well, there was Ron Kupser, Jim Rawlings, Paul Roe, Jeanie Silverson, and John B. Smith.

MR. DALY: And you testified earlier, did you not, that some of the information given to you came from Mr. Black?

MISS MAITRESS: Well, I understood some of it was coming from him, yes.

MR. DALY: He didn't give it to you personally?

MISS MAITRESS: No, he sent it through others. Ron usually brought it. I got the information from Larry Black through intermediaries. Sometimes the documents had "Regards from Larry" typed on them.

MR. DALY: And who were those intermediaries?

MISS MAITRESS: Well, Ron was one, and Mr. Smith was another.

MR. DALY: Mr. Smith brought you documents and other information from Black?

MISS MAITRESS: No, not directly. Ron—would you like me to tell you the details?

MR. DALY: Yes, indeed.

MISS MAITRESS: Well, Ron told me at one point that he was having difficulties with Black. He was getting leery about handing all this material over. Then when I met him the next time, he handed me some documents inside a copy of *Life* Magazine—

MR. DALY: When would this be, approximately?

MISS MAITRESS: Some time in 1943 or maybe 1944.

MR. DALY: Go on.

MISS MAITRESS: So I asked Ron how he was getting along with Black. He said that he was doing all right.

He said that Johnny Smith had talked with Black too and persuaded him to continue to cooperate with us.

THE CHAIRMAN: Let the record show that the witness is consulting with his counsel at this point.

[O'BRIEN: Well, now we know a little more of what we're up against. Did Kupser ever call you "Johnny"? SMITH: Sometimes, but my nickname is "Smitty."]

MR. DALY: Mr. Smith, is the testimony of Mary Maitress which you have just heard true?

MR. SMITH: I decline to answer that question on the ground it might tend to incriminate me.

MR. DALY: Have you ever associated with one Mary Maitress?

MR. SMITH: May I consult, Mr. Chairman?

THE CHAIRMAN: Yes, you may.

[O'BRIEN: You'd better use the Fifth. SMITH: Why, for goodness' sake! I don't know the woman; why? O'BRIEN: Remember Owen Lattimore.]

MR. SMITH: I decline to answer that question on the grounds stated.

MR. DALY: Mr. Chairman, there is one other excerpt I would like to read.

THE CHAIRMAN: You may.

MR. DALY: (reading):

MR. DALY: This study group met where?

MISS MAITRESS: At the apartment, at Paul Roe's apartment.

MR. DALY: And you collected Communist Party dues there?

MISS MAITRESS: Yes.

MR. DALY: From whom did you collect the dues?

MISS MAITRESS: Paul would collect the money and turn it over to me.

MR. DALY: Was there anything else about this Marxist study group which you wanted to tell the committee, Miss Maitress?

MISS MAITRESS: Not that I can think of at the moment.

MR. DALY: Did the members of this cell or study group sometimes play chess after the regular business of the meeting was concluded?

MISS MAITRESS: Oh, yes, frequently. Paul used to describe how mad some of them would get when they lost. Some of them took it very seriously, because it is a very popular game in the Soviet Union, you know.

MR. DALY: Mr. Smith, I will ask you whether you played chess at the apartment of Paul Roe, either during the time when you and he were both employed at the Department of Agriculture or later when you transferred or were shifted to the Treasury Department.

MR. SMITH: May I consult, Senator?

THE CHAIRMAN: You may.

(Witness consults his counsel.)

[SMITH: Another multiple question? O'BRIEN: No, it's in the alternative. You have already testified that you play chess, so you will have to refuse to answer. SMITH: Oh, no! O'BRIEN: Sorry, John, there's no help for it.]

MR. SMITH: I decline to answer on the grounds previously stated.

THE CHAIRMAN: But you do play the game?

MR. SMITH: Yes, sir.

MR. DALY: Mr. Chairman, I have before me a government paper signed by Ronald Kupser, dated February 24, 1943. Mr. Smith, was Mr. Kupser employed by the Treasury Department at that time?

THE CHAIRMAN: You may consult if you wish.

(Witness consults his counsel.)

[SMITH: Answer it? O'BRIEN: Yes, I think so. It is a part of your formal knowledge of the situation in the Department at that time.]

MR. SMITH: Yes, I believe he was.

MR. DALY: Did you know that Mr. Kupser gave you an efficiency rating of "excellent" at that time?

MR. SMITH: No, I didn't.

MR. DALY: You didn't know it. Did you know that Ronald L. Kupser was a member of the Communist Party then?

MR. SMITH: I decline to answer that on the same grounds.

[The committee's counsel then introduced a series of government records showing efficiency ratings, recommendations for promotion, and other personnel documents regarding John Smith signed by Kupser, Black, or Rawlings. In each case he asked the same question, and got the same refusal.]

MR. DALY: Who is your superior at the Council for Economic Research?

MR. SMITH: Mr. Joseph P. Martinson.

MR. DALY: Did you confer with Mr. Martinson after you received the committee's subpoena?

MR. SMITH: May I consult?

MR. DALY: Yes.

(Witness consults his counsel.)

[SMITH: What's this leading up to, Bob? O'BRIEN: Most likely he is going to ask you whether you discussed the situation, whether you denied being a member of the Communist Party, that sort of thing. SMITH: Do I answer? O'BRIEN: This one, yes. Questions on communism, no, because if you do, you will be wide open to all the questions again. Do you understand? SMITH: Yes, don't worry.]

MR. SMITH: Yes.

MR. DALY: You did consult with him?

MR. SMITH: Yes, sir.

MR. DALY: Did you deny to him that you are a member of the Communist Party?

MR. SMITH: I respectfully decline to answer that on the grounds previously given.

MR. DALY: Were you a member of the Communist Party when you conferred with him?

MR. SMITH: I must decline to answer on the same grounds.

MR. DALY: Mr. Chairman, the reason I asked those questions is that witnesses who are subpoenaed before this committee frequently tell their employers that they are not and never have been members of the Communist Party. Of course such statements are not under oath, and the witness, before he is sworn and before he is shown the evidence we have on him or asked questions concerning what we have on him, the witness feels quite free to tell his employer whatever he pleases, because he is not suffering the pains and penalties of perjury when he is in a private conference with his employer.

After testifying some of them even go back and repeat the denial to their employers, and of course there again they can get away with it because they are not going to be held to account in a court of law and they know it.

THE CHAIRMAN: Yes. May I say that we are well aware of that situation.

MR. DALY: Mr. Smith, when you return to New York City, do you intend to confer again with Mr. Martinson regarding this hearing?

MR. SMITH: I suppose I will, yes, sir.

MR. DALY: Do you intend once again to deny to him that you are a member of the Communist Party and were right along during the time you were working for the

United States Government and travelling abroad on important foreign missions for the United States?

MR. SMITH: I decline to answer that question on the grounds given.

MR. DALY: To your knowledge, was there a communist ring operating in the Treasury Department during your employment there?

MR. SMITH: I decline to answer that question on the same grounds, sir.

MR. DALY: Mr. Chairman, that is all I have at this time.

THE CHAIRMAN: Very well. That will be all, Mr. Smith. We will stand adjourned, subject to call.

(Thereupon, at 11:30 a.m., Thursday, May 16, 195-, the hearing was adjourned subject to call.)

Returning to New York, John Smith spent a restless night with his family. The next day, he and Mr. O'Brien talked the situation over with the Council's president, Mr. Martinson, and its attorney, Mr. Overby. The reader, if he wishes, may imagine himself as John B. Smith's boss and decide whether or not to fire him. Not even so devoted a servant of realism as the author has the heart to do it. As far as the author is concerned, Mr. Smith is still working at the Council for Economic Research, though in most such establishments the Queen of Hearts is all too ready to cry: "Off with his head!"

MR. JENNER CHANGES
WHITE INTO RED

"Harry Dexter White was at the center of all this activity. His name was used for reference by other members of the ring . . . He hired them . . . promoted them . . . raised their salaries . . . transferred them . . . assigned them . . . vouched for their loyalty and protected them when exposure threatened. He played handball with them . . ."
—Senator Jenner, concluding the hearing at which Attorney General Brownell and FBI Director J. Edgar Hoover testified.

Somehow Senator William E. Jenner's Subcommittee on Internal Security has acquired a reputation for being different from the committees headed by "Judge" Velde and Senator McCarthy. The American Civil Liberties Union has given Mr. Jenner its good civil liberties housekeeping seal of approval. Mrs. Agnes Meyer, who gave both Senator McCarthy and Mr. Velde their investigatorial come-uppance, has neither praised Mr. Jenner, nor has she damned him. Dr. Buell Gallagher, president of the City College of New York, went further. The subcommittee, he said last year, "had shown meticulous regard for the rights of the innocent."

"Where we find honesty and integrity," the educator declared, "coupled with high principles and sound operation with an absence of headline-seeking and a genuine desire to strengthen free institutions, let us say so."

Yet the most headline-producing hearing of 1953 was the televised appearance in November before Senator Jenner's subcommittee of Attorney General Herbert Brownell, followed by FBI Director J. Edgar Hoover. In many respects, Mr. Hoover's appearance overshadowed Mr. Brownell's, for it is rare indeed that the chief of the FBI gives testimony in a sensational case.

The Senators and the witnesses played to a packed house. In addition to the committee members, the TV and newsreel cameras, and the public, Senator Alexander Wiley, Republican chairman of the powerful Foreign Relations Committee, was on hand. So were the Republican Majority Leader, Senator William F. Knowland of California, and the "golden voice" of the Party from Illinois, Senator Everett McKinley Dirksen. After a tough but victorious battle to get Messrs. Brownell and Hoover as his witnesses, Mr. Jenner was delighted:

"I am happy," he said as the hearing came to order, "that so many of the members of this committee could be present today ... Since April of this past year, the subcommittee has been concentrating on the inquiry into the interlocking subversion in government departments, and has heard more than thirty witnesses whom the evidence amply shows to have been actively engaged in the communist underground, and many even in Soviet espionage."

Then the Attorney General took the stand.

"This afternoon," he said, "I want to discuss the case of [the late] Harry Dexter White and the manner in which it was handled by the Truman administration on the basis of established facts and the records in the Department of Justice."

Dramatically, the Attorney General held up a paper. "The letter I hold in my hand is marked 'Top Secret,'" he said. "I have declassified it and will make it public because it does not reveal any security information which would be damaging ..."

The letter, as published in the printed transcript of the hearing, read:

November 8, 1945

(Top secret by special messenger)

Declassified H. B. November 16, 1953

Brig. Gen. Harry Hawkins Vaughan,
  Military Aide to the President,
   The White House, Washington, D.C.

Dear General Vaughan:

As a result of the Bureau's investigative operations, information has been recently developed from a highly confidential source indicating that a number of persons employed by the Government of the United States have been furnishing data and information to persons outside the Federal Government, who are in turn transmitting this information to espionage agents of the Soviet Government. At the present time it is impossible to determine exactly how many of these people had actual knowledge of the disposition being made of the information they were transmitting. The investigation, however, at this point has indicated that the persons named hereinafter were actually the source from which information passing through the Soviet espionage system was being obtained, and I am continuing vigorous investigation for the purpose of establishing the degree and nature of the complicity of these people in this espionage ring.

The Bureau's information at this time indicates that the following persons were participants in this operation

or were utilized by principals in this ring for the purpose
of obtaining data in which the Soviet is interested:

Dr. Gregory Silvermaster, a longtime employee of the Department of Agriculture.

Harry Dexter White, Assistant to the Secretary of the
Treasury.

George Silverman, formerly employed by the Railroad
Retirement Board, and now reportedly in the War Department.

Lauchlin Currie, former Administrative Assistant to the
late President Roosevelt.

Victor Perlo, formerly with the War Production Board
and the Foreign Economic Administration.

Donald Wheeler, formerly with the Office of Strategic
Services.

Maj. Duncan Lee, Office of Strategic Services.

Julius Joseph, Office of Strategic Services.

Helen Tenney, Office of Strategic Services.

Maurice Halperin, Office of Strategic Services.

Charles Kramer, formerly associated with Senator Kilgore.

Capt. William Ludwig Ullman[n], United States Army
Air Corps.

Lt. Col. John H. Reynolds, of the United States Army, a
former contact of Gaik Ovakimian, former head of the
Soviet Secret Intelligence (NKVD) in New York, is
also apparently involved in the Soviet espionage activities stemming from Washington, D.C.

   In addition to the foregoing group in the Government it appears at this time that Mary Price, formerly
secretary to Walter Lippmann. the newspaper columnist,
and presently publicity manager of the United Office
and Professional Workers of America, CIO, is also associated with the foregoing group.

   The Government documents were furnished to Gregory Silvermaster, who thereafter photographed them and turned over the undeveloped, but exposed, film to a contact of the Soviets in either Washington, D.C., or New York City. In the past, it is reported, the contact man made trips to Washington, D.C., once every two weeks and would pick up on such occasions an average of forty rolls of thirty-five millimeter film.

Investigation of this matter is being pushed vigorously, but I thought that the President and you would be interested in having the foregoing preliminary data immediately.

With expressions of my highest esteem and best regards,

Sincerely yours,
J. EDGAR HOOVER

This was only a preliminary, Mr. Brownell said. On December 4, 1945, the FBI sent General Vaughan a 71-page report on Soviet espionage in which references to Mr. White appeared in three different places. On January 23, 1946, then President Truman nevertheless announced Mr. White's nomination as U.S. delegate to the International Monetary Fund. FBI Director Hoover prepared another letter, this time exclusively on Mr. White, and sent it to General Vaughan on February 4, 1946.

"Information has come to the attention of this Bureau," the letter read, "charging White as being a valuable adjunct to an underground Soviet espionage organization operating in Washington, D.C. Material which came into his possession as a result of his official capacity allegedly was made available through intermediaries to Nathan Gregory Silvermaster, his wife Helen Witte Silvermaster, and William Ludwig Ullmann. Both Silvermaster and Ullmann are employees of the United States

Treasury Department, reportedly directly under the supervision of White.

"The information and documents originating in the Treasury Department were either passed on in substance or photographed by Ullmann in a well-equipped laboratory in the basement of the Silvermaster home. Following this step, the material was taken to New York City by courier and made available to Jacob N. Golos, until the time of his death on November 27, 1943. Golos, a known Soviet agent, delivered this material to an individual tentatively identified as Gaik Ovakimian ... Subsequent to the death of Golos, the courier handling material received from the Silvermasters and Ullman[n] delivered it through an unidentified individual to Anatole Borisovich Gromov who until December 7, 1945, was assigned as First Secretary of the Soviet Embassy, Washington, D.C., when he returned to the U.S.S.R. ... This whole network has been under intensive investigation since November 1945, and it is the results of these efforts that I am now able to make available to you."

The results made available by Mr. Hoover were in the form of the lengthy FBI report accompanying the letter. Although Mr. Brownell declined to declassify this document, he declared that "the essential facts may be disclosed to this subcommittee," and, incidentally, to several million television onlookers. His summary of the report included the charge that Mr. White was "one of the most valuable assets in this particular parallel of Soviet intelligence." As Assistant Secretary of the Treasury, Mr. White, according to Mr. Brownell, could place individuals "whom this group were anxious to have assigned there." Among these, the Attorney General charged, were Mr. Ullmann, William Henry Taylor, and Sonia Steinman Gold. Mrs. Gold, he declared, had been sug-

gested to Mrs. Silvermaster by an unnamed Washington
Communist Party official as someone who could copy
documents obtained from White's office and deliver her
notes to the Silvermasters. Others named by the Attorney
General were V. Frank Coe, Victor Perlo, Harold Glasser,
A. George Silverman, Maurice Halperin, and Irving Kaplan. They were all "close associates" of Mr. White, he said.

"The White case," Mr. Brownell concluded, "illus-
trates that it is not enough for men in high government
positions to be loyal. They must also be vigilant to combat the dangers to our government and to our free institutions."

One of those whose vigilance was conceded was J. Edgar Hoover. The FBI chief followed Mr. Brownell to the
witness chair. Mr. Hoover retold the story that the Attorney General had given the committee, adding a touch
here and there. He spoke of the difficulties of obtaining
corroboration.

"The actual facts," he explained, "were known only to
a limited group whose personal interests dictated conceal-
ment and who conveniently had the Fifth Amendment
as a refuge."

The FBI had been against immediate prosecution of
Mr. White and others, Mr. Hoover implied, because it
lacked "the evidence necessary to sustain convictions"
and because "some of the evidence, while of an irrefutable nature, was not admissible in a court of law." After
Mr. White's death in August, 1948, Mr. Hoover declared,
"events transpired which produced facts of an uncontradictable nature which clearly established the reliability of the information furnished by the FBI in 1945 and
1946." On the committee record, these facts remained
irrefutable and uncontradictable. Mr. Hoover did not
disclose them.

When Mr. Hoover had finished, Chairman Jenner took over the spotlight.

"In its report on 'Interlocking Subversion in Government Departments,'" the Senator declared, "the subcommittee said this:

'Almost all of the persons exposed by the evidence had some connection which could be documented with at least one—and generally several—other exposed persons. They used each other's names for reference on applications for Federal employment. They hired each other. They promoted each other. They raised each other's salaries. They transferred each other from bureau to bureau, from department to department, from congressional committee to congressional committee. They assigned each other to international missions. They vouched for each other's loyalty and protected each other when exposure threatened. They often had common living quarters. There was a group that played handball together. There was another group whose names appeared together in a telephone finder.'"

Although the report from which the Senator quoted had treated Mr. White as a minor character, the Senator moved him to the most prominent role in the drama:

"Harry Dexter White was at the center of all this activity," Mr. Jenner decreed. "His name was used for reference by other members of the ring, when they made applications for Federal employment. He hired them. He promoted them. He raised their salaries. He transferred them from bureau to bureau, from department to department. He assigned them to international missions. He vouched for their loyalty and protected them when exposure threatened. He played handball with them: His name appeared along with those of Frank Coe, Harold Glasser, Harry Magdoff, Lee Pressman, Abraham George

Silverman, and William Ludwig Ullmann in the telephone finder of Nathan Gregory Silvermaster.

"All of these latter were named as participants in the
communist underground conspiracy in government by
either Elizabeth Bentley or Whittaker Chambers, or by
both. All of them, save Pressman, invoked the Fifth
Amendment on grounds of self-incrimination when asked
on the witness stand about the Bentley-Chambers statements. Pressman acknowledged that he had been a communist while serving in government."

The Senator summarized once more the career of
Harry Dexter White as a public servant, and then lifted
the gavel.

"I believe the evidence and the testimony that we
have heard here today will be of great benefit to this
committee in its future work, which we intend to continue
in the same careful manner ..." he said.

The gavel fell. The klieg lights winked out. The ashes
of Harry Dexter White, one time Assistant Secretary of
the U.S. Treasury, confidant of Cabinet officers and
Presidents, and U.S. Executive Director of the International Monetary Fund, were once more laid to rest.

But not for long, for in the chapters which follow we
must sift the whole business once more.

"... I know of differences between the men. I know of differences in the positions that they took on various crucial issues in the government, which are nonexplicable to me on the grounds such as have been brought forward here."
—V. Frank Coe testifying in 1948 regarding those accused as members of a government espionage ring.

IN HIS WELL-TIMED SPEECH four days before election day in November 1953, Attorney General Brownell declared: "Harry Dexter White was known to be a communist spy by the very people who appointed him to the most sensitive and important position he ever held in the government service." Although the FBI records which he de-secretized and read into the record of the Jenner committee hearing did not quite come up to the "spy" charge, the sum total of Mr. Brownell's and Mr. Hoover's testimony left the country gasping. It appeared that, under the Presidencies of Franklin D. Roosevelt and Harry S. Truman, the government fairly swarmed with communists and spies, of whom Mr. White was at least "a valuable adjunct."

This impression was in no way diminished by the undoubted fact that there are Soviet spies in the United

States, the government included. There have been spies
ever since Joshua sent out "two men to spy secretly" with
the command: "Go view the land, even Jericho." Presumably the men in the Kremlin, though not enamored
of the Bible, have never rejected the ancient and dis-
honorable practice of espionage. In fact, experts in the
subject have a high regard for the efficiency and energy
of Soviet military intelligence, regarded, along with Britain's M-5 and France's *Deuxieme Bureau* as among the
world's most competent.

The question still remains, however, whether the dis-
interment of Harry Dexter White and numerous other
former government employees was just an election-time
convenience, or a genuine revelation of an espionage plot.

Beginning in April, 1953 the committee had conducted
a series of some thirty sessions on "interlocking subversion in government." More than four score of witnesses were heard. The witnesses included a 75-year-old
maiden lady from Maine. This dangerous subversive had
been an employee of the Office of Education who served
in the administrations of Wilson, Harding, Coolidge,
Hoover, and Franklin D. Roosevelt. A sprinkling of one-
time employees of congressional committees were called,
but the bulk of the testimony came from assorted laborers in the New Deal and Fair Deal vineyards. Among the
latter were those whom Mr. Jenner linked with Harry Dexter White at the close of the Brownell-Hoover hearing.

The committee filed a report on July 30. The Government Printing Office issued it in printed form in late
August. Members of the Republican National Committee
were so impressed that they arranged for the purchase
of extra copies to be placed in the hands of Party workers
in states where close gubernatorial races were slated for
November. A Texas multi-millionaire and heavy financial

backer of both Senators McCarthy and Jenner in 1952 patriotically paid for 50,000 more. David Lawrence's *U. S. News and World Report* reprinted it verbatim.

The report was a shocker. It declared that the Soviet "international organization" had carried out a successful and important penetration of the U. S. government, extending from the lower ranks to "top-level policy and operating positions." It quoted from a "secret memorandum'" prepared by an "intelligence agency of this government." In the memorandum, the agency referred to itself as "the Bureau." The memorandum dealt with the case of Nathan Gregory Silvermaster which, it said, "first came to the attention of the Bureau on November 8, 1945, when Elizabeth Bentley . . . came into the New York office of the Bureau and stated that for the past 11 years she had been actively engaged in communist activity and Soviet espionage."

The committee also relied heavily on Miss Bentley's testimony, quoting from her appearances before it and earlier congressional inquiries. Almost all of the principal characters in the drama had also testified previously: before the Federal Grand Jury; before other congressional committees; had repeatedly talked to inquiring Civil Service, FBI, and military intelligence investigators. But the committee preferred to report simply that "all of [the accused witnesses] invoked the Fifth Amendment and refused to answer questions regarding communist membership."

With this inference, with Miss Bentley's testimony, and with innumerable insertions of government records showing that the accused in some cases hired, transferred, rated, and promoted one another, and had given each other as references, the committee erected an edifice which scandalized the country.

To create such an impression, the committee had to ignore a good deal of the evidence in its own record as well as previous hearings before other committees. In the matter of the references used by the "interlocking subversives," for example, the report stresses the fact that some of the accused used each other as references. Not mentioned are some twenty-five other persons who were listed as references, including well-known anti-communists; university professors; a United States Senator; an advertising executive; the dean of a famous graduate school of public administration; a vice president of the New York Life Insurance Company; the chief economist of the Interstate Commerce Commission; a vice president of Schenley Industries, Inc.; the administrator of the Defense Production Administration; the president of International Hudson Corporation; a partner in a conservative New York law firm, director of Rockefeller Center, Inc., chairman of the executive committee of the International Basic Economy Corporation, and a trustee of the Brookings Institution; the director since 1949 of the Office of Business Economics, Department of Commerce; a former chairman of the Federal Power Commission, now consultant to the Public Affairs Institute; and the former general counsel of the Federal Power Commission.

One of the references listed by Mr. Silvermaster was David Saposs, former chief economist of the National Labor Relations Board. Mr. Saposs has never made a secret of his outspoken anti-communism. Indeed, he testified before the Jenner committee to the alleged radical influence exerted by two other accused witnesses upon the policies of the Board. At his hearing, however, not a word was said, not a question asked regarding his having been one of Mr. Silvermaster's references.

Many of the accused did receive routine pay increases and even promotions from their accused superiors. One, however, was recommended for a pay decrease. He was Harold Glasser. The recommendation that Mr. Glasser's salary be cut was signed by Harry Dexter White. This fact was, of course, not mentioned in the committee report.

The report also stressed that the witnesses worked for each other, ignoring the fact, for example, that one of Mr. Silvermaster's wartime employees was a lady named Miriam de Haas. Miss De Haas later was forced to resign as a Civil Service Commission Loyalty Review Board examiner because she was giving confidential information to Senator McCarthy. Her name was among a list of former subordinates of Mr. Silvermaster which the committee placed in the record, suggesting that each person listed should be carefully screened for possible subversive background.

The report failed to include the fact that one witness, Professor Maurice Halperin, long after he was accused, received a passport to go to Brazil where he was decorated with the Brazilian Order of the Southern Cross. Returning to his post at Boston University, where he was chairman of the Regional Studies Department, the witness was called before the committee. His invocation of the Fifth Amendment impressed the university less than it did the committee. After the hearing, Boston University announced it was censuring the professor, but would retain him as head of the department. This last item was the only one noted in the committee's report.

Like Humpty Dumpty, Senator Jenner seemed to use documents the way that adamant character from *Through the Looking Glass* employed words.

"When *I* use a word," Humpty Dumpty said in rather

a scornful tone, "it means just what I choose it to mean—neither more nor less."

"The question is," said Alice, "whether you *can* make words mean so many different things."

"The question is," said Humpty Dumpty, "which is to be master—that's all."

The Senator was definitely the master of his own material. The fact that most of the witnesses rose slowly but steadily in government service had sinister implications, he announced. Early in the series of hearings he said for the record:

"I would like to call to the committee's attention that witnesses whom we have had in this phase of our hearings ... clearly begin to establish a definite pattern of a small group of people within the government kept moving from one key job to another ... always moving to positions of greater importance, nearer to the top policy-making persons in our government."

The Senator frowned on the enterprise exhibited by the witness before him at the moment. He found in it, not a slow-motion Horatio Alger story of service to the government, but a pattern of subversion:

"... This particular witness before us here now, started in at a salary of between $2,000 and $3,000 in 1936 and was with the government for ten years, moving from department to department," he exclaimed, adding the shocking intelligence that "he ended up with a salary of almost $10,000."

The Senator chose not to report, however, that another accused witness, Harold Glasser, voluntarily left the Treasury in 1947 where he was earning $10,000 per year to take a *part-time* post with the Council of Jewish Federations and Welfare Funds, Inc., at the same remuneration. The Senator was not above recalling Mr. Glasser to

question him at length regarding what he had told his
employer concerning the charges made against him. The
committee also telephoned Mr. Glasser's employer asking for a statement of his organization's relationship with
the witness. The employer replied stating that former
Secretary of the Treasury John W. Snyder and former
Secretary of State Dean Acheson had recommended Mr.
Glasser highly.

On the day following the Brownell-Hoover hearing,
the Senator took occasion to have all this read into the
record. He was careful to point out that Secretary Snyder
had appointed Mr. Glasser to his $10,000-a-year job after
the FBI reports on Mr. Glasser were, according to Mr.
Hoover, in the hands of the Treasury.

"The information recently given by Miss Bentley to
the Senate committee," Mr. Glasser's employer wrote Mr.
Snyder, "has been very disturbing. I have been informed
that the charges made as they relate to Mr. Glasser are
not new and that Miss Bentley had previously offered
them to various bureaus of the government. I understand
also that Mr. Glasser was thoroughly investigated as a
security risk while he was serving in the United States
Treasury. It would be very helpful to us at this time if
we could receive an additional statement from you bearing upon this aspect of Mr. Glasser's career in government service."

Mr. Snyder was still Secretary at the time. He replied
a week later: "No information regarding Mr. Glasser has
been called to our attention that had not previously been
considered by the Department prior to my letter to you
of December 26, 1947, and all I can do at this time is
reaffirm the appraisal I made of him in my earlier letter.
I am very glad to learn that Mr. Glasser's services have
proven so satisfactory to the council and that he is render-

ing for you the same high type of work he performed
for the Treasury."

To some, these documents might seem flattering to
Mr. Glasser. To Mr. Jenner and committee counsel Morris, they evidently seemed damning to Mr. Snyder. Mr.
Glasser, meanwhile, had tendered his resignation to the
Council, fearing that the publicity attendant on his appearance before the Jenner committee "might be embarrassing to the council." Although the resignation was
accepted, the Council referred to Mr. Glasser's work as
"exceptionally fine . . . objective and impartial." About a
month after the Glasser hearing, the Senator indicated
how he felt about such results of his labors:

"If these people lose their jobs," he said in Boston on
May 7, 1953, "because they refuse to tell if they are loyal
Americans, that is good with me. I have no sympathy
for them."

The Senator also established himself as a master of
the fine art of deleting from quotations at points convenient to his purpose. In his indictment of Mr. White
following FBI chief Hoover's testimony, Mr. Jenner used
with great effect a long series of quotations from Mr.
White's own testimony before the House Committee on
Un-American Activities in August 1948. The quotations
were excerpts from the former Treasury official's candid
and often witty testimony about his association with
Messrs. Glasser, Coe, Ullmann, and the others. The Senator
read a long quotation in which Mr. White described his efforts to assist Mr. Silvermaster "as a friend" when the
latter's loyalty was questioned in 1941 or 1942. From the
quotation, the Senator omitted the following words, spoken under oath by the dead man:

"I can well understand and thoroughly sympathize
with the view that if there is any slightest question of a

man's being a communist, he ought not to be in a position—ought not to hold a position where there was any
confidential information passed; that even though there
was no evidence or proof, a mere suspicion was enough.
We were at war, and there was no need for that. I said
that I was not interested in seeing him [Silvermaster]
get his post back. In fact, I did not think he should."

Mr. Silvermaster did not, in fact, get it back. He was
shifted back to a non-sensitive job in the Department of
Agriculture. Apparently Senator Jenner felt that this too
was not worth mentioning.

Mr. White, who died of a heart attack two days after
the 1948 hearing, testified fully regarding his associations with all of those accused by Miss Bentley and Whittaker Chambers. He even told of going into the Silvermaster basement:

MR. WHITE: Yes, I was at the basement. It was at a
party, and they were playing ping-pong. I fancied myself a little as a ping-pong player, and we played a
few times.

THE CHAIRMAN [former Representative J. Parnell
Thomas, Republican of New Jersey]: Just a minute
right there. Let me see that note. One thing I cannot
reconcile, Mr. White, you send me a note and you say
that 'I am recovering from a severe heart attack. I
would appreciate it if the chairman would give me five
or ten minutes rest after each hour.' For a person who
had a severe heart condition, you certainly play a lot
of sports.

MR. WHITE: I did not intend that this note should
be read aloud. I do not know any reason why it should
be public that I am ill, but I think probably one of the
reasons why I suffered a heart attack was because I
played so many sports, and so well. The heart attack

which I suffered was last year. I am speaking of playing ping-pong, and I was a fair tennis player, and a pretty good ball player, many years prior to that. I hope that clears that up, Mr. Chairman. [Applause.]

✻ ✻ ✻ ✻ ✻

MR. STRIPLING: Getting back to the question, Mr. White, whether you were in the Silvermaster basement, did you ever notice any photographic equipment?

MR. WHITE: I do not recollect. I do not think I would have paid any attention to it. I am not at all interested in photography myself. I do not think I have snapped a picture in 20 years. It might have been; it might not. I do know, though, that Mr. Ullmann was interested in photography. I do know that. He had some splendid photographs in his home, which were, he said, done by him—Silvermaster [sic]—done by him, and they looked quite professional. And I also remember that many years prior to that, or as a result of that, I asked whether he would not take some pictures of my children, which he very generously did, and they are very excellent pictures. We still have them, and they are hanging in my bedroom.

✻ ✻ ✻ ✻ ✻

MR. STRIPLING: Now, Mr. Perlo and Mr. Ullmann, as well as your friend Mr. Silvermaster—

MR. WHITE: Yes.

MR. STRIPLING:—have all been accused.

MR. WHITE: Mr. Ullmann is also my friend.

MR. STRIPLING: Make him your friend, too.

MR. WHITE: Yes.

MR. STRIPLING: What about Mr. Perlo?

MR. WHITE: Not that I would not wish him to be a

friend. I just do not happen to know him very well.

MR. STRIPLING: Regardless of friendship involved, they have all been before this committee and have all refused to state under oath whether or not they were members of the Communist Party. Do you have any attitude on their refusal to answer that very pertinent question since two of them were former employees in your department and the other a very close friend of yours whom you interceded to keep in the government?

MR. WHITE: No, I do not think I would know what the situation is. Apparently they have had the advice of counsel. I suppose it depends on what counsel you have. I do not happen to have any counsel that I would seek advice of that kind from. I do my own thinking.

MR. STRIPLING: If you were still head of the Monetary Research—

MR. WHITE: What is that?

MR. STRIPLING: If you were still Assistant Secretary of the Treasury, would you reemploy these people if they refused to answer that question?

MR. WHITE: Well, I should hardly do so under the circumstances. Of course not. I mean, I would want to know a lot more about it, and want to know a lot of the evidence, would want to turn it over to the proper investigating authorities, and have them be extremely careful. I should not want to injure an innocent man, and I should not take alone myself anybody's word about anybody else being red or a communist, but I certainly should want a thorough investigation made. As a matter of fact, we did that with all cases.

* * * * *

MR. [KARL E.] MUNDT: Do you believe that a member of the Communist Party can be loyal to the American Government as a public servant in a high, important Government post and a member of the Communist Party at one and the same time?

MR. WHITE: I should not think so, Congressman. I would not have employed anybody I knew or suspected to be a Communist to such a post. I might, if I were hiring people, clerks, or something where there was no opportunity to influence policy or to obtain information, I believe. I do not know. I was not faced with that choice.

MR. MUNDT: The difficulty, Dr. White, is that clerks are the type of people who pick up exposed folders and steal them.

MR. WHITE: Yes, but, Congressman Mundt, you are talking about something we know now. If you go back to 1937, 1938, 1939, 1940, 1941, 1942, and those years, that was not in the forefront of our mind. We were concerned with the enemy, not at that time with what was regarded to be our ally, and as a matter of fact, I know one occasion in which there was a suspicion of somebody being in contact with the enemy, and we took such steps as were called for. It proved that the suspicion was unfounded. That is why I would not want to mention the man's name.

Mr. Mundt, then a Representative from South Dakota, explained that he asked the question because Mr. White had previously mentioned that he was not concerned with a man's political convictions.

MR. WHITE: I do not know whether I said that, Congressman Mundt. If I did, I am happy that you corrected the impression. I should have said this: We never asked a man whether he was a Democrat or a Republican ...

Shortly after that, Representative Thomas granted the requested five-minute recess. When the hearing resumed, the questioning reverted to the matter of Mr. Silvermaster's loyalty. Mr. White related that he had been surprised that a question of loyalty had been raised regarding Mr. Silvermaster.

THE CHAIRMAN: Yes, and then I recall your saying that you asked him whether or not he was a Communist.

MR. WHITE: That is right.

THE CHAIRMAN: What was his answer?

MR. WHITE: Definitely not.

THE CHAIRMAN: Definitely not. Then you decided that he was not a Communist, is that correct?

MR. WHITE: Well, that is putting it a little different from the way I would put it. I said that I asked for some more of his background, what were the charges, what were his answers.

Later Chairman Thomas asked the witness whether he did not think any Communist would answer "No" to such a question.

"Probably, but that would not stop my asking," the witness replied drily.

THE CHAIRMAN: How do you feel about Mr. Silvermaster today in view of the testimony that has been given before the FBI and Federal Grand Jury and before this committee, and what you have read in the newspapers? Do you think Mr. Silvermaster was ever a member of the Communist Party?

MR. WHITE: You cannot erase seven or eight years

of friendship with a man that way unless I see evidence, unless the court declares he is, and until they prove he is guilty. I believe he is innocent.

I am sorry, Mr. Chairman, this applause is not my fault.

Neither Mr. Brownell nor Mr. Hoover troubled themselves to refer to this part of Mr. White's lengthy testimony, but Senator Jenner at least summarized it. His summary, in its entirety, was: "White made a blanket denial of all connections with the communist underground when he took the witness stand in 1948."

The Senator also made much of the invocation of the Fifth Amendment by various witnesses. In the "Interlocking Subversion" report, his committee emphasized that "all of [thirty-six witnesses] invoked the Fifth Amendment and refused to answer questions regarding communist membership on the grounds of self-incrimination." Among these was Virginius Frank Coe, until recently Secretary of the International Monetary Fund. In the climactic hearing, not only the Senator, but Messrs. Brownell and Hoover picked up this cue.

"Recently this subcommitee had occasion to inquire of Mr. Coe whether he was presently engaged in subversive activities," Mr. Brownell said. "Mr. Coe replied: 'Mr. Chairman, under the protection afforded me by the Fifth Amendment, I respectfully decline to answer that question.' Coe continued in the employ of the Fund until as recently as December 3, 1953, when he was finally dismissed."

Mr. Hoover also mentioned Mr. Coe in the same way.

"It is particularly significant that he declined to answer questions regarding his relationship with White," the FBI man said ominously.

It is also significant that not a word was said regarding Mr. Coe's testimony before the Grand Jury and the House Committee. He "waived his immunity" from testifying against himself before the Grand Jury, the House Committee record shows. His appearance before the House Committee was at his own request. Not once did he invoke the Fifth Amendment.

"I wish to say that the allegation which Miss Bentley apparently made to this committee about my being a member of a communist espionage group is entirely false," he swore. "I do not know Miss Bentley, and to the best of my knowledge I have never seen or talked with her. I have never been a member of such a group as she has described. I have never been a member of the Communist Party. I have not followed the line of that party nor, for that matter, the line of any political party or group. I have never given official information to any person known to me to be a member of the Communist Party or an agent of the Soviet Union. To the best of my knowledge I have never given official information to any unauthorized person . . ."

Nor did he then decline to answer questions about Mr. White.

MR. STRIPLING: And you know Harry D. White?

MR. COE: Yes, I entered the government at the same time and worked with him at various other times . . . I worked for [him] twice in permanent positions and kept in touch with [him] and saw [him] from time to time at lunches and to a certain extent socially.

Mr. Coe also had a word to say in 1948 on the subject of names, but none of the Republican gentlemen at the Brownell-Hoover hearing took occasion to refer to this testimony:

MR. COE: Mr. Chairman, I wonder if I may say something about the question of knowing [people] in the government. A long list of names has been read to me, as it has been before, and I have previously testified under oath, waived immunity, and testified under oath concerning these things.

MR. STRIPLING: Where was that, Mr. Coe?

MR. COE: That was before a grand jury. I would like to say first that any minor discrepancies in my statement on various occasions are unintentional. I am speaking now as to my best recollection. I cannot recall details about persons or dates about persons.

MR. MUNDT: I take it that wouldn't hold for your printed statement? [The gentleman from South Dakota was referring to Mr. Coe's point-by-point denial of Miss Bentley's charges against him.]

MR. COE: No, sir. I thought about that quite carefully. The second point I want to say, especially in view of the allegation that these people comprised a group, is that so far as I can see these were never a group in any shape or form. They never acted as a group. As the testimony before you shows, some knew each other and some did not. The nearest they ever came to being a group, to my knowledge, was in the playing of volley ball. They used to meet, or a number of these people used to go out Sundays and play volley ball. I personally didn't do it because I didn't get up that early. On the one or two occasions I did go out, I saw some and not others. I could, if it were of any relevance—

MR. STRIPLING: Just a moment, Mr. Coe, I would like to ask you: Are you thoroughly familiar in detail with the lives of these people? Can you testify as to whether or not they are a group?

MR. COE: I am testifying as to my knowledge and experience of them.

Mr. Stripling interrupted to ask a long series of questions regarding Mr. Coe's acquaintanceship with some eighteen accused individuals. The committee's investigator then stated his conclusion:

"Mr. Chairman, I would say that with eighteen names on the list his acquaintanceship with them was very casual," he declared. This was hardly the same view of the matter as is now held by Senator Jenner, but it suited Mr. Stripling's purpose at the time. Mr. Coe remained undeterred, however, when Mr. Stripling asked him: "Now, do you want to continue your statement about the group, Mr. Coe?"

MR. COE: Yes, sir. I would like to say a couple of more things, if I may. I noticed that there was introduced here a telephone device for recording numbers which indicated that my name was on a telephone device which Mr. Silvermaster used. Following that I dug out or had my secretary dig out the same devices which were used in my office in 1945 and 1946. That is a time subsequent to Miss Bentley's apparent activity. I found on that list Silvermaster's name. I also found on one such device which was used in our office, 266 names, on another 200.

The point I am making is that some of these people, according to my knowledge, were friendly to each other, some were not, some were thrown into juxtaposition by the nature of their work, some were not, and that inevitably in Washington, as everybody knows, you meet and know a great many people. In saying that I do not wish to imply that in any way any of these people ever gave me any cause to doubt their loyalty to the United States government.

On the few occasions when he did play volleyball, Mr. Coe swore, "the one that I did not see there was Silvermaster . . . I personally am unable to account for the behavior known to me of a number of these persons if they were members of a group in any such sense as alleged here. I know of differences between the men. I know of differences in the positions that they took on various crucial issues in the government, which are nonexplicable to me on the grounds such as have been brought forward here."

All this was sworn testimony. Not a word of it was adverted to by Mr. Brownell, Mr. Hoover, or Senator Jenner. Because Mr. Coe later tired of what Elmer Davis has called the "perpetual jeopardy" to which congressional committees subject witnesses, the Attorney General, the Director of the FBI, and one of the Senate's most powerful committee chairmen make believe that he never uttered a word on the subject except their favorite phrase: "Under the protection afforded me by the Fifth Amendment, I respectfully decline to answer that question."

No mention was made either of the fact that Mr. Silvermaster, although he invoked the Fifth Amendment in 1948 as to questions involving communism, swore that "the charges made by Miss Bentley are false and fantastic. I can only conclude that she is a neurotic liar. I am and have been a loyal American citizen and was a faithful government employee. I am not and never have been a spy or agent of any foreign government."

Similarly A. George Silverman denied under oath Miss Bentley's accusations.

"You are innocent of the charge of espionage, you state specifically?" he was asked.

"Yes," he testified. He also denied giving restricted government documents to "any unauthorized person." In a dramatic confrontation scene, Representative F. Edward Hébert, Louisiana Democrat, asked both Mr. Silverman and Miss Bentley to stand and face each other in the crowded hearing room.

MR. HÉBERT: I tell you, Dr. Silverman, that this lady standing here, whom I have described by name, accuses you in open court before the American people of being an espionage agent, or rather of having given her secret documents, confidential documents, which you, Dr. Silverman obtained through your connections with the Army Air Forces. She accuses you of disloyalty to your government, and she tells you that you were untrue to your trust. You face your accuser, Dr. Silverman. What is your answer? Is she telling the truth, or isn't she telling the truth, and do you recognize her?

MR. SILVERMAN: In my opinion, she is telling a huge web of lies.

MR. HÉBERT: You tell Miss Bentley here—that is contradictory now to the fact that you refused to answer because it might incriminate you. Are you waiving that now?

MR. SILVERMAN: With respect to the charge of espionage and any other criminal conduct, I waive.

The Attorney General made no reference to all this in his testimony. Instead he listed Mr. Silverman as among those of "White's close associates referred to in the FBI reports who were members of the espionage ring who have claimed their privilege not to answer questions on the grounds that it would incriminate them." He also listed William Ludwig Ullmann in the same classification. Yet Mr. Ullmann testified in 1948 that he applied to Harry

D. White for employment in the Treasury; that he knew and lived with the Silvermasters.

MR. STRIPLING: You did not assist in taking pictures of any government documents?

MR. ULLMANN That is correct.

MR. STRIPLING: In the basement of Nathan Gregory Silvermaster's home?

MR. ULLMANN: That is correct.

MR. STRIPLING: Did you ever furnish any informa- to Nathan Gregory Silvermaster?

MR. ULLMANN: Did I ever furnish any documents?

MR. STRIPLING: Any documents to Nathan Gregory Silvermaster.

MR. ULLMANN: No.

MR. STRIPLING: Did you ever furnish any information to Nathan Gregory Silvermaster obtained in your official capacity in the Army?

MR. ULLMANN: No.

MR. STRIPLING: Are you a member of the Communist Party?

MR. ULLMANN: I refuse to answer that question on the ground that it might tend to incriminate me.

MR. STRIPLING: Do you know Elizabeth Bentley?

MR. ULLMANN: I refuse to answer . . .

MR. STRIPLING: Did you ever furnish any information to Elizabeth T. Bentley?

MR. ULLMANN: No.

Still another charge made by the Attorney General testifying before the Jenner Committee was that William Henry Taylor and Sonia Steinman Gold were among those individuals "whom this [espionage] group were anxious to have assigned" to the Treasury by Harry D. White. Mr. Taylor, who was absent from Washington at the time of the 1948 hearings, filed a sworn statement with the committee on his return. In it he declared that he was not and never had been a member of the Communist party, nor a member of any organization affiliated with it, so far as he knew; that he knew some of those mentioned by Miss Bentley but only in a manner "in keeping with my position as a government employee"; and that he had never met or communicated with Miss Bentley in any way to the best of his knowledge.

"As for the third allegation [by Miss Bentley]," he swore, "I deny that I ever transmitted confidential information to any person with the intent that such information should be delivered to agents of the Soviet Union. I deny that I ever transmitted confidential government information or made information available to any person other than as required or proper in my line of duty as a government employee." He asked for, but never was accorded "the opportunity of appearing before the committee to deny these charges in person." Mr. Brownell, *et al.*, made no mention of this denial, of course.

As for Mrs. Gold, Attorney General Brownell asserted that she had been suggested by an unnamed Communist Party official as someone who should be placed "as a secretary to White in order to facilitate the obtaining of information from his office for delivery to Soviet espionage agents." She obtained a position, Mr. Brownell said, "as one of the secretaries."

"As a result of this employment, Mrs. Gold obtained documents from White's office, which she copied and made her notes available to Mrs. Helen Witte Silvermaster . . ." the Attorney General told the committee.

In 1948, Miss Bentley testified as follows concerning a "William" Gold:

MR. STRIPLING: Was he a member of the Communist Party?

MISS BENTLEY: Yes.

MR. STRIPLING: Did he furnish information to your group?

MISS BENTLEY: Yes, he did.

MR. STRIPLING: Is there anyone else you haven't named?

MISS BENTLEY: Yes, his wife Sonia Gold.

MR. STRIPLING: Was she an employee of the government?

MISS BENTLEY: Yes, in the Treasury.

Despite the fact that he had been named "William" Gold by Miss Bentley, a man named Bela Gold and his wife, Sonia, telegraphed the committee asking to testify. "Charges by Miss Bentley apparently directed against us are shocking and completely untrue," they wired.

When Mr. Gold took the stand, he swore: "I have never seen the witness who has apparently put forward the completely unfounded charges reported by the newspapers last week. I am not and have never been a member of the Communist Party or of any organizations associated with it. I deny without qualification that I have ever disclosed any government documents or their contents to any unauthorized individuals."

Mr. Gold said that N. Gregory Silvermaster had helped him in the preparation of an economic study. "Although I have not seen Dr. Silvermaster for more than three years now," he testified, "I remain grateful for his generous help at that early stage in the undertaking. In all fairness to him, especially in view of the grave charges which have been so widely publicized, I want to emphasize under oath that he never made any suggestion or expressed any view to me that any reasonably responsible person could possibly consider subversive or disloyal . . ."

Committee investigator Stripling then began the questioning:

MR. STRIPLING: You never furnished any information to Mr. Silvermaster?

MR. GOLD: Never.

MR. STRIPLING: Which you obtained in your official capacity in the government?

MR. GOLD: Never.

* * * * *

MR. STRIPLING: You don't know Elizabeth T. Bentley?

MR. GOLD: No.

Mr. Stripling read Miss Bentley's sworn testimony regarding Dr. Gold.

MR. HÉBERT: You heard those charges, Mr. Gold?

MR. GOLD: Yes.

MR. HÉBERT: You categorically deny them as being untrue?

MR. GOLD: Yes, sir.

MR. HÉBERT: That is all.

[Representative JOHN] MCDOWELL [Republican of Pennsylvania]: Dr. Gold, have you ever used any other name than Gold?

MR. GOLD: No, and never any other name than Bela either. The William J. comes as an alias without foundation.

Mrs. Gold also took the witness stand. She told the committee that she had done graduate work in economics and had "matriculated for my Ph.D. degree in economics at Columbia University." As a research assistant she

wrote a report for the House Select Committee on Interstate Migration in June 1941. Later she worked as a labor
market analyst for the War Manpower Commission and
finally "wishing to broaden my work experience and to
add another specialization to my academic qualifications
and work experience, I applied to the Division of Monetary Research [of the Treasury]." She said she stayed
with the Division, except for a period of maternity leave,
until she resigned in August 1947 to accompany her husband to Pittsburgh. "During my employment at the Division I was assigned to work on a variety of technical
monetary and financial problems: inflation, exchange
rates, and so forth," she testified.

"I too wish to declare under oath that I have never
seen the witness who has apparently put forward the
completely unfounded charges against us reported by
the newspapers last week," she swore. "I am not and have
never been a member of the Communist Party or any
organizations associated with it. I deny without qualification that I have ever disclosed any government information to any unauthorized individual."

Had she been "one of the secretaries," as Mr. Brownell asserted, she would have been the best bargain the
taxpayers ever got. But she was not. As a matter of fact,
the well-educated Mrs. Gold was employed as a research
assistant. She subsequently accepted a post teaching
economics at a Pennsylvania college.

MR. HÉBERT: *Was he* [White] *considered as a source of information to the communist cell?*

MR. CHAMBERS: *No. I should perhaps make the point that these people were specifically not wanted as sources of information . . .*

—House Committee Hearings, 1948.

THE STRONGEST EVIDENCE put into the record of the Brownell-Hoover hearing was that found in photostats offered by Attorney General Brownell. They were reproductions of eight hand-written sheets of paper. According to Mr. Brownell, they were "written by [Harry Dexter White] in his own handwriting for delivery to agents of the Red Army Intelligence." They had been "recovered," he said, "in the fall of 1948." Under questioning, Mr. Brownell subsequently conceded that what he meant was that they had been produced by Whittaker Chambers after Mr. White's death that fall.

Even in this instance, the revelation was nothing new. Vice President (then Representative from California) Richard M. Nixon had read the notes into the *Congressional Record* in January, 1950, almost four years earlier.

Mr. Nixon took the papers very seriously indeed. A government expert, he asserted, had authenticated the documents as having been written by Mr. White. The congressman singled out one quotation for special consideration, implying that he thought it the most damaging:

"We have just agreed to purchase 50,000,000 more ounces of silver from China," he read. "China will have left (almost all in London) about 100,000,000 ounces of silver. Her dollar balances are almost gone."

Mr. Nixon told his colleagues that a man whose judgment he valued had informed him "that that information in the hands of individuals who desired to embarrass the Chinese government would be almost invaluable." The item is dated January 9, 1938. The individuals most anxious to embarrass the Chinese government at that time were the Japanese, with whom China had long been locked in undeclared war. Periodically, Japanese troops were raiding the Manchurian-Siberian border in force. If Mr. Nixon was suggesting that Mr. White was a spy for Nippon and Mr. Chambers a courier for the Japanese, he did not say so.

Mr. Nixon is a shrewd, cautious man, who proved to be an able examiner of the witnesses he questioned in the "Hiss case" hearings before the House Committee on Un-American Activities in 1948. Unlike Mr. Brownell, he refrained from any direct accusation against Mr. White. He was content merely to remark that "Mr. Chambers, a confessed espionage agent, had the documents in his possession." The gentleman from California was merely bringing them to the attention of the House because they "may be of interest to you" and because "the public is entitled to see and consider the evidence."

Mr. Brownell's consideration of the evidence led him, as we know, to conclude that they were "written ... for delivery to agents of the Red Army Intelligence." Assum-

ing that the handwriting expert is correct, the Attorney
General's conclusion is based wholly on Mr. Chambers'
assertion that Mr. White turned over "information" to
him which he (Chambers) then passed on to Red Intelligence. Other than that, there is nothing in the record
to show that Mr. White wrote them "for delivery" to anyone. There is nothing to suggest that they were not stolen
without Mr. White's knowledge. There is, on the other
hand, quite a little to suggest that they were. Such things
happened. One theft of papers from the Treasury in 1943
was briefly discussed when Mr. White appeared before
the House Committee in 1948.

Unfortunately, the opportunity to ask him about these
eight sheets was forever lost. Mr. Chambers, who testified
twice a week prior to Mr. White's appearance, declared:
"I can't say positively that he was a registered member of
the Communist Party, but he certainly was a fellow traveller so far within the fold that his not being a communist
would be a mistake on both sides."

The witness offered no papers in corroboration, however. Then came a response to a question put by Representative F. Edward Hébert of New Orleans which
may explain why:

MR. HÉBERT: Was he considered as a source of information to the communist cell?

MR. CHAMBERS: *No. I should perhaps make the point
that these people were specifically not wanted to act as
sources of information.* These people were an elite
group, an outstanding group, which it was believed
would rise to positions—as indeed some of them did—
notably Mr. White and Mr. Hiss—in the government,
and their position in the government would be of very
much more service to the Communist Party—(My emphasis.)

At the moment these words were spoken, Mr. White was very much alive and, as he later demonstrated, in a highly contradicting mood. He denied Mr. Chambers' charges—such as they then were—specifically and *in toto*. Only after he died were the papers "recovered"—to use Mr. Brownell's term—from Mr. Chambers' archives. Only later did Mr. Chambers declare that he had been mistaken, that, on second thought, Mr. White *did* give him information.

Mr. Nixon, though he was present at the 1948 hearing, did not allude to these petty discrepancies in his 1950 Senate speech. Nor, naturally, did Mr. Brownell. Indeed, the Attorney General had apparently not troubled to prepare himself for the White case hearing before Senator Jenner. Asked by Democratic Senator Olin D. Johnston of South Carolina whether he had read the report on the 1948 hearing, Mr. Brownell replied: "Not recently, but I imagine I have."

Senator Johnston also pointed out that Mr. White "along with about one hundred others" testified before the grand jury.

"He was investigated," the Senator said, "and they did not see fit to find at that time sufficient evidence to make out a probable case . . ."

The Attorney General had a ready explanation: The evidence against Mr. White, he declared, included "wiretap" evidence which could not be given the grand jury. Mr. Brownell did not give it to the committee either. He ended his explanation with these curious words:

". . . When the pressure came, when the conclusive evidence came of these papers in 1948, shortly after his death, of course that had not been discovered at that time [of the grand inquest]."

Earlier Mr. Brownell referred to the papers as "re-

ports." The information they contained, he declared "was
... of great importance at the time White wrote them ..."

One of the eight sheets contains the cryptic notation:

65 big sheets
4 little slips

Another page bears a single, hardly earth-shaking sentence: "The Van Zeeland report was not taken seriously
here."

The remaining six pages of scribbled notes are not
easily interpreted as "reports." They consist of a miscellany
of fact, rumor, gossip. Some of them refer to events of
a wholly public character. Others deal sketchily with the
inner workings of international monetary doings. There is
one item which might cause a man less wise than Mr.
Brownell to scratch his head in puzzlement. It reads:

"(What is behind Taylor's, and possibly Feis' desire
to press M into a debt settlement arrangement of that
character at this time? Why didn't Taylor try to convince
Secretary directly instead of surreptitiously via Feis?)"

Did Mr. Brownell and friends suppose that "M" here
refers to Malenkov instead of Morgenthau? In reporting
to "Red Army Intelligence," was Mr. White seeking to get
answers to these parenthetical questions, perhaps in exchange for the tidbits he supplied? Did he expect the
Kremlin to read the minds of "Taylor" and "Feis"?

Or is there some other explanation for these notes?
The paragraph of questions and the fact that the entries
begin with a date noted in the margin (thus: "1/10/38")
are suggestive of another possibility. Let us suppose, for
the moment, that the following notes were also posthu-
mously produced by Mr. Chambers:

"Saturday, September 9, 1939: Saturday evening,
September 2, six of us including the President, had a
stag dinner and poker party at the White House ...

"At cabinet on Monday we discussed the question of neutrality. It was decided to issue at once the customary neutrality declaration that follows any outbreak of war. The President was not in so much of a hurry to issue the proclamation required under the Neutrality Act. He wanted England and France to have all the opportunity possible to export munitions of war, none of which could be exported after this proclamation was once issued. We also discussed the issuing of a declaration of emergency. The President disclosed that by issuing such a declaration the executive branch of the government would have greatly enhanced powers. He was in some doubt whether to issue it almost at once or to wait until there was a greater evidence of public sentiment in the country . . .

". . . The President thought that it might be advantageous both to the French and to us if the French should turn the *Normandie* over to us at its present value, which he estimated to be about $20,000,000, to apply on war debts to us. We could then sail the *Normandie* under the American flag and could use it principally to bring back Americans who found themselves stranded in Europe when war was declared.

"He instructed Henry Morgenthau, who had just landed in Washington after racing back across the North Atlantic in a Revenue cutter that had been sent over to bring him back, to negotiate with France, and he also authorized similar negotiations with Great Britain with respect to the *Queen Mary*. It happened that when I was in the President's office on Wednesday, Undersecretary Welles of the State Department got him on the telephone, and I could tell from what I heard at the President's end that Bonnet, of the French cabinet, had apparently not taken in good part the suggestion with respect to the *Normandie*. The President told Welles to assure Bonnet that our intentions were strictly honorable and to explain to him the purposes to which we intended to devote the *Normandie* in the event that it came under the American flag. But the deal was off."

The *Normandie* burned and sank at her dock in New York not long afterwards. There was talk of sabotage. The author of these words was a Cabinet officer who, in another such dated entry remarked *á propos* of the Nazi Soviet Pact: "I am not surprised at Russia's action, but I am disappointed . . . England could have made terms with Russia long ago. She kept hoping against hope that she could embroil Russia and Germany with each other and thus escape scot-free herself." These words are to be found in the *Secret Diary of Harold L. Ickes.*

Let the reader ask himself what a scandal would have rocked the country had notes of this nature been produced as evidence of espionage. Practically every high government official, cocking an eye on his old age and on posterity, made notes for future memoirs or a diary. If Mr. White, too, was making notes for subsequent memoirs, he had plenty of company, including Fleet Admiral Nimitz, Harry Hopkins, Mr. Ickes, Generals Omar N. Bradley and Dwight D. Eisenhower.

While the papers hardly make a spy or even a giver of information out of Mr. White, the fact remains that they found their way by whatever route into Mr. Chambers' hands. Did somebody lift them from Mr. White's desk drawer and pass them on? Far be it from the author to say Nay. To elaborate a vast intrigue, hatched by Red Intelligence in Moscow, on the basis of such material alone, however, places an equal strain on logic.

Estimates of the Russians' skill at intelligence operations are usually lofty. For example, when General Walter Bedell Smith left the directorship of the U. S. Central

Intelligence Agency, he told the National Security Commission of the American Legion on January 25, 1953, that he hoped the CIA "in a few years will become the best in the world."

"We are now about as good as any country in the world," he said, "with the possible exception of the Soviet Union."

General Smith ought to know, if anybody does. If Red Intelligence is that competent, would it not insist, at the very least, on its agents taking a few elementary precautions? The "interlocking" spies of Messrs. Jenner, Brownell and Hoover cannot be said to have behaved in the approved style of agents of one of the best, if not *the* best, intelligence service in the world. They were as indiscreet, as inept, as convivial a collection of spies as history has ever brought forth. They were downright sloppy.

Either Mr. Brownell and Mr. Hoover have not bothered to examine the record, or the "irrefutable and uncontradictable" proof which the latter declined to disclose is so overwhelming as to brush aside the picture revealed by the testimony of accused and accuser alike. Lacking access to Mr. Hoover's asserted proof, we will turn to the public record, as disclosed in the testimony of the witnesses.

On the Washington end of the committee's trail of stolen secrets was a party-loving, hand-ball-, soft-ball-volley-ball-, ping-pong-, and tennis-playing group. Ignoring the elementary rules of the espionage game, Arch-spy White nonchalantly played volley-ball and soft-ball with one fellow-spy, ping-pong in the home of another, and tennis with a third.

For agents of the NKVD or Red Intelligence, they were unconscionably lackadaisical in their attitude toward their assignments. Instead of remaining where they could

do the most good for the Kremlin, they left their posts
in droves, some after only a year or two of service, others
at the worst possible time: just as the "cold war" began.
One quit because he refused to accept a salary cut; another for a mere triviality: an offer of more salary in
private employment. Mr. Coe, rather unbecomingly for
an agent of Red Intelligence, kept bouncing in and out of
the Treasury, as one questioner put it, as if he were caught
in a revolving door. Instead of manning his post for Stalin,
he bustled off to this or that academic pursuit in various
universities.

Agent White, meanwhile, was not in top NKVD form
when he gave an overseas assignment to "interlocking"
subordinate Harold Glasser in 1940. At the time, Russia
had invaded Finland, having signed a treaty of non-
aggression with Hitler. Relations between Washington and
Moscow were particularly strained. This was the moment
when Mr. White, according to Senator Jenner, chose to
send Mr. Glasser to that nerve center of military secrets,
the Republic of Ecuador. There he remained, slyly keeping Moscow up-to-date on the cacao situation, until sometime after July, 1942, by which time U.S.-Soviet relations
were approaching the utmost cordiality.

Conviviality reigned if not supreme, then in a manner most improper for well-trained spies. Mr. Coe seems
to have been especially fun-loving. He told the House
Committee he had socialized with Messrs. Silverman, Silvermaster, Adler, White, and Lauchlin Currie. Mr. Currie said he had been to parties at the Silvermaster home
and had brought his son there to view Mr. Ullmann's
power tools in the famous basement.

Miss Bentley herself described the strange situation
of one of the supposed Red agents, Irving Kaplan.

"He was in a very peculiar position," she told the

House Committee probers in 1948, "because he was paying his dues to the Perlo group and giving his information to the Silvermaster group. Somehow the two groups got a little scrambled at that point."

It is difficult to choose between the Silvermasters and Mr. Ullmann for the title of Most Indiscreet Spy in History. They committed the cardinal intelligence sin of living in the same house. Mr. Silvermaster went on to other follies. When he left the government, like a good executive, he turned over to his WAA secretary a telephone index from which she later read to the House Committee the names of about a dozen of his co-espions.

To top it all, when he left Washington, Mr. Silvermaster decided to sell his house. Secure, we suppose, in the knowledge that the vigilance of the FBI would never extend to reading the real estate pages of the Washington *Star*, he inserted an advertisement on May 3, 1947. The house was glowingly described in the fashion of such notices. Among its features, Mr. Silvermaster chose to praise the "workshop, gas hot-water heat, detached garage, slate roof, copper tubing, storm sash, beautiful lot 135 feet deep, with highly productive vegetable and fruit garden," and "in the basement an excellent photographic room."

Few persons were able to testify, except the FBI, to having seen this damningly "well-equipped photographic laboratory." Unlike other photographers, it would appear that Mr. Ullmann preversely kept his darkroom dark. If someone should open the door he no doubt planned to explain nonchalantly that he thought visitors might not regard a darkroom as a suitable place in which to play ping-pong. This feeble excuse will get him nowhere with his Red masters. How will he explain his decorating the walls of the house with the product of his work? How will he excuse his taking pictures of fellow-agent Solomon Adler, and how will the latter reconcile his telling the House Committee that Mr. Ullmann was not only a good photographer but took several pictures of him? Mr. White is fortunately beyond the punishment that his Soviet chief would mete out for telling the Committee of Mr. Ullmann's photographic prowess, and, worse yet, of the pictures he had made of his (White's) children.

Mr. Ullmann also loaned Bela Gold a camera. Asked at the 1948 hearing what kind it was, Mr. Gold replied:

"I am afraid I cannot tell you what kind. All I know was it was too involved for me to handle. One with a rangefinder in it . . . I tried it for one or two days, and by the time I got everything focused the picture was gone and finally gave it up."

Still another indiscretion of this underground agent of Moscow was revealed by the Jenner committee last fall. In 1946, Mr. Ullmann, it appears, had had his last will and testament prepared in anticipation of a plane trip to Europe. The address he gave in the draft will was that of the Silvermaster house in Washington. He appointed Mr. Silvermaster as his executor, bequeathing him and Mrs. Silvermaster his interest in the house. This was damning enough, but still worse, he left "my Graflex camera and darkroom equipment" to his sister and brother-in-law.

We will pass over this casual disposition of Soviet property to consider the ultimate folly which he then calmly committed. Incredible as it may seem, secret Soviet agent Ullmann gave all this information to a Treasury Department lawyer who proceeded to prepare the will. Mr. Ullmann apparently kept the original, while a copy was kept on file in the Treasury Department. It was, in the fullness of time, duly discovered there, as the Committee's counsel, Robert Morris, confirmed.

Mr. Ullmann survived his airplane passage to Europe. In the year following his return he resigned his Treasury post. He and the Silvermasters persisted, however, in remaining friends. They went into business together as developers of a rather elegant seaside colony in New Jersey. They located themselves in a house nearby on the Jersey beach. This fact prompted Idaho's unsuspicious Senator Herman Welker to inquire: "Did you ever have any visitors there from any foreign country call on you by marine surface vessel?"

When we turn our attention to the New York end of this apparatus, the picture is one which, if possible, even less resembles an efficient espionage operation. The man the Soviets chose to be spymaster, we are told, was one Jacob Raisin. No doubt to throw the FBI off the scent, Mr. Raisin changed his name to "Golos," the Russian word for "voice." His previous career was one that could be of no possible interest to the FBI:

". . . To anyone who had had a long experience with the communist movement in the United States, Jacob Golos was a famous person. He had been extremely active in the early days of the Party, among other things helping to set up the Technical Aid Society for Soviet Russia . . ." Miss Bentley tells us in her book *Out of Bondage*. "Later on he became increasingly well-known, especially as one of the editors of the Russian [language] communist newspaper *Novy Mir*, published in New York. By the early thirties he was head of World Tourists, a travel agency set up by the American Communist Party in 1927 for the dual purpose of making money and encouraging tourists to go to Russia . . ."

Miss Bentley meanwhile had been an active member of the Communist Party since 1935 and one of its minor officials, according to an FBI report released by the Jen-

ner committee. Switching to the "underground" of the
Party, she wrote, she was introduced to Mr. Golos on a
New York street corner whence one "Comrade Brown"
had taken her from Party headquarters. Thereafter Miss
Bentley and Mr. Golos became lovers, despite intelligence rules strictly forbidding such unspylike behavior.
She also ran in and out of Communist Party headquarters, giving information to Party boss Earl Browder. From
the managing editor of the *Daily Worker*, Louis Budenz,
she arranged to get information. This latter operation
was conducted with the utmost caution, in view of the
desperate nature of their relationship.

"Our rendezvous was near the headquarters of the
Communist Party, a building in which the *Daily Worker*
was also located. After Yasha [Golos] had gone up to the
eighth floor and brought Budenz down, I was introduced
under the name of Helen and we adjourned to a bar
and grill on the corner of University Place and 12th
Street."

This hush-hush meeting place was perhaps five doors
from Communist headquarters.

"There we settled ourselves in a wooden booth where
we could not be overheard, ordered coffee, and began to
discuss our business," Miss Bentley continued. " . . . It was
arranged that Louis and I would meet in the future in the
same bar and grill. There would be no prearranged meetings. Instead, when I wanted to see him I would call the
Daily Worker (if he was not in, I would leave word that
'Helen Johns' had called); when he had information to
be passed on he would call me at World Tourists, leaving word in my absence that 'Mr. Louis' had called."

Meanwhile, Spymaster Golos had his eye on Washington.

MR. STRIPLING: Did Mr. Golos ever ask you to perform any special duties for him in connection with any work that he was doing for the Communist Party in behalf of the Soviet Union?

MISS BENTLEY: Later on, yes.

* * * * *

MR. STRIPLING: When was that?

MISS BENTLEY: At about the start of the Russian-German war which would be around June or July of 1941.

MR. STRIPLING: What did he ask you to do?

MISS BENTLEY: He asked me to take charge of individuals and groups. This was a gradual process, not all at once. It was to take charge of individuals and groups who were employed in the United States government and in positions to furnish information.

MR. STRIPLING: What kind of information?

MISS BENTLEY: All sorts of information—political, military, whatever they could lay their hands on.

MR. STRIPLING: Was he operating or had he set up a so-called espionage organization to obtain information from government employees and government officials to be transmitted to the Soviet Union?

MISS BENTLEY: I think that he set it up. I rather doubt that he had operated it before that. Of course, I can't state definitely.

* * * * *

MR. STRIPLING: Would you tell the committee how this espionage organization operated and your participation in it?

MISS BENTLEY: It started with actual government employees in about July 1941, when he told me that he had received from Earl Browder the name of a man

working for the United States government who was interested in helping in getting information to Russia
and who could organize a group of other government
employees to help in this work.

Miss Bentley then identified this person as Nathan
Gregory Silvermaster. The arrangement sounded rather
informal in this part of her testimony, but a moment
later, Miss Bentley corrected this impression.

[REP. JOHN E.] RANKIN [Democrat of Mississippi]:
He [Silvermaster] was a member of the Communist
Party, you say?

MISS BENTLEY: That is correct.

MR. RANKIN: And an agent of the Communist International?

MISS BENTLEY: Probably an agent of the NKVD
would be more correct.

MR. RANKIN: That is the Russian Communist secret
police?

MISS BENTLEY: That is correct.

A few minutes later, Miss Bentley referred, not to an
individual, but to a group formed by Mr. Golos.

MR. STRIPLING: Were there other people in the
government in this group that Mr. Golos referred to?

MISS BENTLEY: This was the first group of government employees, the first government employees which
Mr. Golos had taken on, and which I, in the position
of courier—

MR. STRIPLING: You were a courier?

MISS BENTLEY: I was the person who made trips to
Washington and picked up the material and brought
it back to Mr. Golos.

The committee investigator then had Miss Bentley run through a list of names of individuals which she identified with the group. Then he asked her how she operated.

MISS BENTLEY: It was my policy to come down almost regularly every two weeks. I would go to the Silvermaster home, very often have dinner with them, spend the evening, and collect from them the information which they had previously collected from the members of the group.

MR. STRIPLING: Where did he live?

MISS BENTLEY: I can't remember the exact street. It was out just before you get to Chevy Chase Circle. I think it was Thirty-fourth or Thirty-fifth Street. I have forgotten the address right now.

* * * * *

MR. STRIPLING: What did you do with the photographs or documents once you received them?

MISS BENTLEY: I gave them to Mr. Golos.

MR. STRIPLING: I mean, how did you take them back to New York?

MISS BENTLEY: Well, whatever way was practical. If I had a large pocketbook and there was room in that, I took them, or in a knitting bag or a shopping bag or whatever was handy, depending on the size of the collection.

MR. STRIPLING: Did you have large packages of material to take or were they usually small?

MISS BENTLEY: Yes, toward the end, yes. Toward the beginning it was just starting, as you realize, and there was not too much material ...

Such is the picture of the workings of the "ring," with

Miss Bentley tripping to the Silvermaster home every two
weeks from July 1941 to September 1944. Yet she could
not remember the address after visiting the house more
than seventy times. We have the word, however, of J.
Edgar Hoover that Miss Bentley is thoroughly reliable
as a witness.

"All information furnished by Miss Bentley, which was
susceptible to check," he told the Jenner committee, "has
proven to be correct. She had been subjected to the most
searching of cross-examinations; her testimony has been
evaluated by juries and reviewed by the courts and has
been found to be accurate."

This observation suggests that Mr. Hoover, like his
superior, is unfamiliar with Miss Bentley's previous committee testimony. In her appearance before the House
Committee, Miss Bentley was contradicted by no less
than ten witnesses.

One of these was a former aide to General William J.
Donovan, wartime chief of the Office of Strategic Services. A lifelong Republican, General Donovan brought
with him to OSS a young member of his New York law
firm, Duncan Lee. Miss Bentley declared that Mr. Lee
had furnished her with secret information regarding OSS.
Mr. Lee said he had met Miss Bentley. He indignantly
denied that he was a communist, a spy, or that he had
given her an iota of information. His testimony was so
diametrically opposed to Miss Bentley's that Representative Hébert felt called upon to point it out to her.

MR. HÉBERT: So we get down to it, either you or Mr.
Lee is lying today.

MISS BENTLEY: I guess that is the only conclusion
you can draw.

MR. HÉBERT: Both of you cannot be telling the truth.

MISS BENTLEY: It would seem so.

Recalled to the stand, Mr. Lee was asked whether he denied or affirmed Miss Bentley's testimony.

MR. LEE: I deny it, and in every respect in which it is contrary to the testimony I have previously given.

* * * * *

MR. HÉBERT: Now, looking back in retrospect, you think Miss Bentley had a purpose in following you up?

MR. LEE: That may be, sir.

MR. HÉBERT: What do you think?

MR. LEE: I am frankly completely bewildered, Congressman, by Miss Bentley's testimony. I know one thing, that from her testimony of today she has an extremely vivid imagination. As to how far her description of activity is true, I really cannot say. I know they are not true as far as I am concerned.

MR. HÉBERT: Then I will ask you the same question I asked Miss Bentley. You have both told diametrically opposed stories, and one of you is lying.

MR. LEE: That is right, sir.

Another witness also contradicted Miss Bentley during the 1948 hearings. He was Robert T. Miller III. Miss Bentley did not say in so many words that she had obtained information from Mr. Miller when he was employed in the office of the Coordinator of Inter-American Affairs, though her testimony implied the charge. She did declare that Mr. Miller was a member of the Communist Party.

MR. MUNDT: Did you collect dues from him?

MISS BENTLEY: Yes.

When Mr. Miller took the stand he denied membership in the Party and also denied having given the lady information. He said he had been introduced to her in New York by a man calling himself "John Friedman." "Friedman," he supposed, was the late Mr. Golos. Mr. Miller said that "Friedman" had approached him when he was publisher of a news-letter on Latin American affairs, stating that he was in the export-import business.

MR. MUNDT: What did he say about Bentley when he introduced you?

MR. MILLER: That she was a friend of his, and it was apparent that she was. [Laughter]

When he moved to Washington, Mr. Miller said, Miss Bentley frequently called him at his office or his home. Eventually, like Mr. Lee, the Latin American expert decided he had had enough.

"Actually, Miss Bentley became more or less of a nuisance to me after I had known her a couple of years..." he told the committee. "Miss Bentley would telephone me when she was down here from New York, and I would go to have dinner or lunch with her, and it got to be pretty much of a nuisance. Also she was under some nervous tension of some kind apparently, and she had begun to drink, and she showed up at a couple of these meetings in not a very happy condition."

The committee did not recall Miss Bentley to rebut Mr. Miller. Nor was he, Mr. Lee, or Miss Bentley subsequently prosecuted for perjury.

Though one would never know it from the Jenner committee's hearings or report, other witnesses also contradicted Miss Bentley. Lauchlin Currie, an Administrative Assistant to President Roosevelt, appeared at his own request in 1948. He specifically denied each of Miss Bentley's accusations regarding him. So did Bela and Sonia Gold, V. Frank Coe, and William H. Taylor. The Golds,

Currie, Taylor, Lee and Miller were never called by Senator Jenner to be heard publicly.

Mr. Silvermaster invoked the Fifth Amendment in 1948 in answer to specific questions, but declared, under oath, that Miss Bentley's charges were "false and fantastic." Mr. Ullmann did likewise, but he also specifically swore he had not photographed or helped to photograph government documents nor given information to Miss Bentley or Mr. Silvermaster.

Still another witness who contradicted Miss Bentley was Miss Bentley. In her book, written in 1951, she recalls having taken over contact with Mr. Lee because of the ineptness with which another supposed agent had handled him. In 1948, she testified that it was because the agent was "ill with virus pneumonia."

She also told the committee that, thanks to Mr. Ullmann, "we knew D-day long before D-day happened, and we were right." This is a happy coincidence, since General Eisenhower relates in *Crusade in Europe* that because of the uncertainties of weather, the General himself could not know the exact date. Moreover, he kept the Russians up to the minute on his plans for "Operation Overlord" unassisted by Miss Bentley or Mr. Ullmann. He informed Major General John R. Deane, chief of the U. S. Military Mission in Moscow, who in turn passed the word to Soviet Chief of Staff General A. E. Antonov.

". . . We received the necessary instructions on April 7, 1944," General Deane later recalled, "the date for Overlord being given as May 31, 'with two or three days' margin on either side to allow for weather and tide.' . . . As the time of our invasion drew near, I was given several changes of date to impart to Antonov. As I recall, the first was June 2, then June 5, and finally June 6. Even then, for a while, weather threatened to delay the operation for from two to three weeks after June 6 . . ."

On the other rather rare occasions when Miss Bentley has related specific items she obtained, her disclosures proved to be neither precise nor secret. Testifying before the Senate Subcommittee on Immigration and Naturalization, she told the committee that she obtained "information on specific new developments; for example, they [the Russians] were interested in RDX. We got information on RDX."

MR. ARENS: What is RDX?

MISS BENTLEY: RDX is a sort of explosive. I am not a chemist, and I don't know too much about it; it recently appeared in the papers. Particularly on the B-29—the B-29 was a new development during my days, and we had a man who was a specialist in B-29. He was sent out to Dayton Field [Wright Field, Dayton, Ohio], to do work on them, as a result of which we knew how they tested, how they stood up, we even knew about projected raids on Tokyo and so on—that type of information. . . . Mr. Ullman[n] was the one who went to Dayton on the B-29.

MR. ARENS: Did you have any information respecting the Doolittle raid on Tokyo which you transmitted as a courier?

MISS BENTLEY: Yes, we knew about that raid, I guess a week or ten days ahead of time; yes.

MR. ARENS: From whom did you secure the information on that raid?

MISS BENTLEY: That was from William Ludwig Ullman[n], who was a specialist, as I understand it, in the B-29 program.

RDX is one of several nicknames for an explosive polysyllabically known as cyclotrimethylenetrinitramine. It was first prepared in 1899 by a man named Henning, according to the *Encyclopedia of Chemical Technology*. Thus far, Moscow has not claimed that Henning was a Russian. It was "used on a large scale by all major participants" in World War II.

As for General James Doolittle's Tokyo raid, it took place on April 18, 1942. Weeks earlier the State Department asked and was refused Soviet permission to allow our bombers to land in Siberia. Twin-engined B-25 bombers were used. The four-engined B-29 "Super-Fortress" did not see action until June 1944. Mr. Ullmann entered the Army as a draftee in October 1942. He was graduated from Officer Candidate School in April 1943 and was not assigned to aircraft production work in the Pentagon until after that date.

In another hearing, she said that all but two of her contacts were native-born citizens. In fact, eight of those she named were foreign-born.

Miss Bentley is also one of those witnesses whose memories become more lucid as time passes. Nowhere in her five appearances before the House Committee did she mention a German occupation currency plates transaction which took place in 1944. Yet in a 1953 hearing before Senator Mundt, sitting as a one-man subcommittee of Senator McCarthy's committee, Miss Bentley testified in detail regarding the transaction. She asserted Mr. Ullmann had loaned her samples of the occupation marks for counterfeiting purposes. When her Soviet bosses reported that they could not be counterfeited, she swore, she arranged for Harry D. White to apply pressure to turn over duplicate plates to the Russians. Treasury records show quite clearly, however, that the decision to turn over the plates was made, not by Mr. White, nor even the Secretary of the Treasury, but by the joint agreement of the State, War, and Treasury Departments, prodded by the Combined Chiefs of Staff. Sample marks, meanwhile, had been officially given to the Soviet Ambassador by the Bureau of Printing and Engraving with the request that he obtain his government's approval of their design.

To risk exposure of a valuable secret agent in order to obtain samples of currency which the Soviet Ambassador had either already received or had been promised, does not seem like the policy of one of "the best" intelligence services in the world.

But Miss Bentley stoutly maintained that that is what happened. It was dangerous, dramatic work, she tells us. Long before these events, she wrote in her book, the FBI picked up the scent:

"... As I left World Tourists where I had been conferring with him [Golos], I noticed it was getting late, so when I walked out of the lobby into Broadway I quickened my steps. Then I stopped very suddenly. The street, as usual at that hour, was deserted except for two young men, one on either side of the next corner, where they could effectively block my progress up Broadway. My heart felt as if it had stopped. This was it!"

Miss Bentley's description of how she dashed about, eluding her pursuers by "a frantic dash" through the "Ladies" room of Pennsylvania station, is too heartrending to reproduce here. Safe at last at her apartment, anger swept over her:

"What right had these people to persecute us like that?" she described herself as thinking. "... Now the chips were down and it was they or I. I said to myself quite savagely that if the F.B.I. thought it was going to find out anything from me it had another think coming."

According to the "intelligence agency" report released by the Jenner committee, Miss Bentley's determination lasted some four or five years longer. It is difficult to be exact, for Miss Bentley does not often mention dates.

"This case first came to the attention of the Bureau on November 8, 1945," the report declared, "when Elizabeth Bentley, an official of the United States Service and Shipping, Inc., N.Y.C. came into the New York office of the Bureau...."

The FBI went into action at once. The letter to General Vaughan was dated the same day. It struck, as committee counsel Morris noted, "an emergency note."

"As I indicated," Mr. Hoover told the committee, "when the letter of November 8, 1945 was written, that was the so-called preliminary flash of the fact that there was a risk to the security of the country...."

The letter itself bears Mr. Hoover out. In his opening sentence he told General Vaughan that the letter's contents were based upon "information recently developed from a highly confidential source." The FBI chief could hardly have stated more plainly that the period around November 8, 1945. was the first time he became aware of the White-Silvermaster-Bentley-Golos "apparatus."

This is the oddest circumstance in the whole affair. More than six years before that, representatives of the United States Attorney's office in New York City, of the State Department, and the United States Marshal swooped down upon the offices of World Tourists, Inc. in New York City. They served a subpoena on Jacob Golos. The subpoena required him to produce immediately before the Grand Inquest for the Southern District of New York all books, records, papers, documents, etc. in any way pertaining to the business and management of World

Tourists. To make sure that nothing would be removed in the meantime, armed guards were stationed in the hallways of the World Tourists offices. Almost at once the story leaked out. Recognized by reporters as he entered the Grand Jury room in the court house at Foley Square, Mr. Golos was headlined as a suspected Soviet agent. He testified repeatedly before the Grand Jury in October, November and December, 1939.

But this was not all. On January 2, 1940 Attorney General Frank Murphy filed letters in the Federal District Court for the District of Columbia in which he accused Mr. Golos of espionage activities in behalf of the Soviet Union.

Some weeks later, a special Grand Jury in Washington handed up an indictment against "Jacob Raisin, also known as J. N. Golos," and against World Tourists, Inc. They were charged with failure to register under the Foreign Agents Registration Act. Mr. Golos pleaded guilty. He was sentenced to four months to one year in jail, and fined $500. World Tourists, Inc. was fined $500. Mr. Golos' sentence was changed to probation and the fine against World Tourists, Inc. was suspended.

A year later, according to Miss Bentley's testimony, she and Jacob Golos set up the "Silvermaster ring." From that time until September 1944, she and her bulging knitting bag were "almost regularly" to be seen en route to or from the home of "NKVD agent" Silvermaster. At the other end of the line she was delivering the bag's contents to a man now registered at the Department of Justice as a Soviet agent. She met with Louis Budenz in a bar and grill around the corner from Communist Party headquarters; with Earl Browder, after he was released from jail, *at* the headquarters.

If Mr. Hoover's young men did not pick up the trail

in New York, they had ample opportunity in Washington, and not only by following Miss Bentley. In 1939, Whittaker Chambers had been to see Adolph A. Berle, then Undersecretary of State. He mentioned at least four of those later named by Miss Bentley as ring members. Mr. Berle at once called in the FBI. In 1940 the Bureau interviewed Mr. White regarding Mr. Glasser's loyalty. Mr. Silvermaster's loyalty was questioned in 1942, and he was removed from a sensitive to a nonsensitive job. During the same period, the FBI was receiving derogatory reports on at least two others of the accused.

Mr. Hoover has said that it is the FBI's method to "first find out who the spies are ... and then, carefully keeping them under scrutiny, ascertain ... the identity of their associates ..."

Picture the situation from 1939 to 1945, if you will:

Following Mr. Golos' arrest and conviction, there could hardly have been a more obvious need or a more convenient opportunity for the FBI to practice this technique. Yet six years passed before Mr. Hoover was able to dispatch to the White House a "preliminary flash" marked "(Top secret by special messenger)." Between July 1941 and September 1944, Miss Bentley, according to the FBI, transported every two weeks an average of forty rolls of film containing twenty to thirty-six photographs of classified government documents. In other words, Mr. Hoover's men, if they kept Miss Bentley under scrutiny, were watching the transmission of anywhere from 60,000 to 70,000 photographed government papers, not to mention the actual documents which Miss Bentley says she sometimes delivered. Life must have been hectic indeed in what Mr. Hoover's February 1, 1946 letter described as the Silvermaster's "well-equipped photographic laboratory."

Is it possible that Mr. Hoover's men never once yielded to the temptation to peek into Miss Bentley's bulging knitting bag? Did they never glance around Mr. Golos' or Miss Bentley's apartments? And what of the stream of original documents flowing in and out of the Silvermaster basement at the rate of four hundred or more pieces of bureaucratic paper per week? Why were Messrs. Silvermaster and Ullmann never caught lugging this incriminating torrent of grist for their intelligence mill?

Films and documents are extremely tangible evidence, admissible before any grand jury and in any court. Where are they?

Senator Jenner did not ask these questions, but Mr. Hoover volunteered the information that the FBI lacked "the evidence necessary to sustain conviction." No one should be very much surprised.

THE INVESTIGATORS' VERSION OF HISTORY

". . . The Democrats in 1952 had no national party to speak of then. Their party had been taken over in bits and pieces by the socialist planners who were imitating the bankrupt governments of Europe. As the hands of the socialists fumbled because the power was too great for them to manage, the grip grew firm again—the hidden communists on the fringe of our government moved in and took over at the weak points."
—Senator Jenner speaking on Lincoln's Birthday, 1954.

As the hearings on the White case droned on, the committee staff began handing one press release after another to reporters. "It was as if they were installments in a mystery," one newspaperman observed.

Among the batches of mimeographed sheets laid on the press table was one which seemed the most mysterious of all. During late November, 1941, the release declared, Harry Dexter White had been opposed to an effort to establish a *modus vivendi* with Japan. Such an effort, it asserted, might have postponed the outbreak of war the following month. Instead of finding its way into the news stories of the hearings, the release apparently landed in the wastebaskets of most newspapers. If this additional charge against Mr. White seemed rather pointless to editors, it did not to Mr. Jenner. Since 1950 the Senator has publicly entertained the suspicion that recent history has been tampered with by the forces of darkness—in other words, by Messrs. Roosevelt, Truman, Acheson, and other prominent Democrats. The keystone of the plot, in the Senator's mind, is Pearl Harbor. It was not an unprovoked act of aggression against us by the Japanese. The men of Nippon were deliberately provoked by President Roosevelt, Prime Minister Churchill, and General George C. Marshall, and as an afterthought, Harry Dexter White. For what conceivable reason? To assure that America would be allied in the war with communism and to make certain that the anti-communist Axis powers would be destroyed.

The Senator declared himself to this effect in September, 1950. The occasion was a Senate speech in opposition to President Truman's nomination of General Marshall to be Secretary of Defense.

Mr. Jenner conceded that General Marshall was held in great esteem "across the country and around the whole world." But it was all "propaganda," all a deliberate "build up" to conceal the truth.

". . . The true historicity of this period," he declared, "has been torn up by the roots, locked in State Department and Hyde Park vaults and in the deep freezes of the White House and distorted perverted and rifled and destroyed."

Happily for our nation, however, the Senator had penetrated the secret. The truth was that we had entered World War II on the wrong side:

"The awful casualty lists and heroic deaths of American G.I.'s . . ." he declared, "had been sacrificed on the bloody altar of power politics and treason—not to win the war for America—but to destroy the only two powers able to stop the advance of communist conquest. This meant that American G.I.'s were . . . betrayed by their own chief of staff and used for advancing the cause of communism across the earth."

The wartime chief of staff was the villain of the piece. The Senator pictured him as a kind of apprentice to Sorcerers Churchill, Roosevelt, and Truman.

"General Marshall," he declared, "was an accomplice in a deliberate conspiracy against the American people."

General Marshall knew of the "deceit, duplicity and skulduggery" President Roosevelt and Prime Minister Churchill had "indulged in . . . which set the stage for the Pearl Harbor debacle."

"General Marshall also knew of the plans to invite a Japanese attack," the Senator remarked darkly.

Once America was safely committed to fight "the only two powers able to stop the advance of communist conquest," the plot thickened rapidly. The American people were indoctrinated with "the vicious propaganda of the Four Freedoms." The conspiracy included an "outrageous plan for the treatment" of that other anti-communist power, Nazi Germany.

The creation of the United Nations was part of the same scheme, Senator Jenner said:

"But General Marshall was not content to go half way with his treasonable conspiracy. He has gone the whole way. He knew that the United Nations was being set up as nothing but a ruthless instrument of power politics to enforce not peace, but the outrageous *status quo* that would result from the secret agreements of Teheran, Yalta and Potsdam . . .

"The American people do not yet realize how desperate this administration is to cover up its bloody tracks of treason," he declared. Desperation was also the explanation of General Marshall's behavior: "Unless he, himself, were desperate, he could not possibly agree to continue as an errand boy, a front man, a stooge, or a co-conspirator for this administration's crazy assortment of collectivist cutthroat crackpots and communist fellow-travelling appeasers." The reason why President Truman had named General Marshall for the Defense post was clear. It was "for the frightening purpose of providing the front of respectability to the vicious sellout, not only of Chiang, not only of Formosa, which is vital to our security, but of the American G.I.'s who are fighting and dying even now because of one treachery and whose valiant suffering will again be auctioned off on the bloody block of power politics."

A few months later, the Senator again spoke out with undiminished flamboyance. His remarks are helpful in understanding the rationale behind the "careful fashion" with which, as investigator Jenner, he re-exposed "interlocking subversion in government."

"... We are not being governed by the Democratic Party," he told the Senate on April 11, 1951. "We are not being governed by the Fair Deal. I charge that this country today is in the hands of a secret inner coterie which is directed by agents of the Soviet Union ...

"We must cut this whole cancerous conspiracy out of our government at once. Our only choice is to impeach President Truman and find out who is the secret invisible government which has so cleverly led our country down the road to destruction."

Senator McCarthy was not long in picking up the theme. He began in June, 1951 with an attack on General

Marshall in a Senate speech. In the election year which followed, the Senator enlarged and revised it, publishing it as a 70,000-word campaign document.

Mr. McCarthy puzzled a bit over his own assertions that on the morning of Pearl Harbor, General Marshall had been either horseback riding, or at home with his wife, or at the Washington airport, meeting Soviet Ambassador Maxim Litvinoff. The Senator tarried only briefly on this point, however. The essence of his attack on the General was that the latter's policies constituted a "carefully planned retreat from victory." The General's efforts to try to mount an invasion of western Europe across the English Channel were the result, according to the Senator, of "Soviet inspiration." So was the General's alleged opposition to the desire of the British and of General Mark Clark to advance through Italy into the Balkans ahead of the Red Army.

"It was a Marshall-sponsored memorandum," Senator McCarthy wrote, "advising appeasement of Russia in Europe and the enticement of Russia into the Far Eastern war . . . which foreshadowed our whole course at Teheran, at Yalta, and until now in the Far East."

Like Mr. Jenner, Senator McCarthy also discerned the existence of a conspiracy.

"What is the objective of the conspiracy?" he concluded. "I think it is clear from what has occurred and is now occurring: to diminish the United States in world affairs, to weaken us militarily, to confuse our spirit with talk of surrender in the Far East, and to impair our will to resist evil. To what end? To the end that we shall be contained and frustrated and finally fall victim to Soviet intrigue from within and Russian military might from without . . ."

The Senator from Wisconsin has never ceased to elaborate upon this theme. In his televised answer, in November 1953, to former President Truman's remarks on "mccarthyism," the Senator began by casually rewriting the history of the 1952 presidential elections. The Senator referred to the former President as a "defeated politician." Then he returned to tread familiar oratorical ground:

"At the time Truman became President, the number of people under communist domination was 180,000,000. During his term as President, the figure increased from 180,000,000 to 800,000,000 people . . . The pattern of communist conquest has been the same in every country over which the Stygian blackness of communist night has descended. Always first the infiltration of key points in government by communist traitors and then the creeping paralysis of fear to speak out and expose the traitors.

"This fear has been engendered and nurtured not only by communists, but also by phoney deluded, fuzzy-minded liberals in whose book it is a mortal sin ever to expose or criticize a communist . . . Thus, my good friends, the picture has been in Hungary, Czechoslovakia, Rumania, and every other nation taken over by the black death of communism. Thus the picture has been in our country also."

The Senator continued to speak on the "twenty years of treason" theme in appearances he made for the Republican National Committee celebrating Lincoln's birthday in February, 1954. He made nine speeches in eight days. Senator Jenner also did his bit, returning, for the first time since his election campaign, to the hustings. Referring to that contest, he indulged himself in this bit of "true historicity":

". . . The Democrats in 1952 had no national party to speak of then. Their party had been taken over in bits and pieces by the socialist planners who were imitating the bankrupt governments of Euope. As the hands of the socialists fumbled because the power was too great for them to manage, the grip grew firm again—the hidden communists on the fringe of our government moved in and took over at the weak points."

In another address, at Columbus, Indiana, he pronounced his historian's verdict upon the Korean conflict: "The Fair Dealers sent our young men to Korea to fight in a country they had stripped bare of American troops by then. They put every possible handicap on our armed forces. Our brave fighting men did not know they were supposed to be defeated. They went ahead and won the war with one hand tied behind their backs. Then the Fair Dealers and their communist brain trust made one more mistake. They botched the peace our men had bought with their blood. They ordered our military leaders to ask Red China for an armistice."

A fortnight later, Senator Jenner declared the State Department had become, under former Secretary Dean Acheson, the principal agent of the "ideological revolution started by Harry Hopkins, Alger Hiss, Henry Wallace, Owen Lattimore, Harry D. White, Frank Coe and Harold Glasser."

"I may say, Mr. Chairman, that I have instructed a vast number of those [Federal] employees that they were duty bound to give me information even though some little bureaucrat had stamped it 'secret' to protect himself."
—SENATOR JOSEPH R. MCCARTHY at the May 28th session of the "Army-McCarthy" hearings.

EVEN WHEN THEY WERE MEMBERS of a Republican minority in the Senate, Messrs. Jenner and McCarthy did not entirely restrict themselves to condemning the Democratic administration. As far back as 1950, Mr. Jenner laid at the door of "internationalist Republicans" a part of the responsibility for "the tragic predicament in which the nation finds itself." That species of Republican, he said, was as much to blame as the "communist-coddling conspirators" of the Truman administration.

"There is no point in continuing to attack a Democratic leadership that has gone berserk," he told the Senate, "when self-appointed spokesmen for the Republican Party are down on their worshipful knees crawling around and licking the heels of the same false gods."

On another occasion that year, Senator Jenner took

the floor to attack the peace treaty with Japan. The purpose of the accord, he declared, was to remove the guiding hand of General Douglas MacArthur and place "all future relations with Japan directly in the hands of Dean Acheson and his pro-communist conspirators." Among the latter, presumably, was Mr. Jenner's fellow-Republican, the present Secretary of State, John Foster Dulles. Mr. Dulles drafted and negotiated the Japanese treaty.

Senator McCarthy has been even less diffident about attacking individuals who are now central figures in the Republican administration—including General Eisenhower. In his 1951 diatribe against General Marshall, the Senator disclosed an awareness that the future President's role in World War II had not been negligible. He mentioned the subject some nine times. In one reference he said, "Eisenhower . . . invariably sided with Marshall." In another, the senator implied that General Marshall, seeking to block British efforts to invade the Balkans ahead of the Russians, threatened to advise General Eisenhower to resign his command as head of the European Expeditionary Forces, should the British viewpoint prevail. Elsewhere in his nearly three-hour speech, the senator suggested that behind General Eisenhower's negotiations with Moscow something sinister was hidden.

"The Elbe Line was where Eisenhower proposed to Stalin that he would bring the American armies to rest," Senator McCarthy said. "Eisenhower fixed this highly important point, be it noted, with Stalin."

The senator was highly critical of what he called General Eisenhower's plan to halt the Allied Armies and permit the Red Army to capture Berlin.

"It is clear from Bradley's recollections," the senator said, referring to General Omar Bradley's published memoirs, "that Eisenhower acted on this highly political

question without consulting with Churchill ... I continue
to quote Bradley: 'Although Churchill protested Eisenhower's radio to Moscow as an unwarranted intrusion by
the military into a political problem, he reserved his angri-
est vituperation for the plan Eisenhower proposed.'"

Fifteen months later, the General and the Senator
were destined to meet in a hotel room in Peoria, Illinois.
As Republican candidate for the Presidency, General
Eisenhower was campaigning in that crucial area of the
country where the supporters of Senator Robert A. Taft
were still smarting from their defeat at the Republican
nominating convention. Candidate Eisenhower had just
passed through Indiana, where he had given what was
understandably described as an "aloof endorsement" of
Senator Jenner's candidacy. Facing a hard fight for re-
election, Senator Jenner was reported as dissatisfied with
the character of the Presidential candidate's endorsement,
although he felt it wise publicly to thank General Eisenhower for his support.

"Several senators of the Taft wing of the party have
been enlisted in a concerted speaking drive for Jenner,"
the *U.S. News and World Report* informed its readers
on October 10. "Senator McCarthy is among them, and
the Jenner hope is that McCarthy may whip up in Indiana the sentiment that renominated him in Wisconsin."

Judging by a dispatch to the New York *Times*, Senator
McCarthy must indeed have been feeling his political
oats. *Times* correspondent W. H. Lawrence reported the
scene in the Peoria hotel room. The General, Mr. Lawrence wrote, indicated that he was willing to give his endorsement to Senator McCarthy, despite the slurs the
latter had cast upon the reputation of General Eisenhower's former military superior and old comrade-in-arms,
General Marshall. The Presidential candidate then read

to the senator an excerpt from a speech which the former General intended to make in Milwaukee. The excerpt was a paragraph in which General Eisenhower generously praised the character and record of General Marshall.

"Defiant as always, the senator told the Republican nominee he could say whatever he wished," reporter Lawrence wrote, "but he suggested Milwaukee or Wisconsin was not the place to say it. He said the candidate might, in fact, be booed."

At Milwaukee, Senator McCarthy grinned knowingly at his followers while General Eisenhower delivered his campaign speech. A storm of applause broke out when the candidate read a lukewarm endorsement of Senator McCarthy. If the audience was primed to boo any favorable reference to General Marshall, the preparations were unnecessary. The Republican candidate omitted any mention of the one-time chief of staff, Secretary of State, and Secretary of Defense.

The presence, for the first time in twenty years, of a fellow-Republican in the White House proved to have a negligible effect on the senator's investigatorial sense of smell. As soon as the 83rd Congress convened, as was mentioned in Chapter five, Senator McCarthy began to interest himself in or to investigate assorted governmental departments headed by such Presidential favorites as Secretary of State John Foster Dulles, Central Intelligence Agency Director Allen W. Dulles, and Mutual Security Administrator Harold Stassen.

In July, 1953 an incident occurred which roused the ire of the President himself. The senator, without consulting his fellow committee-men, had appointed one J. B. Matthews as staff director of the Subcommittee on Investigations. Dr. Matthews' professional ex-radicalism goes all the way back to the days of the Dies Committee, of which he was chief investigator. Almost simultaneously with his appointment, an article entitled "Reds and Our Churches" authored by the new staff chief appeared in the July issue of *American Mercury*.

"The largest single group supporting the communist apparatus in the United States today is composed of Protestant clergymen," Dr. Matthews had written. "Since the beginning of the First Cold War in April 1948, the Communist Party of this country has placed more and more reliance upon the ranks of the Protestant clergy to provide the Party's subversive apparatus with its agents, stooges, dupes, front men, and fellow-travelers.

"Clergymen outnumber professors two to one in supporting the Communist front apparatus of the Kremlin conspiracy . . . The Communist Party has enlisted the support of at least 7,000 Protestant clergymen in the same categories — party members, fellow-travelers, espionage agents, party line adherents, and unwitting dupes."

A bitter executive session of the subcommittee took place. Senator McCarthy told his colleagues and later the press that Dr. Matthews had offered his resignation on July 2, but that he had no present intention of accepting it. The committee by a single vote upheld the chairman's power to hire and fire staff members who were not rated as "professional." The senator promptly announced that Dr. Matthews, as a "temporary" employee, was "nonprofessional." As promptly the three Democratic members resigned from the committee.

Meanwhile, the President, though slow to anger, had reached the boiling point. The three co-chairmen of the Commission on Religious Organizations of the National Conference of Christians and Jews, Monsignor John A. O'Brien, Rabbi Maurice H. Eisendrath, and the Reverend Dr. John Sutherland Bonnell, had sent him a telegram.

"The sweeping attack on the loyalty of Protestant clergymen and the charge that they are the largest single group supporting the communist apparatus is unjustified and deplorable," the clergymen wired. "... We fully recognize the right of Congress to investigate the loyalty of any citizen regardless of the office he may occupy, ecclesiastical or otherwise. But destroying trust in the leaders of Protestantism, Catholicism or Judaism by wholesale condemnation is to weaken the greatest American bulwark against atheistic materialism and communism."

Two days after Senator McCarthy announced he was retaining Dr. Matthews, the White House released, at 5:29 P.M., both the clergymen's telegram and the President's reply.

".... I want you to know at once that I fully share the convictions you state," Mr. Eisenhower telegraphed. "The issues here are clear. Generalized and irresponsible attacks that sweepingly condemn the whole of any group of citizens are alien to America. Such attacks betray contempt for the principles of freedom and decency ..."

At 6:35 PM, Senator McCarthy announced that he had "very reluctantly" accepted Dr. Matthews' resignation. In his letter Dr. Matthews declared: "I hereby reiterate the accuracy of my statements."

By a curious coincidence, the Senator also made an announcement on the floor of the Senate on that day. Allen W. Dulles, he declared, had been guilty of "the most blatant attempt to thwart the authority of the Senate I have ever heard of." Mr. Dulles' sin was in refusing to permit members of his ultra-secret CIA to testify before the subcommittee.

From that time forward, the senator's inquisitorial curiosity seemed more and more directed toward the government department closest to the President's interest: the Army. Late in August he began a series of hearings on "Communist Infiltration in the Army." The hearings lasted through September, and in October the senator turned his attention to the Army Signal Corps.

The hearings were first held behind closed doors. By making a series of announcements to the reporters excluded from the hearing room, Mr. McCarthy was virtually able to write his own headlines. The results included such typographical barrages as: ARMY RADAR DATA REPORTED MISSING; ESPIONAGE IN SIGNAL CORPS FOR TEN YEARS IS CHARGED; McCARTHY HINTS OF SPY PLOT HITTING WHOLE SIGNAL CORPS; RADAR WITNESS BREAKS DOWN, WILL TELL ALL ABOUT SPY RING.

Below the last item, which appeared in that paragon of journalistic moderation, the New York *Times*, there followed a page-one story. It said that "an 'important' employee at the Army's Fort Monmouth radar laboratories, a close friend of Julius Rosenberg, executed atom spy, broke down yesterday and agreed to tell all he knew about espionage rings."

"This 'most important development' at a hearing of the Senate Permanent Subcommittee on Investigations was reported by Senator Joseph R. McCarthy, Republican of Wisconsin and subcommitee chairman. He immediately placed the witness in 'protective custody' because, he said, the latter 'is afraid for his own personal safety.'"

A month later, the *Times* carried another story, this time on an inside page. In an interview with the Asbury Park (N. J.) *Press*, the *Times* reported, Carl Greenblum, 37, an electrical engineer at the Fort Monmouth Evans

Radar laboratory, had identified himself as the witness. His decision to disclose what had actually occurred was prompted by the fact that "his family was being persecuted by neighbors." He had not "told all," had never been suspended from his radar work, still held a clearance permitting him access to information classified as "secret." Far from having been the "intimate friend" of Julius Rosenberg, he had been his classmate at the City College of New York.

"Mr. Greenblum denied that he had lied at any time and declared he always had been a loyal American. He said the reason he had broken down was because his mother had died two days before the hearing and he was unprepared for the rapid barrage of questions," the *Times* article said. "Senator McCarthy was asked last night in the United States Courthouse, Foley Square [New York City] about Mr. Greenblum's denial of any connections with the Communist Party. 'I would not want to comment on that,' Mr. McCarthy said."

One by one the other charges, true to military tradition, "just faded away." The "missing data" scare turned out to be a re-hash of a story investigated and discarded as false by FBI and Army investigators a year earlier. The senator himself discredited his own charges that there was espionage at the Signal Corps installation. He declared on October 12 that the situation "has all the earmarks of extremely dangerous espionage [which] may envelop the entire Signal Corps" and that "it looks very much like a case of current espionage." Nine days later he was backing off: "I am not saying whether there is espionage or there is not..." the Washington *Post* quoted him. "It would be improper for me to evaluate the testimony..." By November 5, he was busy evaluating the testimony: "There is no question now, from the

evidence, that there has been espionage in the Army
Signal Corps," he told a reporter from the Washington
Evening Star. But a month later, the December 10 issue
of the New York *Times* quoted him as saying he had
"no real hope" of proving espionage. ". . . We don't expect to come up with anything more than contempt or
perjury. It is not our function to develop cases of espionage."

Meanwhile, Fort Monmouth was being turned into an
administrative madhouse. Frightened Army officials
suspended nineteen scientists and other workers without
pay as "security risks." Others were removed from work
they had been doing on our radar warning defenses and
placed on non-classified work in a group popularly—or
unpopularly—dubbed the "leper colony." In all, some
forty persons, thirty of them professional scientists, were
directly affected by the investigations. One of those suspended was charged with having been enrolled by his
mother in the left-wing Young Pioneers of America at a
time when the suspended man was twelve years old. Another was accused of favoring the "leftist" policies of
Max Lerner, a decidedly anti-communist liberal columnist for the New York *Post*.

The New York *Times* assigned one of its top men,
Peter Kihss, to study the situation at the Signal Corps
base. Summarizing his findings, Mr. Kihss reported:
"Such charges—none involving espionage or disloyalty,
and all vigorously rebutted by the employees—are generally a far cry from the headlines of possible Monmouth spying raised by Senator McCarthy."

Writing in the New York *Herald Tribune*, Walter
Millis declared: "The Fort Monmouth situation is truly
scandalous. It is so scandalous that some who have looked
into it, thoroughly conservative in outlook and Republi-

can in politics, are talking about demanding a Congressional investigation—not into the alleged espionage (of
which on Secretary Stevens' word, no evidence has been
discovered by the Army) but into the processes of witch-
hunting, bigotry, cowardice, race prejudice, and sheer
incompetence which have turned one of our top-level
military-scientific operations into a mare's nest of exasperation, fear, and futility . . ."

As the senator persisted, outcries against the inquiry
began to come from every quarter. The Washington *Post*
ran a series of articles by Murray Marder demolishing
the senator's claims and describing the resulting chaos
at Fort Monmouth. The Federation of Atomic Scientists
investigated. After perusing a report of its committee
which looked into the situation, the Federation concluded
that Mr. McCarthy's inquiry had severely damaged mo-
rale at the installation. A real danger existed, the scientists warned, that many of the most important scientists
working on our defense against air attack might resign
rather than submit to the perpetual jeopardy of recur-
rent subcommittee-security inquiries.

"Investigations which are characterized largely by sensational headlines and wholesale suspensions can, by crip-
pling our defense research, actually result in a net gain
for those who work against the interests of the United
States," the scientists warned. "The effect on our national security would be extremely serious if such investigative methods are allowed to spread to other areas
of this country's scientific effort."

In blunter language, General Telford Taylor told an
audience of cadets and officers at West Point on November 27 that "most of the McCarthy accusations are in-
defensible fabrications." The senator "will stand con-

demned as a dangerous adventurer who does not hesitate to gamble with the national security."

The senator's gamble was for big stakes indeed. As
the Signal Corps and other Army Red hunts continued,
matters finally reached an open break between Mr.
McCarthy and Army Secretary Stevens. The official bone
of contention concerned whether the senator, his chief
counsel Roy Cohn, and his staff director Francis P. Carr,
a former FBI man, had used improper and undue influence in attempting to obtain an Army commission
and other favors for former unpaid committee staff member Pvt. G. David Schine. The senator and his aides
countered with charges that Mr. Stevens, Army Counsel
John G. Adams, and Assistant Secretary of Defense H.
Struve Hensel had attempted to halt the Monmouth
investigation using "blackmail" and Pvt. Schine as a
"hostage."

On the first day of the much-publicized airing of the
charges, the senator declared that his fire was not so
much directed at Secretaries Stevens and Hensel as it was
elsewhere. The senator was asking General Reber one of
the marathon questions for which he soon became famous.

SENATOR MCCARTHY: At that time we asked you—as
I recall, I repeated the question a number of times—
asked you whether or not you felt that the committee
should be entitled to the names of individuals in the
Pentagon who had protected and covered up Communists. At that time I had difficulty getting an answer from you on that. I ask you this question today
because I am firmly convinced the reason we are
here spending our time on the question of whether or
not Private Schine received special consideration is
because we are getting close to the nerve center in
the Pentagon of the old civilian polticians over the

past ten or twenty years who have covered up . . .

SENATOR MUNDT: The Senator's time has expired.

But the senator's time had expired only in the parliamentary sense. Messrs. McCarthy and Cohn continued to fray executive nerves in one way or another. That afternoon, retired General Walter Bedell Smith, Undersecretary of State and former head of the CIA, read a letter he had written to Secretary of Defense Charles E. Wilson in which he described Mr. Cohn's efforts in behalf of Pvt. Schine. After outlining the substance of two telephone calls, the General's letter ended with these revealing words:

"Mr. Cohn then asked if the CIA could not arrange to have Mr. Schine commissioned, as he had investigative experience. I replied that CIA drew a few commissioned personnel by detail from the armed services, but gave them additional training and required a longer tour of duty. However, I offered to telephone Mr. Allen Dulles, Director of Central Intelligence, and ask him about the possibilities. Mr. Cohn said that I need not do this. The CIA, he said, was too juicy a subject for future investigation, and it would not be right to ask them to get Mr. Schine commissioned and then investigate the organization later."

As the forty-day hearings droned on, the senator repeatedly indicated his continuing interest in inquiring into the CIA, the Pentagon, and the Eisenhower administration. Near the end of the hearings, he declared that the CIA embodied the country's "worst situation" from the standpoint of "communist infiltration." His remarks became increasingly hostile toward the administration itself.

"It so happens, it so happens that he is in name the

boss over there," he said of Army Secretary Stevens on May 6, "but I am interested in the individuals who have been there [in the Pentagon] and who have been clearing Communists for secret work..."

Later that month, Republican Senator Ralph E. Flanders of Vermont lashed out at Mr. McCarthy for his "incredible success in trapping Republicans into a detailed and relentless search for some significant evidence of subversion in the Republican administration." Senator McCarthy had a ready retort which he promptly offered to the television audience watching the hearings.

"Mr. Chairman, I am sure that the chair of the committee... will agree that when you get to the issue of treason you can't start drawing party lines," he intoned. "I am sure that the very able chief counsel... will agree that when we get to the question of subversion there should be no party line."

A fortnight earlier, Mr. McCarthy took exception to the President's order forbidding witnesses to disclose what took place in a high-level meeting involving officers of the executive branch.

"This is the first time I've ever seen the executive branch of the government take the Fifth Amendment," he declared, adding that the administration "must have something to hide."

There was no rebuke from Republican chairman of the subcomittee Senator Karl E. Mundt of South Dakota, nor from the other Republican members of the committee. The Army's counsel, John G. Adams, protested, however, a day or two later when the Senator from Wisconsin repeated the accusation:

SENATOR MCCARTHY:... May I say that I think that if the witness asserts a type of Fifth Amendment privilege here—

MR. ADAMS: I am not asserting Fifth Amendment privileges, Senator.

SENATOR MCCARTHY:—some Presidential privilege, I think the chair should allow him to do it rather than to get into this question which will take us months to decide . . .

MR. ADAMS: I don't like the Senator from Wisconsin inferring that I'm claiming the Fifth Amendment privilege, because I'm not, and I'm not claiming any privilege . . . This is an instruction from the President of the United States, and I consider myself bound by it, sir.

But the senator considered neither himself nor Mr. Adams, nor, for that matter, any of the 2,000,000 employees of the Federal government bound by a mere directive or order of the President of the United States.

"As far as I am concerned," he declared to the television cameras a few days later, "I would like to notify those 2,000,000 Federal employees that I feel it's their duty to give us any information which they have about graft, corruption, communists, treason, and that there is no loyalty to a superior officer which can tower above and beyond their loyalty to their country."

The next day he made the same declaration, but with a slight shift in emphasis: "I may say, Mr. Chairman, that *I have instructed* a vast number of those employees that they were duty bond to give me information even though some little bureaucrat had stamped it 'secret' to protect himself." (My emphasis.) In the same hearing, he casually referred to "the evidence of treason that has been growing over the past twenty, twenty-one years."

The reference to the additional year, which could only refer to the first year of the Eisenhower administration, caused a sensation across the country, but the senator never withdrew the remark. Nor is this surprising. The senator is nothing if he is not logical. He believes firmly that any means justify his ends. If he regards the Eisenhower administration as suspect of treason, he naturally seeks to infiltrate it with sources of information. No one can accuse him of having made a secret of his intentions in this respect.

"It's a daily and nightly occurrence for me to receive information from people in government in regard to communist infiltration," he declared during the hearings regarding Pvt. Schine. ". . . . I often come in possession . . . of reports which apparently originate in the FBI . . ."

Belief in the senator's veracity in this regard was in no way diminished by the fact that, during the course of the hearings, he and Mr. Cohn asked the Army to produce at least eleven FBI reports. They gave the precise date of each report and suggested they knew what each contained.

If viewers of the hearing were startled by this intelligence, attentive students of the senator's career should not have been. The day after the senator made the famous Wheeling, West Virginia speech which launched him as a Red hunter, he spoke over the radio at Salt Lake City, Utah, on February 10, 1950. He said that the House Committee on Un-American Activities' file of dossiers was one of the sources of his information that there were fifty-seven (or 205, or 81) card-carrying communists in the State Department.

"I have many other sources of information, also," he added, "some of them right within the State Department. I might say that there are some very fine men in the State Department. If there were not, I would not be able to have these names tonight."

The senator has never displayed any great degree of shyness about suggesting that he has what his committee would call in another context an "apparatus" within the executive branch of the government. His claims may contain a certain amount of exaggeration, but here they are:

In a Senate speech on February 20, 1950, the junior gentleman from Wisconsin made lengthy references suggesting that he had confidential sources in the State Department and elsewhere:

"... The [State Department] files show that they went into great detail in labelling communists as such ... The files which I have here show the source of the information. I contacted one of the Federal intelligence agencies ... I asked them if they would care to go over what I have to say ... The answer was, 'Well, you have gotten all of it from the State Department files, and the communists within the Department can see those files, and I will show you which commies have the top secret clearance, so if they have seen it, it does not do much damage for the Senate to see them.'" (The Senator is doing the quoting here. Any resemblance to what was actually said by the unnamed official of the anonymous agency may be purely coincidental.)

"... I know the State Department is very eager to know how I have secured all this information," he said on February 20, 1950. "I know that the jobs of the men who helped me secure this material would be worth nothing if the names were given. If it were not for some good loyal Americans in the State Department—and there are many of them—I should not have been able to present this picture to the Senate tonight. . . .

A few days later, he said:

"Mr. President, so that there will be no question in

the minds of any senators or any other citizens, the Senator from Wisconsin will not ever give the names of any government employees who may have helped him secure the information which he presented to the Senate."

In an interview published verbatim in the September 7, 1951 *U. S. News and World Report,* the Senator threw out a few more suggestive comments:

QUESTION: ... Now, one question a lot of people are asking is, "How does Senator McCarthy know more or as much as the government people who have confidential files on these individuals?"

ANSWER: I don't claim to have more information than those in possession of the files.

* * * * *

QUESTION: What I meant was, how do you know as much as is in these confidential files? How can a Senator who doesn't have a committee subpoena [power] and doesn't have any power of commanding information know all these facts? Does it come to you through correspondence or do people in the country who know the facts send them to you? What's the process whereby you get informed about these cases?

ANSWER: Last night an official of the State Department in a nation-wide television show said: "If we learn of anyone who is giving information to McCarthy about communists in the State Department, his job will last about two minutes." Therefore, I cannot very well answer that question.

* * * * *

QUESTION: How many people in government furnished you confidential information?

ANSWER: I wouldn't want to give you that.

(Once again, let no reader suppose that the unidentified State Department official quoted by the Senator necessarily used the words attributed to him. The
Senator is not very precise regarding what he chooses to
put between quotation marks.)

Then there is the case of Miriam M. de Haas, at the
time in question an examiner for the Loyalty Review
Board of the Civil Service Commission. On January 5,
1952, Senator McCarthy gave reporters what he called
the minutes of a meeting of the Loyalty Review Board.
The Commission at once began to look into the leak.
A Commission announcement expressed concern "not only
with the internal management of the executive branch
of the government, but also with our national security."

Asking for the minutes of a grand jury inquiry into
the matter, the Commission told the Federal District
Court in Washington that Miss de Haas' replies to questions put by Commission officials "are not full and complete; in many instances they are evasive, and in numerous instances she refused to answer." Senator McCarthy
had a word to say from Milwaukee on the subject.

"They've hanged the wrong person," he declared.
"This accused person positively gave me no information,
although it is possible that I met her at a gathering in
New York a couple of years ago. The name is somewhat
familiar. But I would have been glad to use her help if I
had known she was inclined against the communists."

Federal District Judge Matthew F. McGuire refused
to permit the Commission to look at what was reported to
be 186 pages of Miss de Haas' grand jury testimony. He
referred rather pointedly to the "zealously guarded" secrecy of such testimony.

The following month, however, the Commission suddenly announced the lady's resignation had been ac-

cepted. She had admitted, the Commission said, that she had "seen to it that pertinent information was made available" to Senator McCarthy and other members of Congress. She had been under suspension for "refusal to give testimony to the Commission concerning unauthorized release of confidential information from the files." Her resignation followed publication of an advertisement in a Washington newspaper. The advertisement was in the form of a letter from Miss de Haas addressed to "my dear fellow-Americans." Still insisting that she did not know Senator McCarthy, she wrote:

"The evidence he has passed on to you has never been successfully controverted, and could not be, because *the information I supplied* was specific, concrete, correct and devastatingly true information from sources described by our Federal Bureau of Investigation as reliable. From my reading of his Senate speeches and other statements I know that his repetition of that information has been accurate and exact. What has been conveyed to the public has, moreover, only scratched the surface of evidence of communism in our government." (My emphasis.)

The day after the advertisement appeared, Mr. McCarthy was asked about it in Appleton, Wisconsin. He did not seem very happy about it.

"I understand now that some of the information I had came indirectly from Miss de Haas," he said. "I never met her, and I frankly was unaware at the time that the information was coming from her. *I do have other sources of information.*" (My emphasis.)

He did. Moreover, further evidence of the fact abounded after the 83rd Congress took over the legislative reins. The State Department was the immediate center of his subcommittee's attentions. According to the New

York *Journal-American,* much of the information regarding the Voice of America was supplied by an "underground" of some seventy-five "Voice" employees. They
were variously reported as calling themselves "the vigi-
lantes" and "the pro-Americans." As the probe began,
the investigators installed themselves in the Waldorf-
Astoria suite of David Schine, who was then a staff member, to keep an eye on the headlines and an ear to the
"underground." The phrase "meet me at the Waldorf"
soon had a changed significance in the Broadway offices
of the "Voice." Some of those who offered to testify were
unwelcome to the investigators, according to the New
York *Times.* One was turned down when he told the staff
that he knew of no communists or waste in the agency.
Another employee who wanted to defend the "Voice's"
record was quickly dissuaded. The committee knew, he
was told, that he had had, many years earlier, an "affair" with a woman. This could not be officially overlooked. He decided it would be wiser not to appear.

"There is a wide-open channel between the organization and the McCarthy committee which has been providing the fuel for the investigation," a VOA official
told *Times* reporter Douglas Dales. "Anything that happens here gets to the committee quickly. The knowledge
of the existence of this pipeline has created an atmosphere of suspicion and tension demoralizing the staff."

The official told Mr. Dales that Senator McCarthy's
promise of protection to witnesses had made lions of civil
service lambs. They had no fear of disciplinary measures, he said.

Any discipline meted out was to those who uttered
criticism of the committee's doings. During the inquiry,
the Department suspended former National Broadcasting Company vice president Alfred H. Morton from his

job as the "Voice's" chief of broadcasting. Mr. Morton
had dared to circulate a memo taking issue with the
Senator's strictures against the VOA's use under any
circumstances of carefully selected material from left-
wing sources. Mr. Morton was later reinstated with a rep-
rimand. Another State Department official was restored
at Mr. McCarthy's demand to his old job. Meanwhile,
an unidentified employee was apparently busy. The chief
of the New York office sent the draft of a policy directive
to Washington VOA headquarters for comment. The inquiry was dispatched on the direct teletype line between
the two offices, a routine procedure. What was not so
customary, as reported by columnist Drew Pearson, was
the fact that a member of Mr. McCarthy's committee
staff called the Washington VOA to ask questions about
the directive before it was received from New York.

The Senator is also reliably credited with the hiring
of one W. Scott McLeod as the State Department's security chief. When the new watchdog's name was announced, the Senator magnanimously praised the action
as a "fine appointment." Thereafter William D. Huskey,
a security officer in the Department for many years
resigned.

"Everyone worked in an atmosphere of fright," he
said. "It was a living hell for anybody who dared question McLeod's wisdom."

This was not just one man's opinion. Theodore Kaghan, former Acting Deputy Director of the Public Affairs Division of the U.S. High Commissioner for Germany, has also described the climate in Washington,
though not in strictly meteorological terms. Mr. Kaghan
was summoned from Germany for McCarthyization.

"It was after the first session with McCarthy that I
began to get the full flavor of the atmosphere in the

State Department," he wrote in *The Reporter*. Fellow employees who heard him speaking about the Senator over
the telephone warned him urgently: "You ought to be
more careful. The phones are tapped, you know."

Mr. Kaghan announced that he would persist in speaking his mind about Senator McCarthy, Mr. Cohn and
Mr. Schine. Such talk, he presumed, was not yet treasonable. He had much to learn.

"One State Department official, a well-placed man
with long years of experience, came to see me between
hearings," he wrote. The official offered to advise Mr.
Kaghan on how to handle the situation. Mr. Kaghan
agreed to listen. "My would-be adviser then picked up a
pencil and wrote on a pad: 'Let's get out of here. This
place is wired.'"

In the bright southern sunshine of Washington the
official endeavored to teach Mr. Kaghan his A B McC's.

"You've been away a long time," Mr. Kaghan recalled his saying. "You just don't know what's happened
here. McLeod has taken this place over for McCarthy.
Nothing happens, nothing is said, that McLeod doesn't
get almost immediately. People don't even talk at staff
meetings any longer. They've discovered that an opinion which is nonconformist, which questions the advisabil-
ity or usefulness of any particular line of argument or
propaganda that may be popular with the inexperienced
new people, is reported to McLeod's office. The whole
organization is penetrated by opportunists who are trying
to buy their way up with bootlicking and informing where
before they couldn't move up without ability and compe-
tence. Nobody trusts anybody, so everybody keeps his
mouth shut and waits."

Mr. Kaghan did not have to wait long. In Germany
he had committed the unforgiveable sin. He had coined

an internationally titillating phrase when he referred to
Messrs. Cohn and Schine on their famous investigating
jaunt through Europe as "junketeering gumshoes." After
his third round in the Senator's hearing room, Mr. Kaghan was summoned by Arthur Kimball, Deputy Administrator of the International Information Administration.
Mr. Kimball had just replaced Reed Harris who had left
the Department after the Senator had given him the
once-over. Mr. Kimball informed Mr. Kaghan that the
Senator was through with him.

"McLeod's office had just phoned, he said, to tell
him to tell me that McCarthy was finished with me," Mr.
Kaghan later related. ". . . . Mr. McLeod, said Kimball,
insists that, unless you resign in writing now, effective
on your return to Germany, the Department will be forced
to bring new security charges against you under the new
security regulations."

Mr. Kaghan resigned.

19 | FEAR, THE ACCUSER

"And that because of false brethren un-
awares brought in, who came in privily
to spy out our liberty . . ."
—St. Paul's Epistle to the Galatians (2:4)

A FAVORED PHRASE of committee chairmen is: "The record will speak for itself." Invariably, however, the distinguished gentlemen find it necessary to lend the record their verbal assistance. In this capacity our solons have no peers. Your obedient servant, the author, will make no effort to compete with them, nor insult your intelligence by pointing out the obvious.

Not that it is impossible to theorize regarding the mass of verbiage contained in the thousands of pages of hearings upon which this book has been—we hope firmly—based. It is quite possible, for example, to work out two or three versions of what "really" may be the story behind the "interlocking subversion" hearings. For their own purpose, that is just what the investigating committees have been engaged in doing, shuffling and re-shuffling the witnesses like so many cards. It is well to heed the advice of seasoned travelers: never play for stakes with strangers. In this case, the stakes—the reputations of men and women—are high.

It is also tempting to point the accusing finger at those, in and out of authority, who are violating our traditional American freedoms. This has been said more eloquently elsewhere. Rather than belabor others, however justly, the author would prefer to flex the muscles of his own right to speak up. The record needs no annotation. In this, the final chapter, the author will speak for himself. Our freedom, like our flesh, requires exercise for strength. By asserting our inalienable rights to think and to act according to our consciences, we may rebuild our hopes with the wreckage of our fears.

America has done so before. At the time of the French revolution, fears of the alien unknown swept the country. Thomas Jefferson was accused of having unspecified "affiliations" with French Jacobinism. The president of Yale College, Timothy Dwight, declared that his election would make of "our wives and daughters the victims of legal prostitution; soberly dishonored; speciously polluted . . . our sons become the disciples of Voltaire, and the dragoons of Marat."

To combat the menace of French republicanism, the Alien and Sedition bills were proposed. Opposing them, Edward Livingston spoke the words from which the title of this book was taken:

"If we are to violate the Constitution, will the people submit to our unauthorized acts? Sir, they ought not to submit; they would deserve the chains that these measures are forging for them. The country will swarm with informers, spies, delators and all the odious reptile tribe that breed in the sunshine of a despotic power . . . The hours of the most unsuspected confidence, the intimacies of friendship, or the recesses of domestic retirement afford no security. The companion whom you must trust, the friend in whom you must confide, the domestic who waits in your chamber, all are tempted to betray your imprudent or unguarded follie; to misrepresent your words; to convey them, distorted by calumny, to the secret tribunal where jealousy presides—where fear officiates as accuser and suspicion is the only evidence that is heard . . . ."

Applied to our own time, Livingston's words are no exaggeration. The Department of Justice now maintains a stable of some eighty-seven paid informers. They roam from committee session to loyalty probe to deportation hearing to courtroom. Their stock-in-trade is made up of names and reputations. They live upon what they may say about their former friends, lovers, ex-husbands, ex-wives. A miserable woman in Seattle, Washington, recently promised to give the House Committee more than three hundred names, including those of her two former husbands.

Such is the fear-breeding atmosphere which causes a motion-picture producer to assure a committee that he no longer "indulges" in "the luxury of individual morality," a distinguished educator humbly to thank another committee for giving him the opportunity to testify that his views on academic freedom and communism coincided nicely with those of Senator Jenner.

Since when has morality been a luxury reserved for the indulgent? Since when have free-born Americans thanked their elected representatives for the opportunity publicly to exhibit their conformity? Where is the spirit of earlier American days when men boasted of their individuality, of their contempt for tyrannical authority?

The investigators of the "philosophical bent" of Americans are not wholly to blame. We are also at fault. We have placed the gavel in the trembling hands of frightened men and pandered to their fears. For it is they who are most afraid. They fear that their belief that America has been going to the socialist dogs since President McKinley was assassinated in 1901 will not stand up outside the hearing room. They are afraid of the very principles which have made this country the greatest, the most free on earth. For freedom, like life, is dangerous. It means change, and they fear change.

But for America, freedom—including the freedom to be moral—is not a mere personal luxury. It is a national necessity. In a changing world, liberty, as Mr. Justice Brandeis said, is not merely a desirable end. It is a means of survival.

We are, fortunately, still free to choose whether we will govern ourselves or be governed by the purveyors of fear. It is customary to speak of our government as having three branches. It is well to remember the trunk of the tree, the American people. To cut off the functions of the trunk is to kill the branches as well. In our way of life, the mechanism in Washington which we call the government has its powers and its duties, but so do we. It is for us to determine, by free discussion and association, the destiny of our beloved country. To exercise these powers, to perform these duties requires courage today, but America, as some one has said, can not remain the land of the free unless she is also the home of the brave.

Notes On Sources

Except where otherwise indicated either below or in the text, references to news events in the text are taken from the New York Times *of the following day.*

CHAPTER 1—The Statement of Henry Ford II appeared in *U.S. News & World Report*, January 25, 1952. Speaker Martin's speech is from the *Congressional Record*, Vol. 99, p. 14. The quotation of Dean Ackerman is from the *New York Times* of April 4, 1953. The incident concerning Mrs. Horton was reported in the *New York Times*, May 22, 1953. The Committee on Un-American Activities' conclusions are from its *Annual Report for the Year 1953*. For Senator Jenner's remarks, see 83d Cong., 1st Sess., Senate Subcommittee to Investigate the Administration of the Internal Security Act, Hearings, *Interlocking Subversion in Government Departments*, Part 16. Spruille Braden's testimony was reprinted in *U.S. News & World Report*, April 9, 1954. Senator McCarthy's Kansas speech was reported in the Washington *Post*, April 21, 1954. *U.S. News & World Report*, September 4, 1953, carried Attorney General Brownell's statement. The figures of FBI employees and appropriations come from the *Democratic Digest*.

CHAPTER 2—The author is indebted to Robert K. Carr's *The House Committee on Un-American Activities, 1945-1950* (Cornell University Press, 1952), for the quotation of Charles Sumner and other material on the history of congressional investigations. Senator Mundt's statement appears in the *Congressional Record*, Vol. 92, p. 5217. The controversy around the investigation carried on by the then Senator Black was reported by the *New York Times* on various days in August, 1935. Frederic R. Coudert's article appeared in 15 *Virginia Law Review* 537, April, 1929. The account of the Massachusetts Nunnery Committee is based on *The Protestant Crusade, 1800-1860* (The Macmillan Company, 1938) by Ray Allen Billington.

CHAPTER 3—The debate of the Senate on the creation of the committee is recorded in the *Congressional Globe* on several days in December, 1859. Senator Simmons' remarks were made on December 7. The full testimony is attached to the report of the "Select Committee of the Senate appointed to inquire into the late invasion and seizure of the public property at Harper's Ferry," 36th Cong., 1st Sess., Senate Rep. Com. No. 278, which also contains the resolution setting up the committee.

CHAPTER 4—The statement of Charles Evans Hughes is quoted in *The Growth of the American Republic* by Samuel Eliot Morison **and**

Henry Steele Commager (Oxford University Press, New York, 1950). Most of the material in this chapter is drawn from Robert K. Carr's book, cited above, (notes for Chapter II), *The Federal Bureau of Investigation* by Max Lowenthal (William Sloane Associates, Inc., New York, 1950), and the Brief for Petitioner to the Supreme Court of the United States in *Emspak* v. *United States*, No. 67, October Term, 1953.

CHAPTER 5—The figures of congressional probes and appropriations therefor are taken from *CQ Weekly Reports*, Vol. XI, No. 7, February 13, 1953, and *Congressional Quarterly Almanac, 1953.* The hearings of the Subcommittee to Investigate the Administration of the Internal Security Act on *Interlocking Subversion in Government Departments* are in sixteen parts, beginning April 10, 1953. The committee report on the hearings under the same title, is dated July 30, 1953. Attorney General Brownell's testimony on November 17, 1953, is in Part 16. Representative Walter's report of Mr. Kunzig's remarks appeared in the *New York Times* of November 11, 1953. Senator McCarthy's reference to "twenty-one years of treason" on May 28, 1954, during the Army-McCarthy hearing was reported in the *New York Times* of the following day. The text of former President Truman's address on November 16, 1953, was reprinted in *U.S. News & World Report*, November 27, and that of Senator McCarthy on November 24 in the same magazine, December 4, 1953.

CHAPTER 6—The facts on Representative Velde's background, his criticism of the Committee on Un-American Activities in 1949, and his charges against Mrs. Roosevelt in 1951 are drawn from the *Democratic Digest*. The testimony of Herbert A. Philbrick appears in 83d Cong., 1st Sess., Committee on Un-American Activities, *Investigation of Communist Activities in the New York City Area—Part 5*. Mr. Philbrick's protest against the release of his testimony was reported in the *Boston Post* and *Boston Daily Globe*, October 1, 1953. Representative Kearney's comment on committee operations was reported in the *New York Times*, March 25, 1954. Artie Shaw's testimony appears in *Investigation of Communist Activities in the New York City Area—Part 1*. The testimony of Jerome Robbins, Lionel Stander, Robert Rossen and Lee S. Sabinson appears in Parts 2, 3 and 4 respectively of the same hearing. That of John H. Reynolds is contained in the hearing entitled *Communist Methods of Infiltration (Education—Part 4)*. The United Press employee testified in Part 3 of this hearing.

CHAPTER 7—Representative Velde's statements on "Reporters Round-up" and the reactions thereto were reported in the *New York Times* of March 10, 1953, and subsequent days. Representative Jackson's refusal to make public the committee's dossier on Bishop Oxnam was reported in the *Washington Post*, April 5, 1953. In the same issue the *Post* published the dossier with the Bishop's comments and the editorial quoted. See *New York Times*, July 8 and 9, 1953, for examples of committee "leaks" of executive session testimony to the press. The testimony of Bishop Oxnam has been published by the committee under the title, *Testimony of Bishop G. Bromley Oxnam.*

CHAPTER 8—Rev. McMichael's testimony is contained in *Hearings Regarding Jack R. McMichael* which also includes that of Mr. and Mrs. Edmiston. The transcripts of the executive session testimony concerning the clergy were published in Parts 5, 6, 7 and 8 of *Investigation of Communist Activities in the New York City Area.* The aftermath of Benjamin Gitlow's charges was reported by Will Maslow in "Case History of a Smear," *Congress Weekly,* October 19, 1953. The Rev. Mr. Irwin St. John Tucker's retort appeared in the New York *Herald Tribune,* September 12, 1953. The hearing of the Rev. Dr. John A. Hutchinson has been published under the title, *Investigation of Communist Activities in the Baltimore Area—Part 1.*

CHAPTER 9—Edward J. Fitzgerald's testimony is contained in *Interlocking Subversion in Government Departments, Part 5.* According to Senate Internal Security Sub-committee spokesmen, the hearing *Communist Underground Printing Facilities and Illegal Propaganda* is "out of print." The testimony of General Zwicker before the Senate Permanent Subcommittee on Investigations has been made public under the title *Communist Infiltration in the Army, Part 3.* The examination of James A. Wechsler before the same committee is in Parts 4 and 5 of *State Department Information Program—Information Centers.* Dean Griswold's address at Mount Holyoke College was printed in *The Harvard Law School Record,* March 25, 1954.

CHAPTER 10—The story of William Bradford was told by Dean Griswold in a speech before the Massachusetts Bar Association on February 5, 1954, which appeared in *The Harvard Law School Record,* February 11, 1954. Jacob S. Hyams' testimony appears in *Communist Underground Printing Facilities and Illegal Propaganda.* Robert Morris' statement is in *Interlocking Subversion in Government Departments, Part 2.* Senator Welker's advice to the witness who worked for the New Theatre School appears in Part 4 of the same hearing. The exchange between Dr. Pusey and Senator McCarthy was reported in the *New York Times.* The New York *Post* of March 4, 1954, recorded Judge Rifkind's remarks.

CHAPTER 11—Barry S. Bernstein's testimony before the Permanent Subcommittee on Investigations is contained in hearings entitled *Army Signal Corps—Subversion and Espionage, Part 1.* That of Wendell H. Furry before the same committee appears in *Subversion and Espionage in Defense Establishments and Industry, Part 1.* The testimony of Alex B. Novikoff and Donald Horton before the Internal Security Subcommittee is in Parts 8 and 12 of *Subversive Influence in the Educational Process.* The report under this title, dated July 17, 1953, is the source for the quotation illustrating the committee's interest in obtaining names.

CHAPTERS 12 and **13**—These chapters are fictitious in their entirety with the exception of the excerpt from the opinion of the Supreme Court of the United States in *Wilson* v. *United States*, 149 U.S. 60, 66 (1893), and the quotation from the testimony of a frightened witness, which is taken from *Communist Underground Printing Facilities and Illegal Propaganda*.

CHAPTER 14—Dr. Buell Gallagher's statement appeared in the *New York Times*, October 6, 1953. The testimony of Messrs. Brownell and Hoover is in *Interlocking Subversion in Government Departments, Part 16*.

CHAPTER 15—The story of Joshua's secret mission was told in Joshua 2:1-24. The facts concerning Professor Halperin are in the Internal Security Sub-committee's hearing, *Subversive Influence in the Educational Process, Part 6*, and the report under the same title, dated July 17, 1953. The 1948 hearing of the House Committee on Un-American Activities was published under the title *Hearings Regarding Communist Espionage in the United States Government*, 80th Cong., 2d. Sess.

CHAPTER 16—Mr. Chambers' testimony is in the above-mentioned Committee on Un-American Activities hearing in 1948. The White papers are reproduced in Part 16 of *Interlocking Subversion in Government Departments*. General Walter Bedell Smith's statement was reported in the New York *Herald Tribune* of January 26, 1953. The material on the behavior of the "ring" members in Washington is drawn from the 1948 House committee hearing and various parts of *Interlocking Subversion in Government Departments*. Mr. Adler testified in *Hearings Regarding Communism in the United States Government—Part 1*, Committee on Un-American Activities, 81st Cong., 2d Sess. Miss Bentley described her relations with Messrs. Golos and Budenz in *Out of Bondage* (The Devin-Adair Company, New York, 1951). The quotation from General John R. Dean is taken from his book *The Strange Alliance* (The Viking Press, New York, 1947) page 150. Miss Bentley's testimony concerning RDX, the Doolittle raid and the nationality of "ring" members is taken from the hearings of the Subcommittee on Immigration and Naturalization of the Senate Committee on the Judiciary, 81st Cong., 1st Sess., entitled *Communist Activities Among Aliens and National Groups, Part 1*. An article on RDX appears in *The Encyclopedia of Chemical Technology* Vol. VI, pp. 39-40 (The Interscience Encyclopedia, Inc., New York, 1951). The hearing before the Subcommittee on Government Operations Abroad of the Permanent Subcommittee on Investigations, *Transfer of Occupation Currency Plates—Espionage Phase*, contains Miss Bentley's testimony on that subject. The facts concerning the occupation marks transaction appear in documents introduced at this hearing and at the hearings before the Senate Committees on Appropriations, Armed Services, and Banking and Currency, 80th Cong., 1st Sess. entitled *Occupation Currency Transactions*. Mr. Golos' difficulties were publicized in the *New York Times* of October 24 and 26, 1939; January 3, March 14 and 15, 1940. Mr. Berle's memorandum of his interview with Mr. Chambers is reproduced in *Interlocking Subversion in Government Departments, Part 6*, and he testified to notifying the FBI before the Committee on Un-American Activities in 1948.

CHAPTER 17—Senator Jenner's Lincoln's Birthday address at Jeffersonville, Ind., was reported in the *New York Times*, February 13, 1954. His Senate speech on General Marshall in September, 1950, is contained in the *Congressional Record*, Vol. 96, pp. 14913-14917. For his statement of April 11, 1951, see the *Congressional Record*, Vol. 97, pp. 3618-3619. Senator McCarthy published his remarks in 1952 under the title *The Story of General George Marshall*. Senator Jenner's speech in Columbus, Ind., was quoted in the *New York Times* of February 12, 1954, and his opinion of the State Department in the same newspaper on February 24.

CHAPTER 18—Senator Jenner's speech in December, 1950 concerning "internationalist Republicans," was quoted in the *New Republic*, July 28, 1952. Senator McCarthy's moves involving Dr. Matthews and President Eisenhower's intervention were reported in the *New York Times* of July 8, 9, and 10, 1953, and *Newsweek*, July 20, 1953. The *New York Times* of October 16, 1953, retailed Senator McCarthy's story of the "breakdown" of a Fort Monmouth employee. The review of the situation at the Signal Corps base by Peter Kihss was published by the same newspaper on January 11 to 13, 1954. Walter Millis' analysis appeared in the New York *Herald Tribune* of December 8, 1953. Murray Marder's reports were in the *Washington Post* on November 9 to 12, 1953. The findings of the Scientists' Committee on Loyalty and Security of the Federation of American **Scientists** were published in mimeographed form under the title *The Fort Monmouth Security Investigations, August 1953-April 1954* (2153 Yale Station, New Haven 11, Conn.). "Communist infiltration" of the CIA was discussed by Senator McCarthy on June 16. Senator Flanders' speech and Senator McCarthy's retort occurred on June 1, 1954. Senator McCarthy's remarks concerning the President's order barring testimony concerning a high-level administration meeting were quoted in the *New York Times*, May 21, 1954. The exchange between the Senator and Mr. Adams on the Fifth Amendment took place on May 24. Senator McCarthy's appeal to federal employees for information was made on May 27. He acknowledged that he received such information on May 5. On May 28, he referred to "twenty-one years" of treason. The quotation from his Salt Lake City, Utah, speech appeared in *The Nation*, May 22, 1954. A compilation of the Senator's statements suggesting that he has confidential sources in the State Department is contained in the report of the Senate Committee on Foreign Relations, *State Department Employee Loyalty Investigation* (81st Cong., 2d Sess., Senate Report No. 2108). The incident involving Miss deHaas was reported in the *New York Times* on September 5, October 8 and November 4, 1952. The reports of the New York *Journal American* and of Drew Pearson were cited in the above-mentioned issue of *The Nation.* The *New York Times* surveyed the situation in the Voice of America on April 15, 1953. Mr. Kaghan described his conflict with Senator McCarthy in *The Reporter,* July 21, 1953. The author has also generally drawn for material in this chapter on the special issue of *The Progressive,* "McCarthy: A Documented Record," April, 1954.

CHAPTER 19—The statement of Timothy Dwight is quoted in *The Growth of the American Republic,* p. 371. The number of informers employed by the Department of Justice was reported in the New York *World Telegram & Sun,* July 12, 1954. The letter of thanks to the Internal Security Subcommittee is reproduced in *Subversive Influence in the Educational Process, Part 11.*

Index

304

MacArthur, Douglas, 92, **269**
McCarthy, Joseph R., 5, 44, 149, 212;
Army and, *see* Army-McCarthy dispute; attack on Republican Party, 50-
51; Eisenhower relationship, 269-274,
281-282; Fifth Amendment attitude,
145-146; public reaction to methods
of, 276-278; reliability of charges made
by, 275, 284-285; sources of information, 214, 282-286, 288; State Department and, 286-290; "twenty years of
treason" theme, 264-267; "twenty-one
years of treason" theme, 48, 281-282;
Wechsler investigation, 131-133;
Zwicker hearing, 130-131
McCarthyism, 50
McCarthy Subcommittee, 5, 268-290;
Army-McCarthy dispute, *see* Army-
McCarthy dispute; Fort Monmouth in-
vestigation, 148-149; Furry investiga-
tion, 155-161; *see also* McCarthy, Jo-
seph R.
McClellan, John L., 46
McCormack, John, 37
McGuire, Matthew F., 285
McLeod, W. Scott, 288-290
McMichael, Jack Richard, 123; testimony
concerning, at Oxnam hearing, 94-
97; Velde Committee hearings, 99-
102, 121-123
Magdoff, Harry, 208
Magnes, Judah L., 112, 113, 114
Marder, Murray, 277
Marshall, George C.: Eisenhower on,
270-271; Jenner on, 262-264; Mc-
Carthy on, 264-265, 269
Marshall Foundation, 86
Martin, Joseph W., 42-43; on Marxism, 2
Marxism, Speaker Martin on, 2
Mason, James M., John Brown investi-
gation, 15-32
Massachusetts, Popery investigation, 12-
13
Massachusetts House Committee on Un-
American Activities, 88-89
Massachusetts State Kansas Committee,
18, 26

Matthews, J. B., 271-273
Methodist Church, Velde Committee
hearings and, 77-98, 99-119
Methodist Federation for Social Action,
106-112
Methodist Federation for Social Service,
93, 94, 96
Meyer, Agnes, 56, 201
Meyer, Eugene, 56
M-5, Britain's, 211
Miller, Robert T., III, 251-253
Millis, Walter, 276
Morgenthau, Henry, 238, 239
Morris, Robert, 124, 138, 217, 244, 257
Morse, Wayne, 1
Morton, Alfred H., 287-288
Moulder, Morgan M., 81, 94
Mount Holyoke College, 134
Moving pictures, *see* Entertainment
Mundt, Karl E., 9, 39, 251-252, 255,
279, 280; in the Thomas Committee
hearings, 221-222, 225
Murphy, Frank, 258
Murray, James E., 86

National Conference of Christians and
Jews, 272-273
National Council of Churches of Christ,
113
National Federation for Constitutional
Liberties, 86
National Labor Relations Board (NLRB),
213
Nazis, pre-World War II investigations
of, 38
New Masses, 80
New Theatre School, 139
New York, council member issue, **68**
Nimitz, Chester, 240
Nixon, Richard M., 234-235, 237
NKVD, *see* Soviet Secret Intelligence
Normandie, 239-240
Novikoff, Alex B., 150-153
Novy Mir, New York, 245

O'Brien, John A., 272
Ohio Youth Conference, 100

305

AH/ R/I88 HR

GILLMOR